HUBRECHT DUIJKER

THE GREAT WINE CHATEAUX OF BORDEAUX

INTRODUCTION BY
Hugh Johnson

CRESCENT BOOKS

Art direction: Van Sambeek Design Associates, Amsterdam
First impression 1975

English translation by Danielle de Froidmont Associates

ISBN 0-517-426056

Printed in the Netherlands

Typeset and prepared by T&O Graphics and Taylor Jackson Designs Ltd, Lowestoft, Suffolk

First published in the U.S.A. by Crescent Books
A division of
Crown Publishers Inc.,
New York

© 1975, 1981 by Het Spectrum B.V.
English translation © Mitchell Beazley Publishers 1983

For Julie, with whom I have shared and hope to share more good bottles than with anyone else.

Photographs in this book by Peter van der Velde. Some additional photographs by Photographie Burdin, Hubrecht Duijker, Château Mouton-Rothschild and Boudewijn Neuteboom. The photograph by Cecil Beaton on page 119 (top, left) is reproduced by courtesy of Château Mouton-Rothschild. The photograph on page 184 (top) is reproduced by courtesy of Château Ausone. Maps, plans and drawings by Otto van Eersel, Jan ten Hove, Jan Klatter, Will van Sambeek and Eddy Schoonheijt. The paintings on page 129 (top) are reproduced by courtesy of Château Lafite-Rothschild.

Contents

Foreword

The great Blaise Pascal once said 'variety which is not ordered into unity is only confusion'. This could well be said of modern science, but I should like to quote these words in quite a different sense, applying them instead to this book about the wines of Bordeaux, which it is my pleasure to introduce.

Lovers of good wines tend to be on uncertain ground where Bordeaux wines are concerned, for there are so many of them! The capital of Aquitaine is surrounded with innumerable names, vineyards and *crus*. This variety can certainly be a cause for hesitation. The beginner does not know where to start and even the connoisseur can occasionally be misled. On the other hand, comparing all these wines, studying their history and discovering those which are most appealing is an absorbing and fascinating task. They display an infinitely subtle range of colours, bouquets and flavours which change from one year to the next and which need to be reinvestigated and experienced again and again.

I am very pleased to invite the reader to take a unique journey around the vineyards of Bordeaux — a tour made possible by this outstanding work by Hubrecht Duijker. Each of the Bordeaux districts has an entirely individual character, which is fully described in this book. The world's best know wine châteaux are concentrated in the Médoc, the Graves, St-Emilion and Pomerol. They have long deserved to be described in such a beautifully illustrated book as this, and having taken the initiative, Hubrecht Duijker deserves the thanks and praise of all wine lovers for the quality and impartiality of his text. This book stands head and shoulders above the many books about wine in general and those concerning Bordeaux wines in particular. In 1824, William Franck published the first edition of his *Traité des Vins du Médoc*. Since then, millions of words have been written on the subject. But apart from the fine albums which were published around the turn of the century by A. Danflou and Ch. de Lorbac — nowadays collectors' items — not a single book has appeared

Introduction

about the great wines of Bordeaux which couples a worthwhile text with illustrations of high quality. This book fills the gap. I am full of admiration for the splendid photographs in the book and the detailed, comprehensive text which in some cases provides information never yet published. Many people in the wine trade will discover new facts, while wine drinkers and wine lovers will find everything they want to know about Bordeaux wines . . . and no doubt develop quite a thirst while reading. I therefore raise my glass and propose a toast to your health and to the success of this book.

Bernard Ginestet
Mayor of Margaux

Regular visitors to the wine regions of France soon become aware that, contrary to British folk-lore, we are not the only, nor even the most active, northern investigators of these Elysian fields. Holland and Belgium, small though they are in man-power, are rich, critical and even more fanatical followers of French wine at every level.

For several years now I have been bumping into a young Dutch writer whose reception by the (often hard-boiled) French producers has impressed me. They like him. They open their bottles, estate records, and even their homes to him. I think it is his cool candour they admire: not always the easiest attitude when tasting the grower's pride under his gaze.

Hubrecht Duijker, this cool young man, has spent the greater part of the last decade in France, methodically tasting, interviewing and photographing to make the most complete album of France and its better wine growers that anyone has yet produced. The first volumes, on Bordeaux, were rapturously received by the Bordeaux growers — not the easiest fraternity to please. The two later volumes, on Burgundy, and on the trio of Alsace, Champagne and the Loire, have had the same reception. Translated into French they have sold like buns.

Hubrecht was kind enough to tell me, when we first met five years ago in Amsterdam, that my World Atlas of Wine was his first inspiration. I am very happy, having read and profited by his books, to have sparked something so thorough, so graphic, and so enjoyable. Duijker's books are the perfect armchair journey through my favourite French provinces: the ideal appetizer to their incomparable wines.

Hugh Johnson
London

Anyone wishing to write a book about the wines, châteaux and the people of Bordeaux is beset by a Hamlet-like doubt. Which wines should you include, and which not? To describe them all is out of the question, unless you confine yourself to very brief notes, as in Cocks and Féret's *Bordeaux et ses Vins.* After consultation with the publishers, we decided to devote this book to those châteaux of Bordeaux that are rated most highly for their red wines. They we shall encounter the *grands crus classés* of the Médoc and Graves, and the *premiers grand crus classés* of St-Emilion; and, not to forget Pomerol (which has no official classification), we have also included two of its châteaux. I have visited each château personally and these are entirely my personal impressions. After all, wine is a highly subjective matter; but I hope that your experiences will coincide, at least to some extent, with my own.

Of course, I owe a tremendous debt of thanks to all the people who helped me by granting me a little of their time, their knowledge and their hospitality. Alas, I cannot name them all, but most of them appear in the text. Even so, I should especially like to thank a few people, notably Thierry Manoncourt of Château Figeac and Jean-Bernard Delmas of Château Haut-Brion who helped me greatly with my programme. Warm thanks too to Bruno Prats of Château Cos d'Estournel, without whose unstinting help this book would never have been written. Finally, I must not forget my good friend Herman Mostermans, one of the most dedicated of Bordeaux devotees that I know.

Hubrecht Duijker

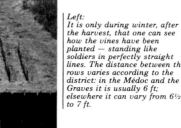

Left:
It is only during winter, after the harvest, that one can see how the vines have been planted — standing like soldiers in perfectly straight lines. The distance between the rows varies according to the district: in the Médoc and the Graves it is usually 6 ft; elsewhere it can vary from 6½ to 7 ft.

Bottom left:
In an experiment at Château Gruaud-Larose, several of the more important grape varieties were put in jars of spirits to see which ripened first. First to ripen of the black grapes was the Malbec, followed by the Merlot and then the Cabernet. The Sémillon was the first of the whites to ripen. This characteristic can greatly influence the quality of the harvest: districts with a lot of Merlot — such as St Emilion — can sometimes be finished picking before a Cabernet district — such as the Médoc — has even begun; perhaps just as the rain has started.

Wine

It is an old wives' tale that all you need is the right soil, the right climate and the right grapes to produce a great wine. Nothing could be further from the truth. Of course, the right ingredients and the right circumstances are vital, but after the grapes have been picked the wine grower cannot simply go off and take a well-earned rest.

Great wine requires people

On the contrary, making wine — the process of vinification — demands all the grower's attention and expertise. The art is, in fact, to transfer the quality of the grapes to the wine to best effect. This sounds easier than it really is. Just one bit of carelessness can have disastrous consequences, consequences which can not only have immediate financial implications but which can also damage the reputation of the estate; because, once a consumer is disappointed by a particular bottle, he will be reluctant to order the same wine next time round.

It is not merely the château owner's dedication and expertise, however, that counts; his whole attitude is vitally important. In the long run it depends on him whether or not a great wine emerges. He it is who decides on the care of the vineyard, the choice of equipment, the number of persons employed, the working methods at all stages of wine-making, the length of maturation, and so on. In each vineyard, it is generally the proprietor or his manager who make or break the wine, because the natural factors at each château are virtually the same. The particular features of the châteaux in this book can therefore be credited — or debited — to the man behind the wine. He is required to devote his time, his money and indeed his life to making as perfect a wine as possible; all the famous *viticulteurs* are therefore, by definition, idealists.

From black grape to red wine

What must be done to transform the grapes, once picked, into a quality red wine? First of all, it is essential that the installations and the buildings where the process of wine-making is done are clean, because a newborn wine is highly vulnerable and therefore easy prey to all kinds of bacteria. When, therefore, the time for harvesting comes and the grapes are picked, they are first tipped into a machine which removes the stems, the *égrappoir*. This ingeniously separates the stalks (to which the pips are attached) from the skins and flesh. During this process, the fruit is lightly crushed but not pressed. In this state the grapes are pumped to the fermenting vats, the *cuves*. Here the first and most important fermentation takes place, the *fermentation alcoholique* or *fermentation tumultueuse* (alcoholic or turbulent fermentation). This is a highly complex natural process in which, amongst

Below:
The first years of a great wine. The series of drawings shows some of the highlights of the vinification process.
A *The black grapes arrive. At a traditionally organized château the fruit has been gathered in wooden douils (one douil produces enough wine to fill a cask of about 225 litres), which are emptied into the égrappoir, or de-stalking machine. This spits the stalks and pips out on one side while on the other it pumps the lightly crushed grapes to the fermentation vats. The skins are not removed as they give the wine its colour.*
B *The first fermentation takes place in oak, concrete or steel vats. The wooden vats are the least practical, but certainly the most attractive. During fermentation the skins and other solid particles rise to the surface to form a solid chapeau, or hat. This is pressed after fermentation (C) and the vin de*

presse obtained is often added in small quantities to the first wine, the vin de goutte, to increase the tannin content.
D *In the meantime, the young wine has been put into oak casks, barriques, where it will be left to mature for at least one and a half years. Many grands crus use a certain percentage of new casks each year; some use them exclusively. This can be expensive, not only because of the cost of the casks themselves but also because each new cask absorbs between 7 to 10 litres of wine. The first fermentation is followed by a second, slow fermentation. The casks in the first-year cellar, or chai, have special glass bungs which allow the gases given off during fermentation to escape. During this first year the wine develops, forming its character. It then begins to mature.*
E *Because between 8% and 12% of the wine evaporates during the year, the casks must*

be topped up at least twice in that time so as to limit — as much as possible — the wine's contact with the air and consequent oxidation. This is known as ouillage.
F *Because the wine continues to throw off deposits, it is pumped into clean casks every three or four months. This process is called the soutirage and is repeated when the casks are moved to the second-year cellar, just before the new harvest.*
G *Usually two or three months before the wine is bottled, but sometimes earlier, the collage takes place. During this process the wine is clarified with the white of fresh eggs, between three and eight eggs being used for each cask. The egg-white is beaten in a wooden bowl — called the bontemps — with a whisk made from twigs and the light and airy mixture folded into the wine. When the egg-white particles sink to the bottom,*

they take all the impurities with them.
H *After the wine has been racked again, the mise en bouteilles takes place, usually with a modern bottling machine but occasionally by hand from the cask. The wine then suffers from bottle sickness for between 8 to 12 months; only after this time is it possible to really taste the final product.*

Some common terms:
Appellation d'Origine Contrôlée, A.O.C., A.C.: *the legally controlled designation of origin.*
Barrique: *Bordeaux-cask of about 225 litres.*
Cave: *underground cellar.*
Chai: *ground-level cellar, typical of Bordeaux.*
Chef de culture: *person responsible for the vineyard.*
Cru: *literally 'growth'.*
Cru bourgeois: *cru below that of the classed crus but often of good quality.*
Cru exceptionnel: *highest of the crus bourgeois.*
Cuve: *fermentation vat or tank.*
Cuvier: *room in which the fermentation vats are situated.*
Fouloir-égrappoir: *de-stalking and crushing machine.*
Gérant: *general manager of a wine estate.*

Grand cru classé: *wine included in one of the official classifications.*
Grand vin: *no official meaning, originally referred to the first wine of a château.*
Maître de chai: *cellar master, responsible for the work in the cellars.*
Mise en bouteilles: *bottling.*
Mise en bouteilles au château: *the wine has been bottled on the estate.*
Négociant: *merchant, shipper.*
Propriétaire: *owner.*
Récolte: *harvest, vintage year.*
Régisseur: *director or manager; the maître de chai and the chef de culture work under him.*
Tonneau: *four barriques, thus about 900 litres. Originally a tonnage unit of sailing ships.*
Vignoble: *vineyard.*
Viticulteur: *wine grower.*

Wine

other things, the sugars present in the fruit are converted by the action of yeasts, also present in the grapes, into alcohol and carbon dioxide gas. The process takes 7-12 days and stops of its own accord when nearly all the sugar has been converted. It goes without saying that the more sugar there is in the grape the more alcohol is produced in the wine, and vice versa. In lean years, a little sugar can be added to the must, otherwise the wine would be too light. This practice, which is legally permitted albeit within very fine limits, is called *chaptalization*. The wine derives its red colour from the skins, which also remain in the vat.

Temperature control

During fermentation heat is released but the temperature should not rise too high. The general rule of thumb is that the fermenting mass ought not to exceed 30°C; 35°C is fatal

to the yeast cells. At many châteaux, 27°-28°C is regarded as the ideal. So that this temperature is not exceeded, the wine at estates with the traditional oak or cement fermentation vats is pumped regularly through a cooling unit. An increasing number of châteaux are changing to stainless steel tanks over which cold water can be run; these are often thermostatically controlled.
When the first fermentation is completed, a second, more gentle fermentation takes place, the *fermentation malolactique*. By then the wine has often already been transferred to casks. This second fermentation greatly improves the wine — the juice of the grape loses something of its hardness, its acidity and its colour. The grape aroma is also transformed into the beginnings of a bouquet; furthermore, the wine becomes far less liable to sickness. The ideal temperature for this fermentation is 18°-20°C. The wine is then transferred to

fresh casks because sediment, *lie*, will have collected. Then follows the *assemblage*, the mixing of the various casks. Most great châteaux, in fact, vinify their grape varieties separately so that the less successful casks can be eliminated. The wine is then left to mature for a long time. Amongst the classified châteaux, the wine remains in the wood for at least one and a half years, but two and a half years is not uncommon. During the maturing period, the barrels are regularly topped up and the wine is racked from time to time into a clean cask. Towards the end of the ripening period in wood, the wine is clarified with egg-white, once again racked, and bottled. All the leading estates now bottle their own wines. The wine continues to mature in the bottle.
People often wonder why it is around Bordeaux that wines are made, as Richelieu said two centuries ago, with *'le gout le plus fin du monde'*. Disregarding the important human factor, what is so special about this

Wine

one spot in the world?
The answer is that Bordeaux provides a unique combination of natural elements. Everything that nature can contribute to help man create a great wine is to be found here; and in such a way, moreover, that everything fits together in perfect harmony — sun, for example, is good but too much sun is not. It is comparable to a perfect symphony written by a great composer in which none of the instruments predominates but each makes its individual contribution towards the total sound.

What Nature does for the wine

Everything starts with the soil. If this does not meet certain requirements, it is useless trying to make a great wine. As a rule, a poor soil with a complex structure is required for a fine wine with many nuances in its bouquet and taste; for it is from the soil that the vine derives its nourishment and the wine its character. These conditions apply to many places in Bordeaux — particularly in the Médoc and the Graves. In the course of centuries, the rivers have carried all kinds of different soils to the mouth of the Gironde, including gravel from the central Pyrenees, from the Massif Central and from the valleys of the Lot and the Aveyron. Sometimes the gravel (*graves*) shows on the surface, but it generally lies in broad layers underground. The drainage too must be exemplary. Nothing is more deadly to the roots of the vine than too damp a subsoil. Here, again, gravel is useful. Many famous vineyards lie on slopes or on plateaux watered by many streams, with more effective exposure to the sun as an added bonus.

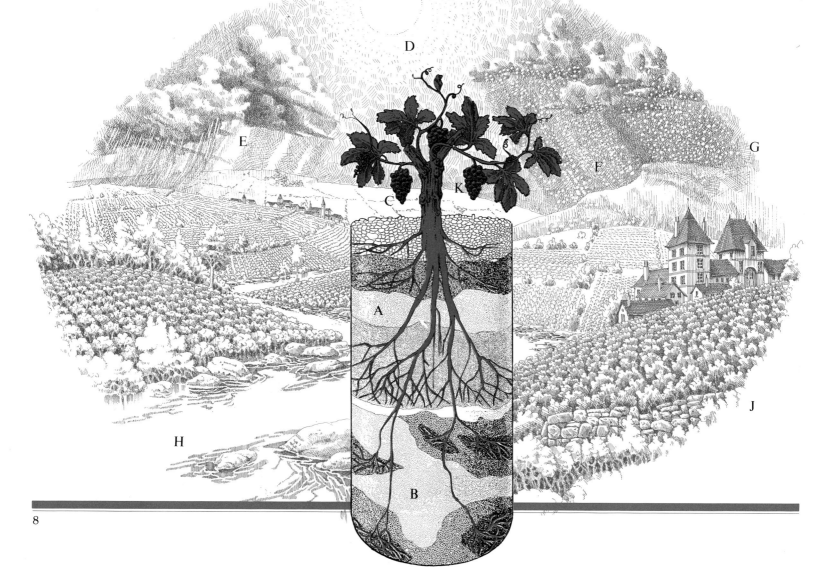

Wine

For a quality wine, the vine must flourish in a mild climate, where extremes of temperature are the exception. Of course, sunshine is needed for the development of vines and fruit, but rain is equally important. A climate which is not quite subtropical is regarded as the ideal. Too many hours of sun mean dull, heavy wine; too much rain weak, thin wine. Bordeaux has a beautifully soft climate with mild winters, gentle springs, dry summers and not too much rain in the autumn.

Only certain types of grape are permitted in the Bordeaux area, namely the varieties which give the best results in this area and on this soil. They are planted in various proportions in the appropriate parts of the vineyard. Selecting the kinds and percentages of grape varieties is thus very important. But choice is not the only consideration. In fact, there are strict regulations and standards for tending and spacing the vines, on the principle that where wine is concerned quality and quantity are in inverse proportions. So not too many vines may be crowded together. The maximum in the Médoc is a little over 4,000 vines to the acre. Then, the soil in which they are planted should be poor, either gravel (e.g. Médoc) or limestone (e.g. St Emilion) are best. Care must be taken that the vine does not bear too many grapes, either, because, with so many bunches, all the good juice would then be too widely distributed. So heavy pruning — a highly skilled operation — must be carried out several times a year, different methods being employed in each district. Finally, the age of the vine is also important. Only old vines have deep roots and can really take from the ground what is in it. 'The vine must suffer' is a common saying. The more trouble it has to take to grow and bear fruit, the better the quality of the grape.

Once it is bottled, all wine must be stored horizontally to prevent the cork from drying out and a consequent rapid oxidation which occurs when wine and air come in contact.

The ideal cellar temperature is 12°C, with as little variation as possible.

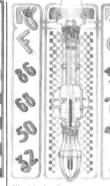

Old wine should be carried carefully. One day before drinking the bottle should be placed in a draught-free place which is not too warm, to allow the lees to settle at the bottom and wine to reach (17-19°C).

The moment to open the bottle has arrived. Cut the top of the lead capsule to one millimetre below the top of the bottle.

Wipe the top of the cork and the rim of the bottle to avoid any dirt getting into the wine.

A good corkscrew should have an open spiral. After the cork has been taken out, the rim of the bottle should be wiped again.

Drinking and enjoying Bordeaux wines

Wine is something quite special. Unlike other alcoholic beverages, wine is not a drink which just sits in the bottle, waiting to be drunk. On the contrary, wine is alive. It is sensitive to air, light, temperature, and vibration. Furthermore, wine, though by no means all wine, can develop in the bottle. There is little point in laying down everyday table wines for years because the end result will probably be more like vinegar than wine. The better red Bordeaux, on the other hand, are excellently suited to maturing in the bottle. In their youth, they are characterized by a somewhat unpleasant hardness, but in the course of time this gives way to a velvety softness.

What is the best way of keeping wine? The juice of the grape is at its happiest in a kind of hibernation, perhaps for years on end. The place where the bottles lie must be cool (about 12°C), dark and free from vibration. That is why a cellar is ideal. There must be reasonable ventilation which must not, however, develop into a strong draught; and the cellar should neither be too dry nor too damp. A bucket of water will help to dampen a cellar that is excessively dry. Conversely, a little sawdust on the floor will dry out a damp cellar. A disadvantage of excess humidity is that the labels will quickly deteriorate and nothing is more frustrating than drinking fine wines without knowing their name or their year. With most Bordeaux, these details are printed on the cork, but then the bottle must first be opened.

If you have no cellar, do not despair. There are places in most houses where wine can be stored. The most important criterion is a constant temperature. Another solution to the storage problem is to use insulated wine bins, which have been marketed for some years. The bottles must be stored on their sides. If this is not done, the cork dries out and oxygen can reach the wine, causing rapid and harmful oxidation.

The right way to serve Bordeaux

Nearly all wine books say that Bordeaux wines must be served 'at room temperature'. The result is that many wine lovers drink their Médocs, St Emilions and Pomerols too warm. So what is the truth of the matter? Bordeaux wine was always found to show its best at room temperature — but that was generations ago, before the days of central heating, when room temperature was generally no more than 17°-19°C. The average room temperature has now risen beyond 20°C but wine has not, of course, adjusted accordingly. It still unfolds at its finest at 17°-19°C. This does not mean that wine served at today's room temperature is disappointing. It is a matter of nuance. A warmer wine will, for example, tend to have rather too powerful a bouquet and a diminished taste.

It goes without saying that wine should never be warmed up quickly. It must be done gradually. A wine which is not sufficiently *chambré* can best be warmed up in the glass

Left:
Cork is expensive, so a good cork is a sign that great care has been given to the wine. The finest clarets should have 'full long', or 2 inch corks, but most now use the 1⅞ inch Bordeaux cork.
From left to right: a still unused (and therefore somewhat thicker) cork from Château Latour; one from Château La Lagune 1964; and for comparison corks of a Burgundy Chambertin Clos de Bèze 1969, an Alsace, an Italian Gattinara, a German Moselle and a Bollinger Champagne.

If the wine is old there is usually some sediment and it should be decanted into a large, plain and spotlessly clean decanter. One accessory needed for this is a candle.

Pour the wine carefully into the decanter, with the burning candle placed below the neck of the bottle to show clearly if any sediment is about to flow with the wine.

Sniff the empty glass to make sure there are no cupboard or detergent smells, then pour enough for a couple of mouthfuls.

Look at the wine and enjoy its scintillating red-brown colour, which the French describe as tuilé, roof-tile brown.

After swirling the wine around in the glass, smell the bouquet. The 'nose' of a wine tells much about its personality.

Then taste the wine, letting it run around your whole mouth. A beautiful Bordeaux always has many nuances of taste.

Drinking and enjoying Bordeaux wines

The glass should ideally be thin — certainly not thick.

The glass should be plain — the colour of the wine should be seen clearly.

The bowl should also be plain. The wine needs no adornment by way of decoration.

The glass should not be too small. In wine regions it is usually only filled about a third.

To swirl the wine round in the glass and enjoy the bouquet, hold the glass by the stem or the foot.

Opposite page, above: Everything ready for the decanting of a fine claret.

Opposite page, centre: There are many types of wine racks available, of metal, wood or plastic.

by holding it with both hands. Nor should the glass be too full; just sufficient for the wine to be swirled around freely, so as to release the bouquet.

As far as the wine itself is concerned, do not be put off by sediment. Many a waiter in a restaurant has received complaints because the wine has a deposit. This is a mistake; in fact, sediment is generally a positive sign. It shows that the wine has not been filtered, and whereas filtering certainly produces a clean drink, it takes away something of the wine's backbone. Deposit is something quite natural which forms as the wine matures. It can be left in the bottle without too much trouble by decanting, as illustrated at the top of this page. The conditions that should be fulfilled by a good wine glass are indicated opposite.

Above: In Bordeaux six bottle sizes are used. From left to right: the half bottle (37.5 cl), standard bottle (75 cl), magnum (300 cl), jéroboam (450 cl), and impériale (600 cl). 1 litre = 100 cl. The first three sizes are the most usual. The larger the bottle, the longer the development of the wine. The classic Bordeaux bottle is in fact used elsewhere as it is admirable for wines throwing a deposit, which can be held back in the shoulder. For comparison, a Burgundy bottle and a flûte d'Alsace.

Gastronomy à la Bordelaise

Now and then you meet people in Bordeaux who swear they do not drink. Even if they knock back 4 litres of wine a day, this is not regarded as 'drinking'; yet one dram of whisky certainly is. But you will never meet anyone who claims he does not eat. In Bordeaux, life is enjoyed and so, therefore, is a well-stocked table. At noon, everything stops for the midday meal and when work starts again depends entirely on the company, the dishes and the wines. This goes without saying at the great wine châteaux, where guests are often received in princely style. In town, people are more time-conscious, but you must still allow at least two hours for ordinary weekday lunch; and Sunday is special, when families dine together at home or in a restaurant. Regional specialities are particularly popular; the true Bordelais, for example, will never weary of his famous *entrecôte* grilled on vine twigs (*aux sarments*).

Five courses and Cognac to boot

Sunday lunch in an unassuming little restaurant is quite an experience. The place is always packed out, often with entire families, from grandfather to toddlers, at the table. A typical meal starts with *hors d'oeuvres*, smoked Bayonne ham, small shellfish, marinated mushrooms and red beetroot. This is followed, perhaps, by half a dozen Arcachon oysters. The main course is either *entrecôte* of gigantic proportions, a leg of lamb, or *poulet maison.* Then there is a choice of cheeses and, finally, ice cream or pastry. These five courses are washed down with, say, a bottle of wine per head, followed by coffee and Cognac — and the bill is usually gratifyingly low. The *décor* at such a restaurant is always very simple, and the same applies to the service; but the quality is impeccable, the place is loud with talk and laughter, and a thoroughly good time is had by all.

Specialities of Bordeaux

In addition to oysters, *entrecôte* and leg of lamb, Bordeaux offers many other tasty specialities. Particularly fine is the *foie gras des Landes* which is equal to any goose liver from Périgord or Alsace. Then there are the *cèpes à la Bordelaise,* large flat mushrooms with an individual, delicate taste. They are generally prepared with shallots and a hint of garlic. The most curious speciality is lamprey, a fish which is served more or less like *coq au vin*, in a red wine sauce with small pieces of bacon. Despite appearances, this primitive, snake-like fish, with its sucker-like mouth, makes good eating. All these dishes are of course generously accompanied by the local wines.

Which wines with what

There are no laws of gastronomy that tell you exactly which wine to be drunk with what food. A good thing too, because experimenting with combinations of wines and foods can be an exciting adventure. Simply drink what you like, and keep experimenting. Nevertheless, there are some general guidelines, namely:
* Attune the wine to the character of the dish (or vice versa). So, with young lamb choose a fine Médoc, and with game a sturdy St Emilion. Neither wine nor food should predominate — good eating is true democracy.
* If you do not skimp on the food, do not skimp on the wine.
* Serve simple wines before the better, young before the older, dry before sweet, white before red.

Bon appetit!

Pâté de foie gras *goes well with a light claret or a dry white Graves, but in Bordeaux it is sometimes served with a great Sauternes.*

In the Bordeaux region, leg of lamb, especially that of Pauillac, is a favourite dish. One of the fine wines of the Médoc is ideal with it.

Steak de veau *in a cream sauce requires a supple, delicate claret, perhaps a Margaux.*

Surprisingly enough, Dutch cheese is often found in Bordeaux. Or, more precisely, Dutch-style cheese which has been manufactured in France. This preference for Dutch cheese goes back to the time a few centuries ago when the Dutch had the largest merchant-shipping fleet in the world — 15,000 ships compared to England's 3,000 and France's 500. The Dutch shipped the wine of Bordeaux all over the world, bringing their cheese to the Bordeaux ports as saleable ballast on the trip from their home ports. The people of Bordeaux have retained their taste for a mild cheese which goes perfectly with all kinds of red Bordeaux wine.

Vast oyster beds — amongst the largest in Europe — exist along the 60 km of the Bassin d'Arcachon on the Atlantic coast. In 1969 they produced 13,500 tonnes. Oysters have been found at Arcachon for centuries — they were known there in the time of Rabelais — but have been cultivated only since 1856. Today's varieties are the small gravettes and the salty portugaises.

A very rare delicacy is the small-grained and subtle-tasting caviar de la Gironde from the sturgeon found in the area.

As well as the red and white wines (dry, semi-dry and sweet), Bordeaux also produces rosé and sparkling wines. The vins mousseux come mainly from St Emilion but also from St André-de-Cubzac and Bourg. A well-known liqueur from the region is Vieille Cure, and a brandy, Fine de Bordeaux, is rapidly increasing in popularity. Growers who find it difficult to sell their white wine — especially in the Blaye district — have great hopes for this brandy. In the past they supplied the brandy producers of Cognac, but since the introduction of the appellation contrôlée legislation this market has been forbidden to them.

Gastronomy à la Bordelaise

Fish is best eaten with dry white wines such as Graves; sole in a red wine sauce is a dish that is better with a fairly light-bodied claret.

Raw ham with a little claret is always popular as a starter — sometimes accompanied by melon. In Bordeaux the jambon de Bayonne is a speciality.

The famous entrecôte bordelaise should ideally be grilled over a fire of vine prunings. It is prepared with shallots, red wine and seasonings.

Dutch cheese with its bland, simple taste shows off any claret to advantage.

Pheasant deserves a fairly full claret, such as a Pauillac or a St Emilion of a good vintage.

Grapes, peaches, pears and nectarines are perfect partners for a sweet dessert wine such as Sauternes, served well chilled.

Robust St Emilions or full-bodied Pomerols or Médocs go well with game.

Blue cheeses, such as Bleu d'Auvergne, need a fairly assertive wine to go with them. A very strong cheese can overpower a delicate red wine.

No meal in France is complete without fresh, crisp bread.

Brie and similar soft cheeses are excellent with a fine red Graves of Margaux, or one of the more subtle clarets.

Wine is adversely affected by vinegar, mustard and anything very strong or piquant, so be cautious with such seasonings.

In the Gironde, oysters are often served with a dry white Graves.

The City of Bordeaux

'Take Versailles, add Antwerp and you get Bordeaux.' That is how Victor Hugo once described this, the sixth largest city of France. Like other major French cities, Bordeaux has its new suburbs with tower blocks and featureless streets, but the fine old town to which the great writer referred continues to flourish. Here are fine examples of 18th-century architecture, such as the Grand Théâtre with its imposing colonnade, the Allées de Tourny and the houses and buildings along the other streets and avenues. Then there is the wide river Garonne, with the quays from which the products of local industry (including wines, of course) are shipped to all corners of the world.

Shops, cafés and restaurants

Bordeaux is the centre of the ancient province of Aquitaine and the capital of the *département* of the Gironde; it is a large city with some 620,000 inhabitants (including the periphery) and within the centre alone you can stroll for hours. The longest and most important shopping street, the rue Sainte-Cathérine, runs straight from north to south and is almost three-quarters of a mile long, enough to bring even the most enthusiastic shopper to the verge of exhaustion (and maybe bankruptcy as well). The street ends at the Grand Théâtre. Opposite this was once the Café de Bordeaux, where everyone used to meet; but this has now disappeared, to be replaced by a modern hotel. One hopes that the management will be sensible enough to provide it with a wide terrace to take on the local atmosphere. Diagonally opposite the Théâtre is the Maison du Vin where all the official bodies in the world of wine are established; and facing this is the Vinothèque, a kind of supermarket where all the *grands crus* and many other wines are for sale, at hefty prices, and where connoisseurs of Bordeaux wines can browse to their heart's content. From here, it is only a short stroll to Le Saint-James, a very famous restaurant where the cooking, on the principles of *nouvelle cuisine*, is fantastic.

There are, of course, many other places where the gourmet will feel at home; often, they are very small bars which you can find only with the aid of a local resident, preferably a wine dealer, because all *négociants* have a few special addresses for their guests!

A love of the arts

Is it mere chance that at the centre of the world's finest wine region a great deal of attention is paid to the arts? Probably not: love of the wines of Bordeaux and of the fine arts often go hand in hand. In Bordeaux, a May Festival is held every year, attracting artists and audiences from all over the world. Prominent soloists who have appeared at the festival include, amongst others, Yehudi Menuhin, Andres Segovia and Marian Anderson. The New York City Ballet and London Festival Ballet have performed here, and concerts have been given by the great symphony orchestras of Philadelphia and Boston. Bordeaux also has an excellent orchestra of its own.

Economic centre

Bordeaux, of course, also has its business side. The city has much industry, including refineries, shipyards, light engineering, foodstuffs and chemical works. It is a busy, active city and traffic jams can sometimes rival those of Paris. Just outside Bordeaux there is an immense exhibition centre, officially opened in 1969. Its largest building is about half a mile long and overlooks a large artificial lake with two luxury hotels on its shores. Education and science are represented by a separate university campus, around which five villages have been built to provide student accommodation.

Some 23 centuries old

Looking at the Bordeaux of today, it is difficult to imagine that around 300 BC a Gallic tribal chieftain called Burdigal decided to establish a settlement on this spot. The name of this obscure warrior lived on, in somewhat adulterated form, as 'Bordeaux'.
Many tribes and nations have tried to occupy the city and the land, including the Visigoths, the Arabs and the Normans, but none with as much success as the English. When, in 1152, Henry Plantagenet married Eleanor, duchess of Aquitaine, he acquired the whole of southwest France. In 1154 he became King of England, and his French possessions continued to belong to the English crown until 1453 when the English were expelled from France. During that period Bordeaux wine was very popular in England, where it was known as claret. Even then, the quality was closely protected — anyone found stealing grapes lost an ear, as did anyone interfering with the wine or making sub-standard casks.

The surroundings of Bordeaux

The districts around Bordeaux are not all vineyards; in fact, only one-third of the agricultural area is planted with vines. To the east there is a varied landscape of rolling hills and plateaux including the valleys of the Garonne, Gironde and Dordogne. Narrow country roads lead to small villages, an occasional old town and to the wine châteaux, sometimes looking like farms and sometimes like real castles, but generally something in between. There is much woodland, too, chiefly to southwest of the city, on the flat region of Les Landes. Here you can wander for hours without meeting a fellow human being. Finally there is the sea coast, with its beaches and the lakes of Carcans and Lacanau. All in all, the surroundings of Bordeaux make up a very attractive area and a holiday in this region is greatly to be recommended. Many Bordelais have a little house in the country where they

The City of Bordeaux

spend the weekend and part of the summer. Shooting is a favourite occupation and in the *département* of Gironde more licences are issued than anywhere else. Roaming the woods can therefore be a risky venture, especially at weekends.

Official classifications and vintages

Below you will find the famous classification of 1855, which at present consists of 5 first growths, 14 second, 14 third, 10 fourth and 18 fifth — 61 altogether. It is noteworthy that up till now only one change has been made — in 1973, Château Mouton-Rothschild made the grade from the *deuxièmes* to the *premiers grands crus* — and that is all. However, this does not mean that everyone is entirely happy with the present listing, because a great deal can alter in 130 years or so. Owners come and go, and the land is exchanged. The existing classification therefore includes many examples of châteaux which deserve a higher place than their present position, and there are others which should be relegated (or perhaps even disappear entirely). Furthermore, time has not stood still elsewhere; in a number of cases wines are produced at unclassified châteaux which at a blind tasting can hold their own against the *grands crus*.

The reason why this classification of 1855 is still maintained is probably due to the virtual impossibility of drawing up a new one. It would therefore be wise not to pin blind faith in the classification or in the sequence of the individual châteaux included. The only really sensible criterion is the quality of the wine, not the name on the label. A good adviser is therefore worth his weight in gold. After all, he knows which wines are worth their high price, and which not.

Breakdown by price

The potential price commanded by the wines was the most important factor on which the 1855 classification was based. It was simply argued that the best wines fetched the best prices. The selection was made by the wine brokers of Bordeaux, and the Chamber of Commerce enforced it for the World Exhibition in Paris, despite the fact that a similar listing had already been adopted by the brokers for many years previously. The first lists, in fact, date back to the beginning of the 18th century. So this was no more

than official recognition of an existing situation.

For the sake of completeness, it should also be mentioned that 21 sweet white Sauternes wines were classified in addition to the Médocs and the Château Haut-Brion (the only Graves château to be included).

Premiers crus

Lafite-Rothschild, Pauillac
Latour, Pauillac
Margaux, Margaux
Mouton-Rothschild, Pauillac
Haut-Brion (Graves), Pessac

Deuxièmes crus

Rausan-Ségla, Margaux
Rauzan-Gassies, Margaux
Léoville-Las-Cases, St Julien
Léoville-Poyferré, St Julien
Léoville-Barton, St Julien
Durfort-Vivens, Margaux
Gruaud-Larose, St Julien
Lascombes, Margaux
Brane-Cantenac, Cantenac
Pichon-Longueville, Pauillac
Pichon-Lalande, Pauillac
Ducru-Beaucaillou, St Julien
Cos d'Estournel, St Estèphe
Montrose, St Estèphe

Troisièmes crus

Kirwan, Cantenac
d'Issan, Cantenac
Lagrange, St Julien
Langoa-Barton, St Julien
Giscours, Labarde
Malescot-St Exupéry, Margaux
Cantenac-Brown, Cantenac
Boyd-Cantenac, Cantenac
Palmer, Cantenac
La Lagune, Ludon
Desmirail, Margaux
Calon-Ségur, St Estèphe
Ferrière, Margaux
Marquis d'Alesme-Becker, Margaux

Quatrièmes crus

St Pierre, St Julien
Talbot, St Julien
Branaire-Ducru, St Julien
Duhart-Milon-Rothschild, Pauillac
Pouget, Cantenac
La Tour Carnet, St Laurent
Lafon-Rochet, St Estèphe
Beychevelle, St Julien
Prieuré-Lichine, Cantenac
Marquis de Terme, Margaux

Cinquièmes crus

Pontet Canet, Pauillac
Batailley, Pauillac
Haut-Batailley, Pauillac
Grand-Puy-Lacoste, Pauillac
Grand-Puy-Ducasse, Pauillac
Lynch-Bages, Pauillac
Lynch-Moussas, Pauillac
Dauzac, Labarde
Mouton Baronne Philippe, Pauillac
du Tertre, Arsac
Haut-Bages-Libéral, Pauillac
Pédesclaux, Pauillac
Belgrave, St Laurent
de Camensac, St Laurent
Cos Labory, St Estèphe
Clerc Milon, Pauillac
Croizet-Bages, Pauillac
Cantemerle, Macau

Red and white Graves

It is odd that apart from Château Haut-Brion no other red Graves is mentioned in the 1855 classification. The vineyards in this district are Bordeaux's oldest. Perhaps they happened to be going through a difficult period and were getting less per *tonneau* than the five *crus* from Médoc, or perhaps there was some discrimination. Be that as it may, the Graves châteaux have now received a classification of their own. After much preparation and an even longer wait, it was enforced by ministerial order on 16 February 1959. Both red and white wines are classified, with the result that certain

Right:
The little town of Pauillac
under extreme weather
conditions — just after a heavy
thunderstorm.

Official classifications and vintages

châteaux have earned a place for both (in Graves both red and white wines are often made). The sensible step was taken of not creating a hierarchy between the châteaux. Haut-Brion is also included among them.

Crus classés: Red

Bouscaut, Cadaujac
Haut Bailly, Léognan
Domaine de Chevalier, Léognan
Carbonnieux, Léognan
de Fieuzal, Léognan
Malartic-Lagravière, Leognan
Olivier, Léognan
La Tour Martillac, Martillac
Smith Haut Lafitte, Martillac
Haut Brion, Pessac
Pape Clément, Pessac
La Mission-Haut-Brion, Talence
La Tour-Haut-Brion, Talence

Crus classés, White

Bouscaut, Cadaujac
Domaine de Chevalier, Léognan
Carbonnieux, Léognan
Malartic-Lagravière, Léognan
Olivier, Léognan
La Tour Martillac, Martillac
Laville-Haut-Brion, Talence
Couhins, Villenave-d'Ornon

St Emilion and Pomerol

St Emilion and Pomerol do not appear, either, in the 1855 classification. As in the case of Graves, St Emilion now has its own classification. However, in Pomerol they have not yet got that far, so there is no official classification as yet in this little district (although there is a semi-official one headed by Château Pétrus). It is clear from the ranking adopted for St Emilion that the classifications for the various districts should never, on any account, be compared with one another.
There is, in fact, no objective criterion for using the term *grand cru*. Every district interprets this in its own way, so that a *grand cru* from St Emilion need in no way be equivalent to a wine with the same title from Médoc or Graves. What exactly is the position at St Emilion? Someone once wrote that this district has so many *grands crus* that you could compare it with a South American Republic — there are almost more generals than soldiers. Since 1969, St Emilion has 83 *grands crus classés* of which 12 are entitled to call themselves *premier grand cru classé* (with Ausone and Cheval Blanc in class A and the rest in class B). In addition, there are also the *grands crus*, a fluctuating rather than a fixed classification. In fact, it is awarded from one vintage to the next, after sampling. In 1971, the examiners tasted 244 candidate wines, 234 being ultimately assigned *grand cru* status. Of the 1970 vintage, therefore, no less than 317 *grands crus de St Emilion* were put into circulation, in three different categories. This accounts for nearly one-third of all the châteaux in the district! The classification is reviewed every 10 years, although those of 1969 still apply in 1983.

Premiers grands crus classés A

Ausone, St Emilion
Cheval Blanc, St Emilion

Premiers grands crus classés B

Beauséjour Duffau-Lagarrosse, St Emilion
Beau-Séjour Bécot, St Emilion
Belair, St Emilion
Canon, St Emilion
Clos Fourtet, St Emilion
Figeac, St Emilion
La Gaffelière, St Emilion
Magdelaine, St Emilion
Pavie, St Emilion
Trottevieille, St Emilion

Grands crus classés

L'Angélus, St Emilion
l'Arrosée, St Emilion
Balestard-La Tonnelle, St Emilion
Bellevue, St Emilion
Bergat, St Emilion
Cadet-Bon, St Emilion
Cadet-Piola, St Emilion
Canon-La Gaffelière, St Emilion
Cap de Mourlin, Saint Emilion (2x)
Chapelle-Madeleine, St Emilion
Chauvin, St Emilion
Corbin, St Emilion
Corbin-Michotte, St Emilion
Côte Baleau, St Emilion
Coutet, St Emilion
Couvent-des-Jacobins, St Emilion
Croque-Michotte, St Emilion
Curé-Bon, St Emilion
Dassault, St Emilion
Faurie-de-Souchard, St Emilion
Fonplégade, St Emilion
Fonroque, St Emilion
Franc-Mayne, St Emilion
Grand-Barrail-Lamarzelle-Figeac, St Emilion
Grand-Corbin, St Emilion
Grand-Corbin-Despagne, St Emilion
Grand-Mayne, St Emilion
Grand-Pontet, St Emilion
Grandes-Murailles, St Emilion
Guadet-Saint-Julien, St Emilion
Haut-Corbin, St Emilion
Haut-Sarpe, St Emilion
Jean-Faure, St Emilion
La Carte, St Emilion
La Clotte, St Emilion
La Cluzière, St Emilion
La Couspaude, St Emilion
La Dominique, St Emilion
Lamarzelle, St Emilion
Laniote, St Emilion
Larcis-Ducasse, St Emilion
Larmande, St Emilion
Laroze, St Emilion
La Serre, St Emilion
La Tour-du-Pin-Figeac (Bélivier), St Emilion
La Tour-du-Pin-Figeac (Moueix), St Emilion
La Tour-Figeac, St Emilion
Le Châtelet, St Emilion
Le Couvent, St Emilion
Le Prieuré, St Emilion
Matras, St Emilion
Mauvezin, St Emilion
Moulin-du-Cadet, St Emilion

The list of official appellations
d'origine contrôlées of
Bordeaux:

Médoc
St Estèphe (red)
Pauillac (red)
St Julien (red)
*Moulis or Moulis-en-Médoc
(red)*
Listrac (red)
Margaux (red)
Haut-Médoc (red)
Médoc (red)
*Wines which do not completely
fulfil the requirements of their
appellation can sometimes be
moved to lower appellations
such as Haut-Médoc, Médoc,
Bordeaux Supérieur and
Bordeaux.*

**Graves, Gérons, Sauternes and
Barsac**
Cérons (white)
Barsac (white)
Sauternes (white)
Graves (red)
Graves (white)
Graves supérieurs (white)

*Wines which do not completely
fulfil the requirements of their
appellation can sometimes be
moved to lower appellations,
such as Cérons to Graves
supérieurs, Bordeaux supérieur
and Bordeaux; Barsac to
Sauternes, Bordeaux supérieur
and Bordeaux; the others to
Bordeaux.*

Right bank of the Garonne
St Croix-du-Mont (white)
Loupiac (white)
*Côtes de Bordeaux-St Macaire
(white)*
Cadillac (white)
*Premières Côtes de Bordeaux
(red)*
*Premières Côtes de Bordeaux
(white)*
*Wines which do not completely
fulfil the requirements of their
appellation can sometimes be
moved to lower appellations
such as Bordeaux supérieur
and Bordeaux.*

Official classifications and vintages

Pavie-Decesse, St Emilion
Pavie-Macquin, St Emilion
Pavillon-Cadet, St Emilion
Petit-Faurie-de-Soutard, St Emilion
Ripeau, St Emilion
Saint-Georges-Côte-Pavie, St Emilion
Sansonnet, St Emilion
Soutard, St Emilion
Tertre-Daugay, St Emilion
Trimoulet, St Emilion
Trois-Moulins, St Emilion
Troplong-Mondot, St Emilion
Villemaurine, St Emilion
Yon-Figeac, St Emilion
Clos des Jacobins, St Emilion
Clos La Madeleine, St Emilion
Clos de l'Oratoire, St Emilion
Clos Saint-Martin, St Emilion

Appellations contrôlées

It is particularly important when buying
Bordeaux wines to note the precise origin
(*appellation*) if only because some quite
famous châteaux have namesakes in other
districts which carry much less weight. For
example, Château Cantemerle in Blaye is
something quite different from Château
Cantemerle in Macau. Similarly, the
Domaine de Beychevelle from St André-de-
Cubzac cannot be compared with Château
Beychevelle from St Julien. Then there are
10 *domaines* incorporating the name
Beauséjour, 19 starting with the prefix
Vieux-Château, 5 with Latour in their name,
and 6 with Lafite or Lafitte. So, look to the
right name and *appellation*. Besides, if a
wine wishes to call itself an *appellation
d'origine contrôlée*, i.e. an officially approved
place of origin, certain legal requirements
must be met. The wine has to come from an
area specifically defined and indicated, from
certain varieties of prescribed grapes,
planted and processed according to certain
methods, and not produce more than so
many hectolitres (100 litres) per hectare (or
acre). In addition, the wine-making
procedure is subject to regulations and the
wine must have a minimum alcohol content.
The *appellation contrôlée* (always mentioned

on the label) is therefore a guarantee of
origin, i.e. the wine is what it claims to be,
and to a certain degree a guarantee of
quality, indicating that the wine has been
made according to the rules applying to its
appellation. At the top of this and the next
page you will find a list of the *appellations* in
the Bordeaux region.

The vintages

A wine dealer in Bordeaux once told me,
'Over here, the growers are nearly always
pessimistic about the next crop. They hope it
will help to raise the prices of previous years.
If you are to believe them, the first quarter of
the crop fails entirely, the second quarter is
lost by night frost, the third quarter a
hailstorm, the fourth you can forget because
it has rotted, and they finally harvest the
fifth quarter . . .!' The talk is all of the the
vintage. Forecasts are made months before
the grapes are picked or have even begun to
ripen, and they increase apace as the
moment of picking approaches. Once the
wine has been made, the public are deluged
with adjectives — and so, for many people,
the vintage concerned is immediately and
irrevocably confirmed or condemned. Alas,
little account is taken of the fact that it is
very difficult to assess a wine for the first
few months after harvesting. Even the
château experts will not commit themselves
so soon.
How difficult it is to assess a wine's true
quality early on is clear from the fact that
many years tend to be initially over- or
under-valued. As examples I might mention
the many 'years of the century' (how many
are still to come before the year 2000?) and
1966, which some experts once considered
inferior to 1967. Of course, the quality of a
particular year is sooner or later correctly
gauged, but it must still be viewed with
great circumspection. Because, after all,
what exactly does such an assessment
amount to? Nothing more, in fact, than a
broad common denominator, an overall
impression, a general average with
exceptions above and below.

This applies particularly to Bordeaux,
because it is France's largest area for quality
wine. Here, some 25,000 growers produce
between 39 million and 65½ million cases of
wine a year within an area of about 260,000
acres, approximately 15 times that of the
Côte d'Or, 9 times that of Alsace and 7 times
that of Champagne. The wine produced is
then distributed among 28 different
appellations for red and 18 for white. It is
clearly impossible, therefore, to group all
these various wines adequately under a
single heading.

Many variants

All this must be borne in mind when
consulting the brief descriptions of the
vintages on the next page. Good wines are
also made in every poor year, and poor wines
in every good one. Grower A, for example,
may have gathered his grapes just before the
rain started, but grower B did not. Grower C,
on the other hand, decides to wait with
picking in the hope that the rain will be over
quickly and the sun shine again. Grower D
has little left to harvest because a hailstorm
destroyed two-thirds of his crop a month
ago. So, each year, there are countless
variations — some growers who have been in
luck, others who have not, some who have
been prudent, others who have lacked
judgment. This applies all the more so in an
année jalouse (such as 1974). The quality of
wines will then differ widely and many
growers are understandably jealous of
neighbours who have fared better. In such
years the utmost demands are made on the
skills of the merchants and importers. They
have to sort out wheat from the chaff to
protect their customers from bad bargains.
The moral of this story is that there are no
years with good wines only and none with
poor wines only. There are always
exceptions, always cases of 'in between'.
The overall assessment of vintages below
has been drawn up with help from experts
from the various districts.

Between Garonne and Dordogne
Ste Foy-Bordeaux (red)
Ste Foy-Bordeaux (white)
Graves de Vayres (red)
Graves de Vayres (white)
Entre-Deux-Mers (white)
Entre-Deux-Mers-Haut-Benauge (white)
Bordeaux-Haut-Benauge (white)
Wines which do not completely fulfil the requirements of their appellation can sometimes be moved to lower appellations such as Bordeaux.

St Emilion and Pomerol
St Emilion (red)
Sables-St Emilion (red)
Montagne-St Emilion (red)
Lussac-St Emilion (red)
Parsac-St Emilion (red)
St Georges-St Emilion (red)
Puisseguin-St Emilion (red)
Pomerol (red)
Néac (red)
Lalande-de-Pomerol (red)
Wines which do not completely fulfil the requirements of their

appellation can sometimes be moved to lower appellations such as Bordeaux supérieur and Bordeaux.

Other wines of the right bank of the Dordogne
Bordeaux-Côtes de Castillon (red)
Bordeaux-Côtes de Francs (red)
Côtes de Canon-Fronsac (red)
Côtes de Fronsac (red)
Bourg or Côtes de Bourg or Bourgeais (red)
Bourg or Côtes de Bourg or Bourgeais (white)
Premières Côtes de Blaye (red)
Premières Côtes de Blaye (white)
Côtes de Blaye (white)
Blaye or Blayais (red)
Blaye or Blayais (white)
Wines which do not completely fulfil the requirements of their appellation can sometimes be moved to lower appellations such as the first four to Bordeaux supérieur and Bordeaux; the Bourg to

Bordeaux; the Premières Côtes de Blaye to Blayais and Bordeaux; and the Côtes de Blaye to Blayais.

Official classifications and vintages

Médoc and Red Graves

1945 Noteworthy year of very high quality
1946 Light wines, now too old
1947 A great year of harmony and fullness
1948 Very successful, with full-bodied wines
1949 Like 1948, but with better reputation
1950 Wines surprising for their keeping quality and class; abundant harvest
1951 Moderate year, doubtful quality
1952 Very sturdy wines, slow development, homogeneous quality
1953 Despite difficult ripening, very balanced wines with both body and subtlety
1954 Average year, nothing more
1955 Powerful, sturdy wines; very good, but lacking body
1956 Year of destructive frost, virtually poor wines only with much acid.
1957 Small harvest of wines which retained their hardness, now maturing
1958 A little below average
1959 Small harvest, great commercial success; excellent now, after a difficult start
1960 Light, easy-going, pleasant wine
1961 Hot summer, undoubtedly the year of the century — the wines are remarkable
1962 Generous harvest which developed to perfection; fine wines now
1963 Very moderate, subject to exceptions
1964 After a fine summer, heavy rain after harvesting, so very irregular — the good wines are balanced and aromatic
1965 Probably the poorest year of the century
1966 A fine summer producing some sturdy wines; very good year
1967 Much larger harvest than 1966, the wine faster-developing and more subtle
1968 Light wines maturing very quickly
1969 Fairly light wines generally which are nevertheless developing very well
1970 An excellent year for quality; a sturdy wine, worth waiting for
1971 Wines with charm, relatively strong; they are developing nicely
1972 A wine with acidity but also much bouquet; maturing well
1973 Irregular, very heavy harvest; subtle, elegant wines, somewhat lacking distinction but with charm
1974 More colour and tannin than 1973 but clearly less body and charm; plentiful and fairly irregular
1975 Excellent harvest with full, concentrated wines requiring much patience, perhaps even better than 1970
1976 An undervalued year after the glorious 1975, with fairly generous, relatively soft

wines to be drunk before the 1975s; they have been compared with 1962
1977 Disappointingly small crop with many moderate, thin wines but some pleasant surprises as well; less acid than 1972
1978 This year is put between 1974 and 1976 for quality; a wet summer was followed by a very sunny autumn
1979 A good, abundant harvest, bears comparison with 1973
1980 Small quantity, rather light wines; undervalued
1981 Colourful, concentrated wines with a lot of charm and class
1982 Exceptionally abundant harvest with even more colour and strength than 1981; low acidity but a lot of tannin

St Emilion and Pomerol

1945 A warm year, very good, rather hard
1946 Lean wine, now too old
1947 A great year, full wine, now at its best
1948 A relatively fine year, often too old
1949 A great year of pure harmony
1950 An average year, now too old
1951 A cramped year, also past its best
1952 Relatively good year, but with variable quality
1953 Certainly a good year but the wines are now past their best
1954 An average year
1955 Fairly irregular, but good bottles to be found
1956 No production of significance
1957 No production of significance
1958 No production of significance
1959 A reasonably successful year but certainly not up to its reputation
1960 Relatively light wines but jaunty
1961 Here, too, an extraordinarily great year with well-bodied, full wines; can mature for 20 years
1962 A happy surprise after the success of 1961, a good year
1963 Minimal in every respect
1964 Seemed promising but relatively disappointing so far; a flat, hard wine
1965 A very weak year
1966 Tending to be heavy, but with a good future
1967 Wines of some charm which are developing faster than the 1966s
1968 Generally a fairly weak year but some agreeable bottles can be found
1969 A year that promised more than it delivered; the wine is on the light side
1970 Really outstanding; very good, powerful, heavy wines, for laying down

1971 Really very good and fine, an excellent, agreeable surprise
1972 A misleading year with acidity; with moderate maturing
1973 An irregular harvest: the wine could be a little more full, but relatively fine
1974 This year, too, shows great differences in quality; the better wines surpass those of 1973
1975 A very great year with long-lived wines
1976 Fruity, subtle wines with charm, maturing faster than the wines of 1975
1977 A disastrous year with a small crop but still better in quality than 1972
1978 The splendid autumn saved many after a sad summer; good quality is in any event expected
1979 A good, abundant year often more successful here than at Médoc
1980 Small yield of varying standard; appears slightly better in Pomerol
1981 A good amount of generous, even great wines
1982 A lot of strength and alcohol in the Merlot and thus also in the wines of this high-yielding, impressive year

The wine trade

Foreign influence on the trade in Bordeaux wines has always been great. Not only were the wines of Bordeaux carried by English and Dutch ships to all corners of the earth, but many foreigners set up in Bordeaux as wine merchants. Many of today's famous trade names have a non-French origin. In his book *Le Vignoble Bordelais*, Philippe Roudie mentions that the house of Beyerman is the oldest. It was established in the first half of the 18th century by a Dutchman. Then came Thomas Barton from Ireland (1725), William Johnston from England (1734) and Jean-Henry Schyler from Germany (1739). The wine trade prospered greatly in the 19th century so that more and more people began to ply the trade of *négociant en vins*. Between 1855 and 1870 hundreds of firms, large and small, most of which still exist, were established in the city.

Guillaume Mestrezat came from Geneva and opened up in 1815, Leon Hanappier from Orleans (1816), Herman Cruse from Denmark (1819), Alfred de Luze from Germany (1829), Jean-Marie Calvet from Tain-l'Hermitage in France (1823), Eschenauer from Alsace (1831), the Frenchman Dourthe (1840), etc. At the end of the 19th century and early in the 20th century they were joined by, amongst others, the Frenchmen Delor, Ginestet and Cordier, and the Dutchman Mahler.

Radical changes in the trade

The rôle played by the trade was particularly important in establishing the international reputation of Bordeaux wines. Initially, the shippers purchased the young wines in wood from the châteaux, and took them to their cellars where they matured them. Such traders were also called *négociants-éleveurs* because they in fact had a double function. The contact between the houses and producers was the *courtier* or wine broker. The position has now changed. The houses no longer have the capacity to finance large stocks for long periods and the leading châteaux now store, mature and bottle the wine themselves. The function of the broker is becoming less important as more direct contact is made between shipper and grower. Furthermore, commission agents are being increasingly successful. They work directly with the growers or through brokers, keep no stocks, and maintain only small stores. The most recent trend in Bordeaux is that of direct sales by the châteaux themselves, either to casual visitors or by mail order. Nobody knows how the rôle of the trade will develop, but those who wish to make headway in the turbulent market for Bordeaux will have to become increasingly aware of modern marketing techniques.

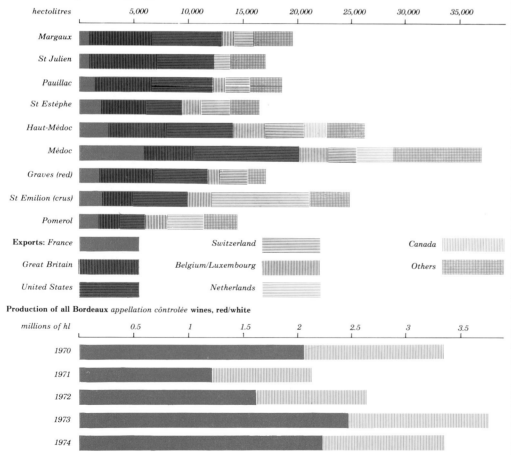

Production and exports in 1973, per *appellation*

Production of all **Bordeaux** *appellation côntrolée* wines, red/white

Production of all Bordeaux wines: 5.5 million hectolitres (1970), of which 48% red and 52% white.

Production of all French wines: 74 million hectolitres (1970), of which 75% red and 25% white.

The Châteaux

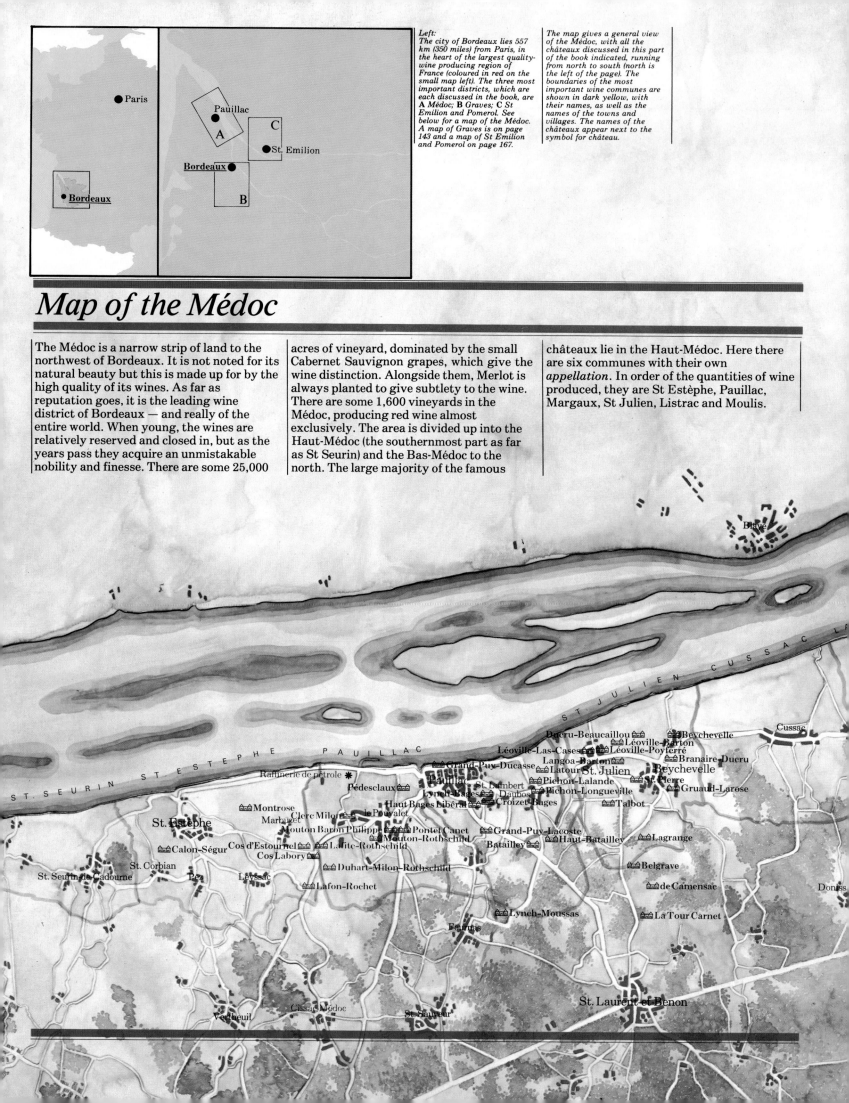

Left:
*The city of Bordeaux lies 557 km (350 miles) from Paris, in the heart of the largest quality-wine producing region of France (coloured in red on the small map left). The three most important districts, which are each discussed in the book, are **A** Médoc; **B** Graves; **C** St Emilion and Pomerol. See below for a map of the Médoc. A map of Graves is on page 143 and a map of St Emilion and Pomerol on page 167.*

The map gives a general view of the Médoc, with all the châteaux discussed in this part of the book indicated, running from north to south (north is to the left of the page). The boundaries of the most important wine communes are shown in dark yellow, with their names, as well as the names of the towns and villages. The names of the châteaux appear next to the symbol for château.

Paris

Pauillac

A

St. Emilion

C

Bordeaux

Bordeaux

B

Map of the Médoc

The Médoc is a narrow strip of land to the northwest of Bordeaux. It is not noted for its natural beauty but this is made up for by the high quality of its wines. As far as reputation goes, it is the leading wine district of Bordeaux — and really of the entire world. When young, the wines are relatively reserved and closed in, but as the years pass they acquire an unmistakable nobility and finesse. There are some 25,000 acres of vineyard, dominated by the small Cabernet Sauvignon grapes, which give the wine distinction. Alongside them, Merlot is always planted to give subtlety to the wine. There are some 1,600 vineyards in the Médoc, producing red wine almost exclusively. The area is divided up into the Haut-Médoc (the southernmost part as far as St Seurin) and the Bas-Médoc to the north. The large majority of the famous châteaux lie in the Haut-Médoc. Here there are six communes with their own *appellation*. In order of the quantities of wine produced, they are St Estèphe, Pauillac, Margaux, St Julien, Listrac and Moulis.

Blaye

ST. JULIEN CUSSAC LA

ST. SEURIN ST. ESTEPHE PAUILLAC

Raffinerie de pétrole ✳

Ducru-Beaucaillou

Beychevelle

Léoville-Las-Cases

Léoville-Barton

Léoville-Poyferré

Cussac

Grand-Puy-Ducasse

Langoa-Barton

Latour St. Julien

Branaire-Ducru

Beychevelle

Pédesclaux

Pauillac

St. Lambert

Pichon-Lalande

St. Pierre

Gruaud-Larose

Lynch-Bages

Daubos

Pichon-Longueville

Haut Bages Libéral

Croizet-Bages

Talbot

Montrose

Clerc Milon

le Pouyalet

Marbuzet

Mouton Baron Philippe

Pontet Canet

Grand-Puy-Lacoste

St. Estèphe

Mouton-Rothschild

Batailley

Haut-Batailley

Lagrange

Calon-Ségur

Cos d'Estournel

Lafite-Rothschild

Cos Labory

St. Corbian

Belgrave

St. Seurin de Cadourne

Pez

Leyssac

Duhart-Milon-Rothschild

de Camensac

Doniss

Lafon-Rochet

La Tour Carnet

Lynch-Moussas

Fonras

St. Laurent-et-Benon

Verteuil

Cissac-Médoc

St. Sauveur

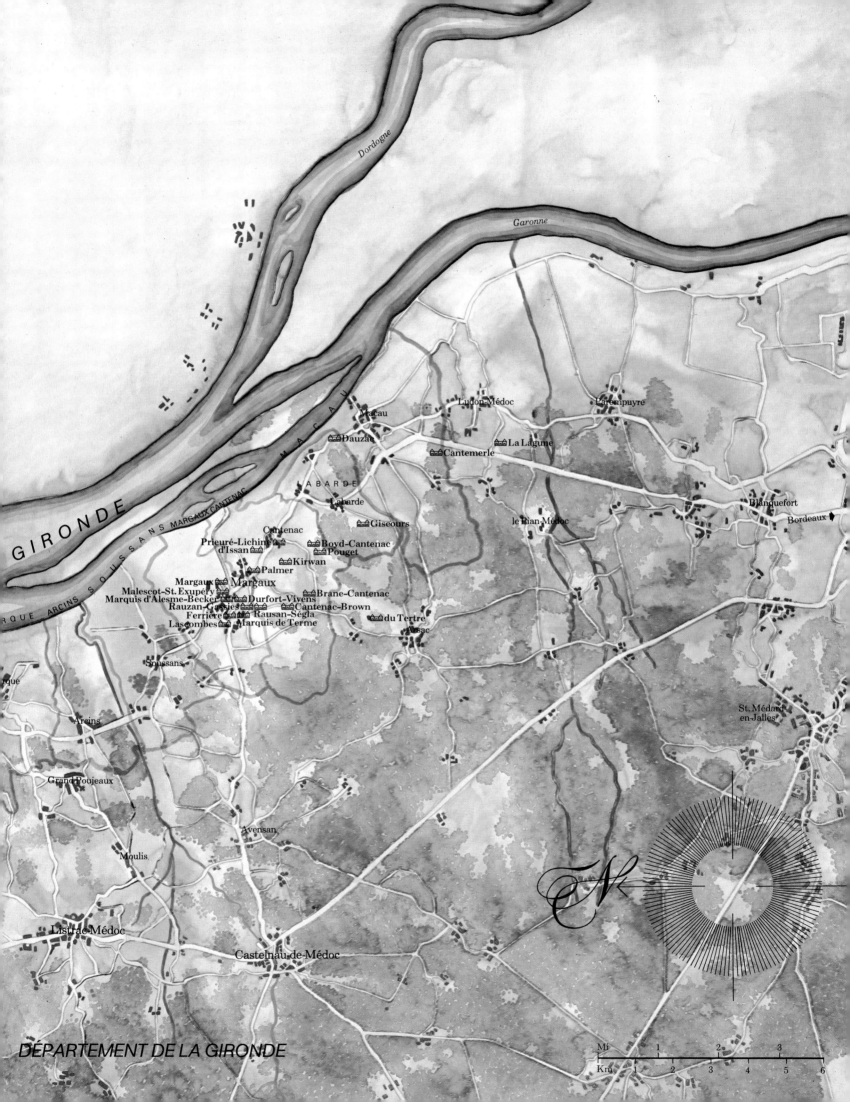

DÉPARTEMENT DE LA GIRONDE

GRAND CRU CLASSÉ

CHATEAU LA LAGUNE
HAUT·MÉDOC
APPELLATION HAUT·MÉDOC CONTROLÉE
1970
SOCIÉTÉ CIVILE AGRICOLE DU CHATEAU LA LAGUNE
PROPRIÉTAIRE A LUDON (GIRONDE) FRANCE

MIS EN BOUTEILLE AU CHATEAU

Château La Lagune

3e Grand Cru Classé

Should you have forgotten what is the most important product of Château La Lagune you will soon be reminded of it by the large wrought-iron entrance gate: real corkscrews are incorporated in it. Other fine examples of the ironwork can be admired inside the perimeter fence, such as the balustrades of the terrace steps and the brackets for the outdoor lamps. Everything is spotless, with not a speck of dirt in sight. Even the woodshed, which ordinary visitors never see, is clean and nicely tidied. But then, it is a woman who has charge of La Lagune. Her name is Mme J. Boyrie and she works from a small office. This tough little lady has been *régisseuse* since 1964, the year when her husband, who managed the vineyard, died. Mme Boyrie does a marvellous job. Not only does she manage 47 permanent staff but she also knows how to make an excellent wine, which often deserves more than its official status of *troisième cru*.

Contemporary approach

That has not always been the case. Although the estate had a great name in the 18th and 19th centuries, a serious decline set in during the present century. Production fell to 15 *tonneaux* and the quality to less than acceptable for a classified wine. Then an idealist, Georges Brunet, bought the dilapidated property in 1958, in order to start making a *grand vin* again. He began replanting on a large scale and installed the most modern fermentation vats. He then organized a system for transferring the wine from vat to cask and racking from cask to cask entirely by means of pipes. Unfortunately, his enormous investment failed to show a profit soon enough and M. Brunet had to sell up in 1961. (It is worth mentioning that he went to live in Provence, where he now produces an excellent red wine, Château Vignelaure.) The present owner of

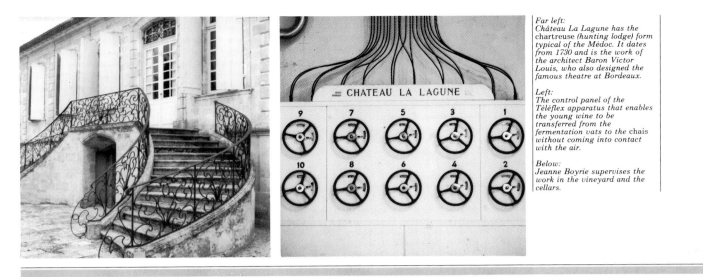

Far left:
Château La Lagune has the chartreuse (hunting lodge) form typical of the Médoc. It dates from 1730 and is the work of the architect Baron Victor Louis, who also designed the famous theatre at Bordeaux.

Left:
The control panel of the Téléflex apparatus that enables the young wine to be transferred from the fermentation vats to the chais without coming into contact with the air.

Below:
Jeanne Boyrie supervises the work in the vineyard and the cellars.

Château La Lagune

La Lagune is the champagne house of Ayala, which has happily fortunately continued Georges Brunet's work in effervescent style, first through *régisseur* Boyrie and, later, his widow.

Sandy soil

La Lagune is the first *grand cru* encountered approaching the Médoc from Bordeaux. The *appellation contrôlée* is Haut Médoc. At some points the vineyard adjoins that of Cantemerle, but even so the wines are quite different. That is due to the particular soil on which the vines grow at La Lagune. It is sandy rather than gravelly; at certain places water is found only one metre down. Also unusual for southern Médoc, this vineyard of 140 acres consists of a single piece and is not scattered over several small plots. The percentage of Cabernet grapes is relatively high — 50% Cabernet Sauvignon, 25% Cabernet Franc, 20% Merlot and 5% Petit Verdot. This undoubtedly helps to give the wines of La Lagune long life. The yield is 128 *tonneaux* (1977) to 300 (1982).

A whiff of woody undergrowth

For the first few years following renovation of the vineyard, the La Lagune wines were much lighter than they are nowadays. The only bottle from this château which I ever found disappointing was in fact a 1960. 1962 was an extraordinarily good year. Since 1966 La Lagune has been producing powerful wines which often require much patience but which is richly rewarded. The abundant yield of 1966 is now gradually becoming drinkable. It has developed into a complex, elegant wine which, in spite of its ripeness, still has a future. It is a characteristic of La Lagune that this château has never put a poor wine on the

market. This was apparent in such vintages as 1974, 1977 and 1980, which were all successful for their year. The great years produce great wines here. Excellent examples of this are the vintages of 1970, 1971, 1975, 1978, 1981 and 1982 (already sold out in 1983). Another feature of the wines from La Lagune is their balance; they almost always have a solid structure and good body. They are usually stronger than other wines from the southern Médoc. In addition to the scents of wood and berries — all the casks are renewed annually there — their perfume also recalls the smell of woody undergrowth after rain. This sound Haut-Médoc is clarified with the white of fresh eggs and is never filtered.

APPELLATION HAUT-MÉDOC CONTROLÉE

1970
CHÂTEAU CANTEMERLE
GRAND CRU CLASSÉ DE MÉDOC

Héritiers Pierre J. DUBOS, Propriétaires   Macau-en-Médoc

Left and below:
The château has been enlarged several times. The earliest part can be identified by the small round turret between the main building and the large tower on the left. Originally Cantemerle was a simple rectangular structure with two wings built at right angles. The two towers were added next, then the large centre section.

Bottom:
In the cuvier heavy equipment can be moved on a trolley that runs on rails between the oak fermentation vats. In this instance the trolley was filled with cases of wine: a sight to make you thirsty.

Château Cantemerle

Cantemerle hides well away from its visitors, for the château cannot be seen from the road and is approached by nearly half a mile of avenue through a thickly wooded park. Even then the main building is difficult to discern on a summer's day, concealed as it is behind two gigantic plane trees. Architecturally, Château Cantemerle is hardly a model of perfect balance since its various owners have added bits ever since the 16th century, according to their own taste and inclination.

Once a bulwark of tradition

When I first visited Cantemerle, I felt as if time had stood still for generations. There

Château Cantemerle

was no sound or glimpse of traffic, the *salons* of the château breathed the spirit of ages past and in the half-light of the *chais* workers were imperturbably topping up the oaken casks. In the *gérant*'s dim, dark-brown office, with its gigantic leather armchairs, there were many old books and several old paintings. I was shown a parchment dating from 1573 — a 15-foot-long deed of sale — one of the château treasures. Cantemerle was once a bulwark of tradition, where the wine was made by ancient, well-tried methods. The grapes were still de-stalked and de-pipped by hand, only timber fermentation vats were used, and all bottling was done manually. The bottles were filled straight from the cask one by one, and there was earth on the floor and grey mould on the ceilings of the ancient cellars.

Large investment

All that is now in the past. In the autumn of 1980 Cantemerle was bought from the Clauzel family by the Goulet-Turpin company (foodstuffs, property, restaurants, etc.), and Jean Cordier also acquired shares in it. In fact, the estate is now managed by the house of Cordier and the wine is marketed exclusively by that firm. A massive renovation programme was begun immediately after the take-over. The vineyard, which had been reduced to 55 acres, was greatly expanded. At present, there are almost 130 acres of vines and it is hoped to increase this area to 155 acres. The grape varieties are 40% Cabernet Sauvignon, 40% Merlot, 18% Cabernet Franc and 2% Petit Verdot. These percentages are almost identical to those at the time of the takeover.

New cellars

The *cuvier* was also renewed. The wine is no longer left to ferment in wooden vats but in rust-proof steel tanks. The vats, however, were kept in case they were needed for wine storage. Completely new cellars were built to a very careful and attractive design. The roof is supported by heavy beams, while the side

walls have been constructed using traditional methods and materials. New machinery was also installed, such as a mechanical *fouloir-égrappoir*, a horizontal press, modern tractors, etc.
In brief, no effort was spared, after the 1970s, during which decade its wines were sometimes a little below standard, to restore the reputation of Château Cantemerle.

A successful start

The revival of Cantemerle has already been reflected in the first two years of its new management. The 1980 vintage has a very deep, dark colour, outstandingly so for the year, and a strong woody presence in both fragrance and taste, with a high level of tannin. The 1981 was almost black when very young; it is a concentrated wine, with plenty of fruit, tannin and suppleness. Finesse and elegance tend to prevail over fatness and fleshiness, although the wines can and must ripen for a long time because of their initial strength.

Last place in the classification

Château Cantemerle was the last of the fifth *crus* in the official classification of 1855 and thus right at the bottom of the tables. Some say that the château had simply been forgotten and that it was quickly added at the very last minute. This sounds likely, for the name of Cantemerle is scrawled in small and untidy lettering at the foot of the original document, while all the other château names are listed in careful, well-rounded handwriting. Cantemerle has always felt this low position to be unjustified, and many unprejudiced outsiders agree. In the *Bordeaux et ses Vins* of 1893, for instance, it states that wine from Cantemerle cost 10% more than wine of the other fifth *crus*.

Two families

The character of Cantemerle has been determined by two families: Villeneuve and

Dubos. It was Jean de Villeneuve, second president of the parliament of Bordeaux, who bought Cantemerle at the end of the 16th century. The estate is said to have remained in the family for almost 300 years. At the end of the 19th century the estate passed first to Théophile-J. Dubos and later to Pierre J. Dubos, a rather remarkable man. The great attention he paid to detail was recognized on 4 April 1949 by a group of Dutch wine importers who presented him with a fine Delft plate bearing his motto, 'Vinification consists of a large number of small problems'. This principle is still honoured in the Cantemerle of today; the wine is produced with great attention to detail and has very clearly risen since 1980 far above the level of that unmerited last place more than a century ago.

Château du Tertre

5e Grand Cru Classé

To reach the Château du Tertre, take the winding road towards Arsac, a few miles into the hinterland of Margaux. At one point a large hill (*tertre* in French) entirely planted with vines suddenly appears on the left beyond the scattering of trees. This is the vineyard of Château de Tertre. The buildings lie at the top of the hill, at the end of a rutted track. The château itself is ash-white in colour and seems almost abandoned; in fact, it is at present unoccupied. The *chais*, on the other hand, look well cared for and the vineyard, too, is neat and tidy. It used to be different, because Château du Tertre is one of the many *grand crus* which went through a difficult period during and after the Second World War. It began to recover its reputation in 1962 when Philippe Capbern-Gasqueton acquired the property. M. Gasqueton is a *viticulteur* through and through. His family has been growing wine in the Médoc since before the French Revolution. Another of Philippe Gasqueton's possessions is the *grand cru* of Calon-Ségur at St Estèphe, farther north, whose wines are world famous. When the Château du Tertre changed owners, M. Gasqueton and his daughter, a qualified oenologist, began to restore the vineyard and renovate the buildings, fermentation vats and other apparatus. He left the main building standing as it was. He and his family were already living in the consummate comfort of Château Capbern-Gasqueton, immediately behind the Church of St Estèphe.

Low yield

The Tertre vineyard covers approximately 115 acres in a single block, a fairly unusual situation for a wine sold under the Margaux *appellation* because the vineyards in this commune are mostly widely scattered. Philippe Gasqueton has planted a great deal of Cabernet Sauvignon, some 80% of the total. The yield fluctuates between 70 and 120 *tonneaux*.
Because it is always a difficult business to restore the reputation of an estate that has suffered a decline, I asked M. Gasqueton

GRAND CRU CLASSÉ

CHATEAU DU TERTRE

—— 1967 ——

APPELLATION MARGAUX CONTROLÉE

MIS EN BOUTEILLES AU CHATEAU
SOCIÉTÉ CIVILE DU CHATEAU DU TERTRE
PROPRIÉTAIRE

Château du Tertre

whether he was doing anything special to publicize his wine. His answer was: 'All our publicity is really based on the *déclaration de la récolte*. If we announce how much wine we shall be selling as Château du Tertre, it gives the impression that we produce 30%-35% less wine per hectare than the other châteaux — indicative that we are placing the emphasis on quality.'

Built-in resistance to sea travel

The Tertre wines are very carefully made; and because the Cabernet Sauvignon plays a major rôle, they tend to retain a certain measure of hardness for a fairly long time. I remember the 1967 which had a fine, delicate bouquet, and a taste which in addition to an element of ripeness still had some rough edges as well. Like everything else with M. Gasqueton, this toughness can be explained. 'I noticed that wine shipped to the United States tended to age 12 months or so within that short period owing to the continuous rocking of the vessel. So I have tried to build a natural resistance into my wines for this ocean trip.' It is obvious from this that America is the Château du Tertre's chief customer. Britain, the Netherlands, France, Switzerland and Japan are also major buyers.

As the average age of the vines increases, a vineyard produces steadily better wine. I therefore left with the clear impression that the Tertre wines set higher standards each year in terms of quality. A striking example was the wine of the anything but superior year of 1972. M. Gasqueton succeeded in making a very pleasant wine with a good colour, bouquet and taste, and also some of charm. For Margaux 1972, the wine also has a fair measure of body, so that it appeared set for a longer life than its contemporaries. The 1971 I found to be simply a good wine with a decent amount of fruit on nose and taste. No particular refinement could (as yet) be noted and the same applies to the much more powerful wine of 1970. This had a very deep colour, a strong fruity bouquet and a closed, rather hard taste. I tasted these

wines at the château itself in 1975. Later vintages, assessed elsewhere, give the impression that the Château du Tertre wines have indeed improved in quality and at the same time lost some of their hardness. Consequently, in September 1980 the 1976 performed particularly well at a comparative tasting of all the classified Margaux wines. The wine had a fairly deep, soft red colour, a refined bouquet with a touch of vanilla, and a similarly refined, elegant taste with just a hint of oak. In terms of quality, 1979 was also a pleasant surprise.

Château Dauzac

In the second half of the 17th century, Ireland was hardly a safe place for the Catholic majority and so tens of thousands of people left the country. They were called the 'wild geese' because they flew off in all directions, though with a preference for France. It is estimated that between 1645 and 1690 some 40,000 Irish people settled permanently on French soil, many of them in the traditionally liberal refuge of Bordeaux. The most famous figure of Irish descent is undoubtedly Count Jean-Baptiste Lynch, who was Mayor of Bordeaux from 1809 to 1815. He was extremely popular locally and when, in 1815, he was promoted by Louis XVIII to membership of the *Chambre des Pairs* (House of Lords) the inhabitants of Bordeaux petitioned to be allowed to keep their leading citizen. The king relented and permitted Jean-Baptiste Lynch to remain honorary major for another 11 months. During his term of office, Lynch often stayed at the Château Dauzac which had come to the family in 1740 as a dowry. However, this was by no means this famous Irish family's only property, for it also owned, amongst others, La Macqueline, Pontac-Lynch, Lynch-Bages and Lynch-Moussas. There was an attempt during the present century to change the name Dauzac to Dauzac-Lynch, but without success.

Lack of control

In 1966 the estate was bought by Alain Miailhe. It was then in a very sorry state, needing a lot of attention, and for a time it seemed that Dauzac might once again become a reputable château. I have the pleasantest memories of the 1966 vintage, which was very fragrant and not without finesse. Unfortunately, there were problems within the Miailhe family and once more no proper control was exercised over the estate for several years. Its already rather dented reputation continued to decline until 1978, when it was bought by a new owner. This was a Frenchman, M. Châtelier, who lives most of the time in Morocco.

Air humidifier

The new owner went to work on the estate with great enthusiasm, building a completely new *cuvier* with a rust-proof steel tank and tiled floor. He also built an enormous barrel cellar which can accommodate 1,000 casks. This space is insulated and equipped with air humidifiers; too dry a temperature would cause the evaporation of too much wine. In principle, the wine should mature for 13-14 months in casks on the Dauzec estate. A third of the casks are renewed annually.

Expanded vineyard

Considerable changes also took place in the vineyards. At the time of the take-over in 1978 only 50 acres were really productive. This has now been increased to well over 75 acres and Dauzac will eventually have some

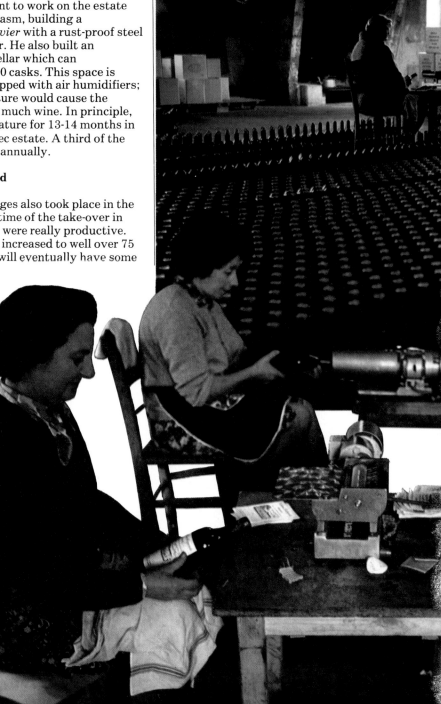

Château Dauzac

110 acres of the Margaux *appellation*. The grape varieties chosen were 70% Cabernet Sauvignon, 20% Merlot, 5% Cabernet Franc and 5% Petit Verdot. The wine from young vine stocks is sold under the second brand of Château Labarde (Médoc). While the pre-1978 Dauzacs include hardly any interesting wines, from that year there is a clear if not dramatic improvement. The 1978 itself is a bit light, while I found the 1979 satisfactory but little more. However, it did impress me with its deep colour, its rather fleshy taste and its elegance. I could smell and taste the oak. The 1980 was slightly lighter again, but very correct. The 1981 was graceful and had a distinct quality, although it did perhaps lack a little depth. The wine of Dauzac can only improve as the vines grow older. The potential for a great wine is clearly present in the soil. Maurice Healy was already convinced of this in 1940 when he wrote in his *Stay Me with Flagons*: 'Dauzac is another wine that I think has been classed much too low. I have never drunk a bad bottle of Dauzac; and the 1920, 1924 and 1926 vintages gave me some very pleasant drinking. I should have imagined Dauzac worthy of promotion to the third growths.'

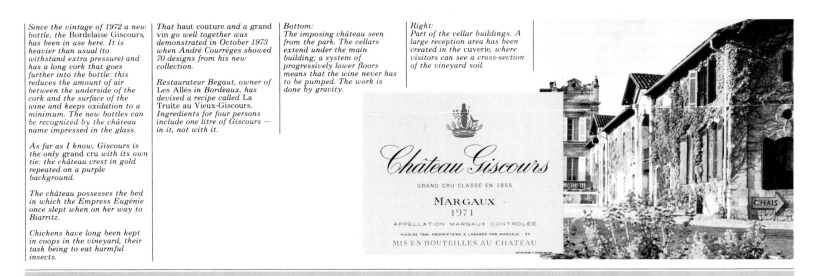

Château Giscours

Giscours is much more than a château with a vineyard — it is a wonderful little world. The estate covers no less than 740 acres, devoted not only to viticulture but also to various forms of agriculture and stock-breeding. Immediately behind the château there is also a splendid wild wood which is maintained by the owners of Giscours as a kind of natural monument.

The present-day vineyard consists of around 200 acres. Another 72 acres of new vines are still being added. These used to belong to the neighbouring estate of Château La Houringue, which disappeared after the Second World War. Only vines which are five years old or more are used on the estate, a Marguaux *appellation contrôlée*. The vines are mainly of two grape varieties; Cabernet Sauvignon (⅔) and Merlot (⅓). The yield varies from 157 *tonneaux* in 1977 to 391 *tonneaux* in 1982. The amount will obviously increase greatly when the new vines become productive. Château Giscours is sold exclusively through the English house of Gilbey and there is no second *appellation*. Giscours does, however, own another estate in Macau, Château Laronde-Desormes.

A lake for better wine

Although the expansion scheme described above is remarkable in itself, there is something else which is equally astonishing. An entirely new lake has been dug just for the sake of the vines. Having seen it myself, I can confirm that it is many times larger than the kind of pond created from a patch of mud often optimistically designated a 'lake'. Ton upon ton of earth has been removed in order to dig a deep hollow for a real, live lake several dozen yards across.
The reason for this gigantic project is purely and simply perfectionism. The intention is to make a *grand vin* at Giscours at all costs, and the new lake can contribute in its own humble way. What, in fact, does it do? Firstly, it is intended to reduce the water table of the subsoil so that the roots of the vines have to probe deeper down in search of food and drink. This will improve the quality of the wine. Secondly, the sheet of water has a moderating effect at very low and very high temperatures which can only benefit the maturing of the grapes. And thirdly, it has replaced trees and scrub which formerly inhibited movement in the air when barometer readings were high, so increasing the risk of a night frost in the spring. These are the reasons for this unique lake's existence — but how many *propriétaires* are willing and able to make that kind of outlay in addition to a new planting programme which is already costly enough?

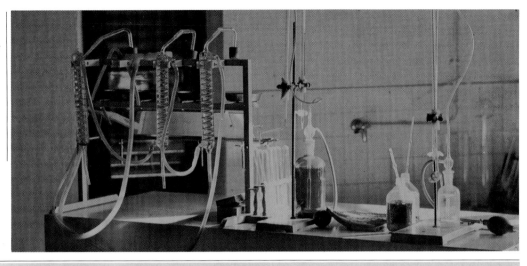

Château Giscours

The man behind the project is Pierre Tari, chairman and director-general of Château Giscours S.A. His family purchased Giscours in 1947. The once excellent vineyard was then in a sorry state. Of the 200 acres, only 17 were under cultivation. Nicholas Tari, Pierre's father, became sole owner in 1952. He still lives at the château but his son has been managing the business since 1970. Perhaps this took Pierre rather by surprise, because as a young man his plans had been quite different. He had first immersed himself in poetry and prose, but had subsequently followed the age-old family tradition and entered the army. On his return from Algeria, however, he decided to become a wine grower. His father and grandfather gave him his initial training, and he then took a university course in oenology. The Pierre Tari of today is a highly dedicated grower who in addition to his busy job as manager of his large estate still finds time for other important functions, including that of travelling ambassador for the great wines of the Médoc. His own journal, *Giscours Réalités* bears witness to this, judging from the many photographs of Pierre Tari taken all over the world.

A slow-developing wine

At Château Giscours the wine is left to ferment in 42 concrete *cuves*. After fermentation, the wine is usually left for about 18 months in oak casks. Depending on the harvest, this period can be extended to 28 months. At least 10% and, at most, 50% of the *barriques* are renewed annually. According to Pierre Tari, the wine produced has 'a complex, elegant bouquet, with nothing in excess'. It also has a solid colour, a firm structure, a pleasant hint of fruitiness, clear presence of wood and perfect balance. Although this wine is not at the very top for complexity and refinement, it is one of the better third growths and is very reliable. At the same time, this Margaux does require a lot of patience; even in the years of relatively supple wines, such as 1973 and 1974, this estate has produced somewhat muscular wines requiring five to ten years of ageing in the bottle. The great years — such as 1970, 1971, 1975, 1978, 1979, 1981 and 1982 — require even more time.

Château Boyd-Cantenac

3e Grand Cru Classé

It is remarkable that two châteaux with different names, different histories and different classifications should for many years have been making the same wine. The Guillemet family have owned Pouget since 1910 and purchased Boyd-Cantenac from the Ginestet family in 1932. After that, the grapes of the two adjoining vineyards were vinified by the same people in the same vats, the same casks and the same *chais*. The difference, M. Guillemet frankly admitted, was purely psychological. Most people felt that the Boyd-Cantenac wines were better, evidently because of its higher classification. Boyd-Cantenac is also much better known because more of it is sold and exported. The Pouget wine is exclusively destined for the house of Dubos Frères which for the most part sells privately to French customers. Consequently the size of the two vineyards had only theoretical significance; in practical terms, there was a single vineyard of approximately 64 acres with an average yield of 100 *tonneaux*, two-thirds of which was sold as Boyd-Cantenac and one-third as Pouget.

Separate ways

This situation finally ended with the harvest of 1982. From the beginning of 1983 the wines of Boyd-Cantenac and Pouget have been vinified separately. Pierre Guillemet has built a completely new *cuvier* and *chai* specially for the new arrangements; these are separated from the other facilities by a road. The new premises house the Château Pouget, while Château Boyd-Cantenac is still made in the existing cellars. According to M. Guillemet, the investment was justified, since Pouget was often undeservedly taken for a subsidiary brand of Boyd-Cantenac. Naturally, there will still be similarities between the two wines, if only because they are prepared in similar ways. Both ferment in concrete, both ripen usually for two years in wood (one-quarter of the casks being renewed for each harvest) and both are filtered. But in spite of these resemblances, there are also perceptible differences, which can be traced to slightly different soils and compositions of grape varieties.

The 44 acres of Boyd-Cantenac are planted with 70% Cabernet Sauvignon, 20% Merlot, 5% Cabernet Franc and 5% Petit Verdot; Pouget has about 20 acres with 66% Cabernet Sauvignon, 30% Merlot and 4% Cabernet Franc. I expect the wine from Pouget to be rounder, while Boyd-Cantenac will be racier and of a slightly higher quality. The latter is, after all, a third *cru*, while Pouget is only in the middle ranks of the fourth *crus*.

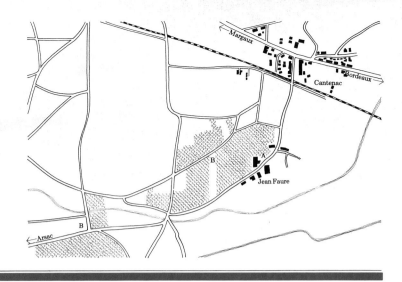

Château Pouget

4e Grand Cru Classé

Tasting impressions

During the period up to and including 1982, the Boyd-Cantenac/Pouget combination produced a relatively supple, but still fairly strong Margaux; it was not strikingly complex but had a strong constitution. I have pleasant memories of several vintages, including 1970, 1971, 1975, 1976, 1978, 1979, not to mention 1982. The last vintage — whether as Boyd-Cantenac or Pouget for I have tasted both — had very concentrated colour, a rather broad, slightly fatty taste, with plenty of flesh, tannin and a strong core of alcohol.

A historical note

There is not, and never has been, a real Château Boyd-Cantenac. The vineyard was in fact separated in 1852 from the neighbouring Cantenac-Brown, without the inclusion of a château. Mr Boyd, who gave his name to the new estate, appears to have been of Irish origin. Pouget, on the other hand, has a château, occupied by Pierre Guillemet. In the early days it belonged to the Benedictines who may be regarded as the pioneers of the Cantenac vineyards. The château derives its name from the Pouget family who held sway from 1650 to 1906.

An early classification

It is worth mentioning that immediately after the French Revolution, Pouget's classification was slightly higher than in 1855. In 1795 a special tax was levied on all the larger châteaux, and the more profitable the wine the heavier the levy. An old document states that the widow Pouget sold her wine for 500 *livres* per *tonneau*, as much as d'Issan and even 50 *livres* more than Palmer, which is now a third *cru*. Boyd-Brown, as it was then called, fetched 550 *livres*, Kirwan 600, Brune-Cantenac 600, Rauzan 700, Durfort 700 and Margaux 900. This was probably one of the earliest classifications for the wines of the communes of Margaux and Cantenac.

Château Prieuré-Lichine

4e Grand Cru Classé

The visitor to the Médoc can hardly miss Château Prieuré-Lichine. Not only does it lie plumb along the *route des grands crus* in the heart of Cantenac (and a large sign points the passer-by to the château) but, what is more, its owner Alexis Lichine has painted his shutters, doors and walls turquoise blue — an unusually frivolous colour for the rather sedate Médoc. Other things, too, show that a great deal of attention has been paid to the overall presentation of the château. When you drive into the forecourt through an arch, you see a wall into which a unique collection of cast-iron firebacks has been set. And when you enter the new *chai*, which was completed in 1974, via the *cuvier* with its nine cement and three wooden fermentation vats, you immediately notice that the tops of the casks have been varnished. This gives a particularly clean impression. None of the other châteaux (with one exception) goes to these lengths, and it results in deep purple stains in the lightish wood. During the first year the *barriques* are topped up three times a week and spilling cannot be avoided; the unvarnished wood immediately absorbs the wine, whereas at Prieuré-Lichine the spillage can simply be wiped off.

The château has been imaginatively furnished and is also very much a home (by no means a common combination in the Médoc). To the left and right of the entrance are two large salons, the one entirely decorated in light pastel tints, the other rather more sober, but both richly adorned with beautiful works of art and a number of splendid paintings in which wine is the centrepiece. Prieuré-Lichine also has an exquisite dining room. This is located in the old kitchen where dark, massive beams support the low ceiling and 40 or so gleaming copper pans provide suitable decoration. There are also several antique stoves, both life-size and in miniature.

Quality rather than quantity

The Prieuré-Lichine vineyard was established some three centuries ago by the Benedictine monks whose monastary stood

Château Prieuré-Lichine

on the site of the château. No wonder, therefore, that the little church of Cantenac is built alongside the château. The house was long called Le Prieuré but that was changed in 1953, when the *Syndicat des Grands Crus Classés du Médoc* approved a change of name to Château Prieuré-Lichine, at the request of Alexis Lichine who had purchased the estate the previous year with some American friends. As Lichine himself writes in his highly praised reference work *Encyclopedia of Wines and Spirits*, neither cost nor effort was spared to improve the quality of the vineyard. Thus two square yards of relatively poor land were exchanged with adjoining châteaux for every one square yard of good ground, quantity being sacrificed for quality. In this costly way, Lichine was able to acquire land from a large number of more highly classified châteaux such as Durfort-Vivens, Brane-Cantenac, Palmer, Ferrière, Kirwan, Giscours, d'Issan and Boyd-Cantenac. In addition, much attention was of course paid to the right way of planting while wine-making methods were also improved. At the present time, the vineyard has some 130 acres under production. A mixture of 52% Cabernet Sauvignon, 32% Merlot, 3% Cabernet Franc and 3% Petit Verdot provides between 100 and 300 *tonneaux* a year. It will surprise nobody that America is the largest purchaser of Prieuré-Lichine, followed by the Caribbean Islands, Canada, Britain and Switzerland.

Worth the trouble

Alex Lichine's effort and investment have not been in vain. For several years, Prieuré-Lichine has been one of the better wines of the Margaux *appellation*. It is almost always a harmonious wine with an elegant taste, neither too heavy nor too light; the amount of tannin is just sufficient and never excessive. Suppleness and sometimes roundness complement breeding and finesse. The wine usually has a good, but not completely dark colour (except in extraordinary years such as 1978 and 1982). Naturally the great classic years have produced excellent wines from this château. I have also been very satisfied with bottles from 1967, 1973, 1974 and 1976.

Before the wine is filtered and bottled, it is allowed to age for 18 to 24 months in oak casks. One-third of these are normally renewed annually. Here, the wine is still clarified in the traditional manner with beaten egg white.

Kirwan lies beside a railway line and on one occasion around the turn of the century when the mayor of Bordeaux gave a party at the château, a train stopped specially to allow the guests to alight.

Below left:
For generations this stone lion, with its slight air of surprise, has guarded the estate.

Right:
The former Kirwan label. The present one is printed in black and gold on a white background, and is horizontal.

Normally the wine matures for 23 months in oak casks. A third to a half of the casks are replaced each year.

The beautiful garden at Kirwan. In the winter the more tender plants are either covered or moved to the large greenhouse beside the château. The interior of Kirwan is equally charming. A fine collection of paintings graces the hall and the salons.

Château Kirwan

3e Grand Cru Classé

It is sheer coincidence that one of the first wells in the Médoc, supplying no less than 65 gallons of water a minute, was dug in the grounds of Château Kirwan. After all, there had been enough good wine to drink for centuries past. Kirwan's history goes back to the time of the Crusades, in 1147, when it was called the Château de Lassalle and then belonged to Raymond de Lassalle.

This lord of the manor bequeathed it to his heirs and they in turn to theirs, so that the castle remained in the family until 1600. It then changed owners several times until a Mr Kirwan, an Irishman, married the daughter of the then owner, Sir John Collingwood, in 1776. Kirwan renamed the château but was unfortunately unable to live out his days there because he was guillotined during the French Revolution. In the 19th century, Kirwan was the property of M. Camille Godard who, so the records say, for lack of heirs left the château to the city of Bordeaux. However, I have the impression that Godard did have a family, but for one reason or another would not leave his relations the property. In *Bordeaux et ses vins* of 1893, it is mentioned that the city of Bordeaux is the owner but that a certain Adolphe Godard had possession and enjoyment. In 1900 the Société Schröder and Schÿler (who are, I

Left:
The château from the vineyard, which starts just behind the main building.

Below left:
The rear entrance to Kirwan. Cellars and other storage areas are on either side of the approach.

Bottom left:
The cuvier, where the oak fermentation vats, so redolent of tradition, have gradually been replaced by new ones of concrete. Quality wines can be made in concrete or steel vats as well as in wood, as many châteaux have proved.

Château Kirwan's present owner is the Société Schröder & Schyler et Cie, established in 1739. This company in turn belongs to the firm of A. Moueix at Libourne.

Kirwan suffered badly from the severe frost of 1956. No fewer than 100,000 vines were lost, but these have all been replaced.

Château Kirwan

think, the Bordeaux's oldest wine firm) purchased the exclusive rights from the city of Bordeaux to sell the wine for a period of 99 years. However in 1926, Schröder and Schÿler bought the property and have continued to be the exclusive distributors of Kirwan wine.

Fine furniture

Curiously enough, this wine was sold for many years without mention of a vintage. Jean-Henri Schÿler told me that Château Kirwan began selling vintage wines only in 1934. It is he who, together with his family, lives in the 18th-century manor from July to November. The interior was restored throughout in 1973 so that the growing number of foreign visitors could be properly received. Particularly notable are the decorated tapestries in the salon and the fine Charles X furniture carved out of lemonwood. One of the valuable cabinets contains the key to the small family cellar, which is only exceptionally shown to outsiders. It accommodates an ample quantity of estate wine dating back to 1943. Right behind the château is the vineyard, or at least part of it, because the land is much split up. About 76 acres are productive, while an expansion project should add a further 10 acres or so. The varieties of grape are Cabernet Sauvignon (45%), Merlot (25%) Cabernet Franc (20%) and Petit Verdot (10%). Production is 90 to 145 *tonneaux*.

A flowery bouquet

The Schÿler family have always made a special effort to provide the château's fine front garden with a beautiful show of flowers in the summer. It has even won prizes on several occasions. Maybe that is why I find this Margaux so flowery, both in nose and in taste. This was particularly noticeable in the 1973 (which was elegant and full of distinction, more so than the 1972) and also the 1959 Kirwan. Fifteen years after harvesting, the latter wine had a velvety, red-brown colour, a splendid spring-like nose and a fine elegant taste, Kirwan at its best, a bouquet of flowers without a hint of excess. The 1975 was also a fine wine, with the scent of flowers, powerful yet refined. I found the 1976 disappointing. This wine, tasted in 1983, certainly had a charming personality but could have been more exciting, finer in aroma and taste. The wines of Kirwan are at their best and most elegant when they come from good but not exceptional years. If there is excessive sun, their finesse tends to be subdued by their strength. For this reason, I prefer the Kirwan from years such as 1971, 1979 and 1981, rather than from, say, 1970, 1978 and 1982. Obviously, though, this is a matter of personal taste.

Château Brane-Cantenac

The bouquet of Brane-Cantenac has always enjoyed a high reputation. Once, when the soft west wind carried the first scents of spring to the hamlet of Cantenac, people said 'Le Baron de Brane soutire ses vins' (Baron de Brane is racking his wines). Nowadays, the Brane-Cantenac wines still have a very fine bouquet, even though they do not emerge until the wine has aged a bit and not, as the anecdote would have it, while it is still in cask. Of all the vintages which I have tasted, the bouquet of the 1961 is the most marked. That was really splendid. I drank this wine with a trio of international cheeses (Edam from Holland, Cheddar from England and Gruyère from France) after a family luncheon at the château. It was a lively meal in more than one respect because it included the owner Lucien Lurton, his wife and their ten children. At this meal we also enjoyed the 1960 Brane-Cantenac which formed a worthy accompaniment to the grilled entrecôte. The wine was uncommonly powerful for a 1960 and an unqualified success.

Lucien Lurton told me that to start with nobody had a good word for this vintage, himself included. It was considered hard and mean, and so almost the entire harvest was declassified to an ordinary Bordeaux and sold under Brane's subsidiary brand, Château Notton.

Fortunately, this did not prove too serious because the entire yield did not exceed 4,000 bottles. By pure chance, some 10 years later M. Lurton tasted the wine from this apparently quite unsuccessful year — to be bowled over by a full, agreeable wine which bore no resemblance whatever to that threadbare wine of yesteryear. Nature continues to surprise!

Soft and elegant

Often, luck also plays a rôle. In 1964 Lucien Lurton had engaged a group of Spanish pickers who were to come and harvest for him on a particular day. They arrived a week or so early and had little inclination to go off to another château first. Consequently, Lucien Lurton set them to work picking immediately. In fact, the day after the grapes had been gathered the rain started and continued for several weeks on end. Throughout almost the entire district the 1964 vintage was very moderate, but at Brane-Cantenac a very good wine was produced with a luxuriant fragrance.

Is it possible for wine to reveal something of the maker's personality? This would certainly appear to be the case at Brane-Cantenac. Lucien Lurton is a friendly, quiet, erudite man, and his wine is soft, elegant and distinguished; this is a Margaux with no obvious or pronounced taste, but it is stylish. The colour is rarely deep, though the tannin content is sometimes disturbingly strong. Even when relatively young, Brane-Cantenac is often an approachable, attractive wine. It is not subjected to excessive ripening in the wood — usually about 18 months (one-third of the casks being new). Among the recommended vintages are 1966, 1967, 1970, 1971, 1974 (for that year), 1975, 1978, 1979, 1981 and 1982. Fruit, juiciness, charm and style are the characteristics of this last vintage. Brane-Cantenac is clarified with fresh egg white and undergoes very light filtering before bottling.

Château Brane-Cantenac

The plateau of Cantenac

One of the secrets which enables Brane-Cantenac to make its excellent wine is strict selection. Only the very best is good enough to be sold as Brane. The remainder, as in 1960, is marketed under the Château Notton label. This immensely important decision must be made each year but it is not Lucien Lurton's to make alone. He is assisted by an expert, objective outsider in the person of Professor Peynaud. Together, they rejected the entire crop in 1960, 1963 and 1968. In 1965, 80% was found not good enough and in 1974 approximately 35%. These few examples show what has often to be sacrificed commercially in order to make a consistently great wine.

Another aspect which has a decisive influence on the quality of the wine is, of course, the location of the vineyard. The vines are planted on the great plateau of Cantenac which is ringed about with a number of famous estates. From its highest point (75 feet above the Gironde) you can see not only Brane-Cantenac but also Cantenac-Brown, Rausan-Ségla, Palmer, Prieuré-Lichine, Kirwan and Pouget. The Brane-Cantenac vineyard is 210 acres in extent, of which an average of 185 acres are in production. The grape varieties are as follows: 70% Cabernet Sauvignon, 13% Merlot, 15% Cabernet Franc and 2% Petit Verdot. In normal years, production is 220-230 *tonneaux*. The wine is sold to some 40 different shippers and therefore appears in the catalogues of a great many merchants in many countries throughout the world.

Château Cantenac-Brown

Although the history of Cantenac-Brown goes back to the 16th century, the name is of more recent date. The château was in fact called Château de Cantenac for centuries, until the property was bought in 1826 by John Lewis Brown who joined his name to it soon afterwards. Mr Brown, of British origin, was a Bordeaux *négociant* with a hobby of painting horses. He purchased the estate from the widow of François Coudac, an Amsterdam wine merchant who had in turn inherited it from Louis Massac, also of Amsterdam. Through these two Dutchmen, a fund of good will was created in Holland and the country was long one of the chief customers. In the meantime, however, America, Britain, Belgium, Switzerland and Japan have also become worthwhile markets for the export of this wine (which is sold as *appellation contrôlée* Margaux). One gets the impression that Mr Brown over-extended himself somewhat with this and other acquisitions because in 1843 he was declared bankrupt. Via his creditors the estate then passed to M. Gromard, a banker. He was apparently more interested in money than wine because he seriously neglected the vineyard. He sold Cantenac-Brown in 1860 to Armand Lalande, already the owner of Château Léoville-Poyferré.

Château Cantenac-Brown

Mock-Stuart in the Médoc

Lalande, an energetic and enterprising man, immediately began replacing the vines, improving the *chais* and reviewing wine-making methods with a view to restoring past glories.

Feeling that the existing château did not match the grandeur of his wine, he commissioned an entirely new château, to be built immediately behind it, in a more imposing style. It seems that the architect (or perhaps his patron) had a somewhat bizarre taste, because the completed structure is strongly reminiscent of a very large, very British, country house in the Stuart style. A silent homage, perhaps, to Mr Brown's ancestors — or maybe just an attempt to attract the important English market? We shall never know. The old château still stands on its original site, a simple, angular building, linked to the new château by a store room.

M. Lalande's family continued to own Cantenac-Brown until 1968. In that year it was taken over by the du Vivier family, also the owners of the Bordeaux firm of A. de Luze & Fils. This company has since 1980 formed part of the house of Rémy-Martin (Cognac), but Cantenac-Brown remained in the hands of the du Viviers with Bertrand du Vivier (who also retained his post as chairman and director-general of de Luze) as manager. Although Bertrand du Vivier does not live at the château himself, part has been let and is occupied. One of the ground floor salons has been made into a stylish reception room. Entered through a bar with several fine works of art, this room is entirely furnished in 19th-century style.

A classic wine for laying down

Perhaps the penchant for the traditional also plays a part in the preparation of the wine. My impression is that it is still made without many concessions to present-day methods. The thought that passes through my head whenever I taste Cantenac-Brown is: 'That's how all Bordeaux wine must have been made in the past.' When young, the wine usually tastes very hard (in strong contrast to neighbouring Brane-Cantenac) and it takes many years before this ruggedness is converted into softness and charm. The bouquet, too, requires considerable time. Cantenac-Brown was a classic wine for laying down. I use the past tense advisedly, since I have the impression that, since 1976, the wines have become more supple, slightly less hard and tannic and can therefore be drunk earlier. Their structure also seems to have become more loose: this was apparent in the wines of 1978, 1979 and 1982. In spite of this, it is undoubtedly a very good, though reserved Margaux, which has to be given time. In the past I have drunk several vintages of Cantenac-Brown and found them extremely satisfactory, both from great years such as 1966 and 1970 and from less noteworthy years, as 1962, 1969, 1972. Nowadays, the wine is left to mature for 16 to 20 months in wood; one-sixth of the casks are new. Production is about 150 *tonneaux*.

Wooden vats for atmosphere

When you enter the presshouses of Cantenac-Brown, you see a neat row of gleaming oak fermentation vats. They are quite in keeping with the traditional image of this château, but in this instance all is not as it seems. Behind the first *cuvier* there is, in fact, a second, with steel vats, and this is where the wine is made. Bertrand du Vivier has kept the old ones intact to convey the bygone atmosphere of the cellars. There is also a great deal of wood in the area where the wine is bottled. Here, the walls are made up of actual packaging crates.

The Cantenac-Brown vineyard was much larger before Boyd-Cantenac was hived off. Now, the 79 acres are planted with 70% Cabernet Sauvignon and 30% Merlot.

Château d'Issan

The British have always been very partial to Château d'Issan. Back in 1152 this was the wine served at the wedding celebrations of Henry Plantagenet — later Henry II of England — and Eleanor of Aquitaine. However, the wine of those days cannot be compared with that of today; the knack had not then been discovered of keeping wine in sealed bottles and so only the fairly light-coloured 'clairet' of the most recent crop was drunk.

The English had another opportunity of showing their preference for d'Issan in 1453, after the battle of Castillon, which put paid to two centuries of English supremacy in Guyenne. After this decisive battle, the English retired but still had sufficient wits about them to put up a rearguard action to gain time while they emptied the cellars at d'Issan. The English army left Pauillac with more than enough wine to drown their sorrows for the time being. Britain is still an

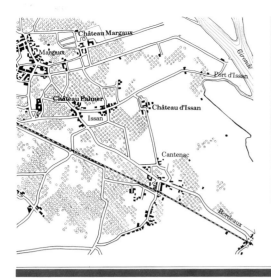

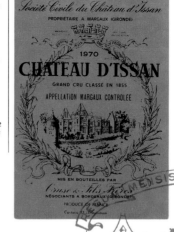

Château d'Issan

important customer for this *troisième grand cru classé*, although Japan, United States, the Netherlands and Canada have also become leading export markets. The *appellation* is Margaux, as with the other fine wines from the commune of Cantenac.

Complete restoration

As a token of this appreciation, the victorious King Charles VII awarded the barony of d'Issan to that scourge of the English, the Comte de Foix, and his family remained owners until early in the 19th century. During the early generations of the de Foix family, the new estate was not that attractive because the English, as a final gesture, had burned the château down. Only in the 17th century was the present magnificent mansion built on the foundations of the old stronghold. Desite its angular shapes, it makes a handsome impression.
The château was almost ruined again during the Second World War when the Germans took it over. It is largely thanks to the late Emmanuel Cruse that d'Issan has now been entirely restored. This remarkable man purchased the estate in 1945 and spent almost the rest of his life restoring the old lustre to the vineyard and château. It took a tremendous amount of work because, judging from post-war photographs, trees were literally growing from the windows. Emmanuel Cruse was also joint owner for a time of Rausan-Ségla, and on the sale of the latter château in 1956 many works of art were transferred to d'Issan.

Reliable

The gatehouse to d'Issan boasts the legend '*Regum Mensis Arisque Deorum*' or 'For the Kings' tables and the gods' altars'. This motto is not as arrogant as it may seem because the d'Issan wine was indeed the favourite drink of the crowned heads, including Emperor Franz Joseph of Austria, who preferred d'Issan to all the other wines of Bordeaux and persuaded his court to

follow suit. You do not need to be a head of state to enjoy d'Issan although if you drink enough of it you may well feel like one. The d'Issan wine has a fairly modest reputation for its 3rd *grand cru* status, and I think that is understandable. Generally speaking, the greatest virtue of the d'Issan wines is their reliability; even in moderate years such as 1972 the château produced an acceptable wine. Apart from this, d'Issan is a wine which becomes drinkable quite quickly, is relatively lightweight, and possesses few nuances. I regard it as a fairly elegant but not very complex Margaux. In 1980 I tasted 15 vintages of d'Issan, from 1961 to 1978 inclusive. Only 1963, 1965 and 1968 were missing. The best wines were those of the traditionally great years — 1961, 1966, 1970, 1971 and 1975. The 1978 had been bottled a few months before and was still very 'bottle sick'. In the second range were the wines of 1962, 1967, 1973 and 1976. The rest followed.

Château bottling since 1972

Since the 1972 harvest, the estate has been bottling its own wine. There were other radical changes, too, during the 1970s. In 1979 the château acquired an entirely new battery of stainless steel fermentation tanks and around the same time a start was made on planting an additional 7 acres. With the new section, the château d'Issan vineyard covers some 87 acres. The vines consist of approximately 75% Cabernet Sauvignon, a very small quantity of Cabernet Franc, and the remainder Merlot. The owner is Mme Cruse, the widow of Emmanuel. The annual yield of 90 to 150 *tonneaux* usually matures for 15 months in oak casks, one-third of which are renewed before each harvest.

Palmer is one of the very few estates where the stalks are removed by égrappage à main. This is done in a very labour-intensive fashion by seven workers to each of the large wooden grilles. The task is done by machine almost everywhere else.

In the past not all Palmer wine was bottled at the château. Wine that was not bottled there was distinguished by a white label with a line drawing. The last bottle I saw with this label was the 1962. The wine was relatively cheap — but there was no comparison with its greatly superior château-bottled counterpart.

Below:
The château as it appears on the nicely produced black label.

Bottom:
Glasses ready in the reception hall. As at all the Médoc châteaux ordinary visitors are only given wine from the casks to taste, which is a disappointment for many of them as they are unaccustomed to sampling such young wine. Only a few fortunate special guests of the owner are allowed to taste older vintages. Guests so privileged should remember that Palmer's most successful vintages since the Second World War have been the 1945, 1959, 1961 and the 1970 (still too young at the time of writing).

Château Palmer

3e Grand Cru Classé

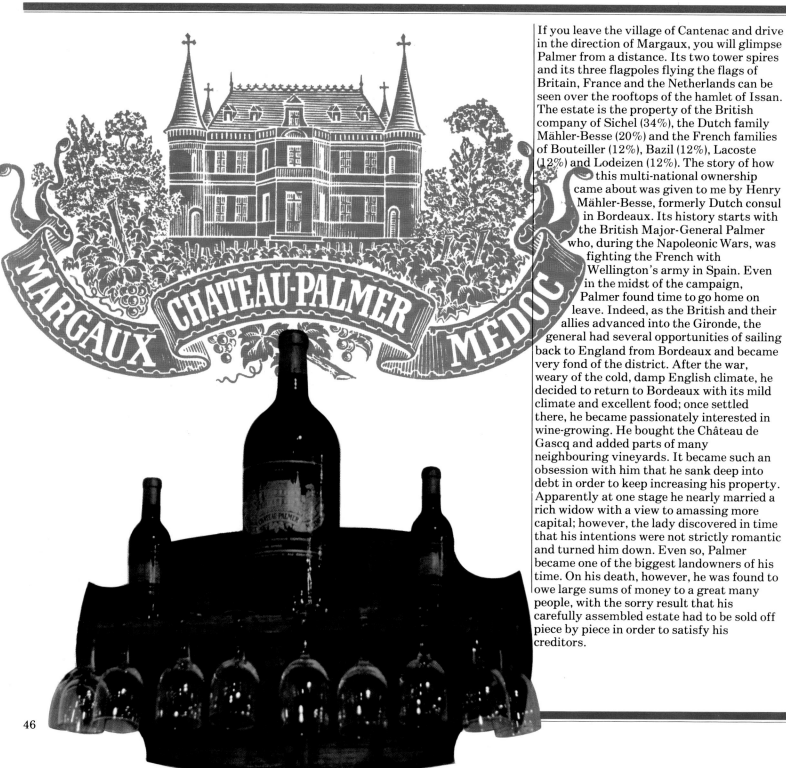

If you leave the village of Cantenac and drive in the direction of Margaux, you will glimpse Palmer from a distance. Its two tower spires and its three flagpoles flying the flags of Britain, France and the Netherlands can be seen over the rooftops of the hamlet of Issan. The estate is the property of the British company of Sichel (34%), the Dutch family Mähler-Besse (20%) and the French families of Bouteiller (12%), Bazil (12%), Lacoste (12%) and Lodeizen (12%). The story of how this multi-national ownership came about was given to me by Henry Mähler-Besse, formerly Dutch consul in Bordeaux. Its history starts with the British Major-General Palmer who, during the Napoleonic Wars, was fighting the French with Wellington's army in Spain. Even in the midst of the campaign, Palmer found time to go home on leave. Indeed, as the British and their allies advanced into the Gironde, the general had several opportunities of sailing back to England from Bordeaux and became very fond of the district. After the war, weary of the cold, damp English climate, he decided to return to Bordeaux with its mild climate and excellent food; once settled there, he became passionately interested in wine-growing. He bought the Château de Gascq and added parts of many neighbouring vineyards. It became such an obsession with him that he sank deep into debt in order to keep increasing his property. Apparently at one stage he nearly married a rich widow with a view to amassing more capital; however, the lady discovered in time that his intentions were not strictly romantic and turned him down. Even so, Palmer became one of the biggest landowners of his time. On his death, however, he was found to owe large sums of money to a great many people, with the sorry result that his carefully assembled estate had to be sold off piece by piece in order to satisfy his creditors.

Château Palmer

A long uninterrupted reputation

The greater part of the vineyard was bought up by the enormously wealthy, perhaps slightly *nouveau riche,* Pereire family. In Paris, the name is still to be found on a boulevard and a metro station. The Pereires proved to be good owners who invested heavily so as to enhance Palmer's reputation, approaching it rather in the manner of breeding racehorses — as a status symbol. The Pereires' exemplary attitude proved its worth only after the crash of 1929. Few could still afford fine wine, but the

Pereires continued to spend money on producing a first-class product — not the case with many other *grands crus* which deteriorated sharply during the depression. Yet even the powerful bankers Pereire suffered losses and the day came when the two brothers who managed Palmer reported to the family that the last penny had been spent, and invited all shareholders to make a hefty contribution. That, however, was an unpopular proposal. People were happy enough drinking the wine but not to pay extra for it. The two brothers then suggested that they should buy Palmer — but here,

again, the family were opposed to their having the château. So the brothers were forced to sell the property on the open market, at a period when a number of estates were up for sale. The price was disappointingly low, not more than one year's upkeep. The purchasers were the father of Henry Mähler-Besse and two brokers (brothers of the Miailhe family) the legendary Allan Sichel and Fernand Ginestet (the father of Pierre Ginestet).
Although the *cru's* reputation was maintained intact the new owners still had to spend money for many years, particularly as

Left:
The first-year cellar. Note the bands of scrubbed wood on the casks — a special feature at Palmer. The religious statue at the back cannot be that of St Vincent, patron saint of wine, as there is no cross in his hand.

Below:
The lees left after the fairly violent first fermentation are pressed by means of this small, round wooden press. Small quantities of the wine from this first pressing are often added to the grand vin to increase its tannin content.

Bottom:
One of the cellar workers in his huge apron.

Henry Mähler-Besse's father was simply called Mähler. However, he married a Mlle Besse from a well-known Bordeaux family. To give his enterprise more prestige, and make it sound more French, he added the name of Besse to his own. Everyone started to call him M. Mähler-Besse and his son Henry later changed officially to this form.

The 1934 vintage was particularly abundant, but because this was a time of economic crisis, most châteaux had been sparing in their orders for new casks: except for Palmer. Henry Mähler-Besse still recalls how many owners, in desperation, came and offered him one full cask of wine in return for two empty ones.

Palmer is in the hamlet of Issan, which belongs to the commune of Cantenac, but its wine carries the Margaux appellation.

Château Palmer

the Second World War soon broke out. The present distribution of the shares resulted from one of the Miailhe brothers selling his portion to Sichel, and Mähler-Besse and then Ginestet selling his entire share to Mähler-Besse alone (Sichel lacking funds at the time). Later, the Mähler-Besse family sold some shares to other private individuals.

Tradition and painstaking care

Today, under the skilful guidance of the manager Bertrand Bouteiller (who also runs Pichon-Longueville-Baron), some 20 staff work on the estate. Nearly 100 acres have been planted with 40% Merlot, 55% Cabernet Sauvignon, 3% Cabernet Franc and 2% Petit Verdot. Until a short time ago the Merlot constituted 60%, but gradually much of this variety was repaced by Cabernet Sauvignon in the course of replanting in order to give the wine a little more strength. The yield is an average of 120 *tonneaux* (*appellation* Margaux), mainly shipped to the USA, Britain, the Netherlands and Belgium. Vinification is by strictly traditional means in red-brown oak casks. According to Bertrand Bouteiller, the oak adds just a dash more tannin to the generally supple wine, especially because the fermentation vats are regularly renewed. Furthermore, in excellent years (such as 1970) entirely new casks are used for storing the wine. In years of moderate quality, about one-third of the *barriques* are renewed. Needless to say, the partners of Château Palmer select their wine very carefully, particularly in a year such as 1974, with wide differences in quality. The wine is tasted several times, and there is no great hurry to make a decision. Better to wait a month than be sorry later. For Henry Mähler-Besse, difficult years are the greatest challenge, 'because then you really have to know your business'. M. Mähler makes his final decision as to which wine may be offered as Palmer not at the château itself but in his own tasting room in Bordeaux where he tests a range of wines almost daily. And why? The reason is that only here does he feel 100% confident about his business.

The wine of the century?

The most memorable Palmer which I have ever drunk was that of 1961. The wine was still far too young but was already so overwhelming in colour, taste and aroma that the accompanying food paled in consequence. After a good ten years, the magnificent bouquet still held a great deal of fruit, and the taste had a creamy, almost-sweet strength. By chance, not long after drinking this tremendous wine, I met John Elliott, the expert cellar master at London's Café Royal. He knew the vintage well and considered it so outstanding that he pronounced it 'the wine of the century'. The class of this wine was confirmed in 1978 at a tasting of some 20 wines of 1961, when Palmer ended up first, ahead of Lafite, Mouton, Latour and Margaux, amongst others. I also greatly enjoyed the 1959 Palmer, stronger than most of that year. Other, almost legendary successes are the 1962 and 1966. They are perfectly balanced wines in every respect, with a rounded, supple taste and a lingering aftertaste. I should also love to have bottles of the 1970, 1975 and 1978 lying in my cellar. The vintages of 1976, 1974 and 1973 produced relatively soft, pleasant and still aristocratic wines, which will be ready for drinking quite soon.

Desmirail, a vanished treasure

In 1957, the third *cru* Desmirail disappeared after Palmer sold the vineyard and château. However, the estate has now resurfaced. The buildings and name were taken over by Lucien Lurton who has been producing Desmirail again since 1981. This is an especially elegant, stylish wine with a lot of finesse. The vineyard covers 27 acres and is to be further increased to 45 acres. The grape varieties used are Cabernet Sauvignon (80%), Merlot (10%), Cabernet Franc (9%) and Petit Verdot (1%). The wine matures for 18 months in casks, a quarter of which are new.

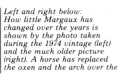

Château Margaux

1e Grand Cru Classé

Château Margaux is so many things. Perhaps more than any other *grand cru*, it leaves the visitor with such a broad range of impressions that it creates a picture as complete and as complex as the wine itself. At Margaux, thoughts turn to art, architecture, hospitality, craftsmanship, history, gastronomy, culture — all those things that make life worth living. Perhaps that is why this château has often served as a symbol of French civilization. For example, immediately after the Second World War, when the first ship with flour arrived at a French port as part of the American Marshall Plan, the French wanted to thank the Americans with wine and took them by train from Paris to Margaux for a banquet sponsored by this château. Similarly, to celebrate its 500th anniversary, the University of Bordeaux chose Château Margaux as the place for a dinner with the world's most famous scientists. In 1962, the West German Chancellor, Dr Adenauer ('I'm no beer drinker!'), asked to visit Château Margaux and thoroughly enjoyed it. Ex-owner Pierre Ginestet said: 'Margaux represents an élite, perfection. It has been a pleasure for me that my wine has always been closely linked with culture and intellectual life — with civilization.'

Acme of finesse

It is obvious from these remarks that, in the heyday of the Ginestet period — the 1950s and 1960s — Château Margaux was an

Château Margaux

outstandingly fine and civilized wine. Margaux of this period was the acme of finesse; no other Bordeaux rivalled it for delicacy. It recalled tender flowers, fragile china, soft satin or the finely strung sounds of the harpsichord. The 1967 struck me with its fine bouquet, an almost sultry perfume with fine, flowery overtones. The structure of the wine was on the light side, while the aftertaste was slightly shorter than usual. The 1966 had a brilliant, deep colour, a fragile, exciting perfume and a taste rich in variation and subtle nuance. In 1964 — the year when the rains came in the middle of the Médoc harvest — Château Margaux was still able to make a good wine thanks to strict selection, for only grapes picked before the rain were used. The wine possessed great vitality and many surprising nuances of taste and aroma. The colour was excellent. 1962 was also a fine year for Margaux. The bouquet was reminiscent of violets, but of many other flowers as well. It was deep, distinguished, pure. Taste was on the light side, but still in perfect harmony with the rest. The harvest of 1961 produced a glorious wine at Margaux; it was remarkable for its rich nuances and satiny taste. The 1959 was also a success: light bouquet and soft, delicate taste. I was extremely surprised by the vintage of 1957; 17 years after its harvest, this wine showed no sign of tiredness and could even still be described as reserved. The oldest Margaux I have drunk was the 1928 (in 1981). It had a deep, dark, concentrated colour and still retained a currant-like fragrance and a surprisingly lively, firm, somewhat fruity taste. A harmonious wine, impressive in every way.

Difficult times

Château Margaux unfortunately had its problems in the early 1970s. All kinds of personal and financial difficulties prevented the Ginestets from following sound policies. Thus, in 1977, the vintages of 1973, 1974, 1975 and 1976 were all still lying in the cellars. Of these, the 1973 was a complete disappointment. The 1974 wine was relatively lean, short on bouquet and thin in taste. The 1975 had a so-called *goût de lie*; the wine had undoubtedly been racked to a clean cask a few months too late. The still very young 1976 did have a pleasing perfume and a soft taste with more than a touch of fruitiness, but it lacked the class of a *premier cru*.

The crisis that beset the Ginestets reached its climax when, at the end of 1977, Château Margaux was sold. This had been preceded by many months of negotiations with, among others, the Cognac house of Rémy-Martin. Another potential purchaser was the American National Distillers Group. It offered 82 million francs, but the French Government would not approve the transaction. Eventually, André Mentzelopoulos, a Greek living in France and leading shareholder in the Félix Potin grocery chain, paid 72 million francs to become the new owner of Margaux. But this was by no means the end of his outlay. The entire Château was renovated. A totally new *chai* was built, with an underground cellar, and expensive work was put in hand in the vineyard, including the renewal of part of the drainage system. André Mentzelopoulos had no time to witness more than the rebirth of Château Margaux, for he died in December 1980. His work has been continued by his wife Laura, his daughter Corinne, and the director Philippe Barre.

Back at the top

Immediately after taking over, André Mentzelopoulos took another important decision, giving Professor Emile Peynaud a free hand to bring Margaux back to the level of *premier grand cru*. The Peynaud-Barré partnership scored a notable success in 1978, the wine of that year being of far higher quality than any of previous vintages of the decade. Tasting the 1978 was a revelation. It was deep red in colour, with a rich perfume containing plenty of fruit, wood and a multitude of other nuances. It had a concentrated, complex taste, fleshy and succulent, and an aftertaste which lasted for

Château Margaux

several minutes in the mouth. The Château Margaux of 1978, together with the Château Latour, was probably the best wine in the whole of Bordeaux: once again, Margaux was back at the very height of excellence. Subsequent vintages have only reinforced that position. The 1979 was also a magnificent wine, and at least as good as the 1978. Even in the much criticized year of 1980, Margaux produced an imposing wine, dark coloured, with strong hints of wood and fruit and a good structure. The wine had slightly less length than those of 1978 and 1979, but was still one of the best of that vintage. Style and culture are still present in today's Margaux, though the delicacy, sometimes even fragility, of earlier vintages appears to have disappeared for good. This does not bother me personally, since the wine has gained in quality as well as strength. The grape varieties used are Cabernet Sauvignon (75%), Merlot (20%) and Petit Verdot (5%). In all, the vineyard covers 183 acres, with expansion up to 200 acres possible. Production is between 150 and 250 *tonneaux*.

Two other wines

Not all the red wine is sold as Château Margaux. Less successful *cuvées* — usually from young vine stocks — are marketed under the name of Pavillon Rouge. The wine is slightly lighter in colour and constitution than the *grand vin*, but is nevertheless of very high standard. There is also a Pavillon Blanc, using grapes from a separate 24-acre vineyard in the neighbourhood of Castelnau (and thus has no right to the Margaux *appellation*). This vineyard is exclusively Sauvignon Blanc. After pressing, the wine is left to ferment in wooden casks, half of which are new. In quality, this is an excellent Sauvignon, neither grassy nor aggressive, but civilized, very fruity and pure — suitable for keeping a few years.

New casks

All the red wine from Château Margaux — including Pavillon Rouge — matures in new

Château Margaux

oak casks. The first-year *chai* is 300 feet long and 70 feet wide; the ceiling is supported by 18 white pillars. The second-year cellar has been in service since 1982. The new *cave* has a capacity of 2,400 casks, plus 50,000 bottles. Near the château is a small village where the vineyard workers and their families live. The village is almost totally self-supporting and can even supply its own water and electricity. In addition to the cellar workers and other employees directly concerned with the production of the wine, Château Margaux also employs a work force to look after the house and the outbuildings. Other members of the staff include a cooper who makes and repairs the casks. The Margaux estate is thus almost as impressive as the wine it produces.

Château Durfort-Vivens

2e Grand Cru Classé

When Thomas Jefferson, future president of
the United States, visited Bordeaux in 1785
he lumped Durfort together with Rauzan
and Léoville as red wines 'of second quality',
after Lafite and Margaux which he regarded
as first-class wines. His judgement proved to
be correct because in 1855 Durfort-Vivens
was included amongst the second *grands
crus*. The estate passed out of the hands of
the Durfort and Vivens families in 1866.
After several owners, including the wine
house of Delor and the Ginestets, the
vineyard and cellars were purchased in 1961
by Lucien Lurton of Brane-Cantenac. The
château itself remained in the possession of
the former owners, the Ginestets. Bernard
Ginestet and his family now live there.

I have drunk several vintages — from the
1960s, 1970s and 1980s — of Durfort-
Vivens, which clearly prove that the wine
differs in style from that of Brane-Cantenac.
Even though both wines share the same
commune, the same classification and the
same owner, they are quite distinct. It is
possible to detect more Cabernet Sauvignon
in Durfort-Vivens and it therefore appears
more reserved. I also find it slightly less
refined than Brane-Cantenac and having
slighty less charm. It is still a very good
wine, although I have reservations about its
present classification as a second growth
(though certainly not as a third). It is vitally
important for this Margaux to be allowed to
mature properly. Even in rather light years,
it tends to be a strong wine (except for the
rather weak 1972, 1973 and 1977). The

following vintages of Durfort-Vivens are to
be recommended: 1967, 1969, 1970, 1971,
1974, 1975, 1976, 1978, 1979, 1981, 1982. My
oldest bottle was from the 1904 vintage; the
wine was still lively after three-quarters of a
century, with a relatively mild taste.

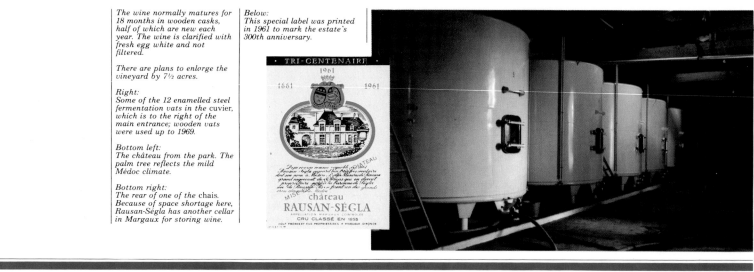

Château Rausan-Ségla

2e Grand Cru Classé

Now that Mouton-Rothschild has been promoted to the first *grands crus classés*, Rausan-Ségla stands at the head of the second group. It is followed immediately by Rauzan-Gassies, which is only logical because the two châteaux originate from one and the same estate. Although many well known Médoc vineyards date from the 18th century, that of Rausan goes back to 1661. The property was then owned by Pierre des Mesures de Rausan, a wine merchant. The vineyard was split up at the time of the French Revolution, about two-thirds going to the heirs of the Baroness de Ségla, the remainder to the politician Gassies. Rausan-Ségla was purchased in 1866 by the father-in-law of Frédéric Cruse, and his family were to keep the château for 90 years. The Cruses did much to the château and to the vineyard. They constructed an entirely new main building and also transferred all kinds of fine objects from a château which was being pulled down close to Bordeaux. On walking round Rausan-Ségla and through the garden, one comes across odd stones which are clearly much older than the remainder of the château. Many bear inscriptions, sometimes in Latin; there is probably no château that offers so much to read on its walls than

Rausan. There is a charming and authentic inscription stating that 'the Baroness Rausan-Ségla, 1761-1828, took pleasure in growing hydrangeas on this spot'. After 1956, the château was for four years the property of M. de Meslon who sold it in 1960 to the British John Holt Group (which also owns the firm of Eschenauer). The château is not occupied permanently but has been tastefully fitted out to receive guests.

Throw it in the Thames!

Britain has always been an important market for Rausan-Ségla. This was already the case a few centuries ago, until demand suddenly dropped. Unable to understand why, M. Rausan decided to do something about it himself. The problem was that the English no longer wished to pay the price that M. Rausan considered his wine was worth. Writing did not help and so one day the owner left for London on a ship laden with casks. But even that failed to impress. The English remained imperturbable. M. Rausan then became so cross that he shouted at the importers that he would never sell them his wine at their cut-throat prices; he would sooner pour all his wine into the

Thames. And this he proceeded to do. The first day an entire *tonneau* disappeared into the river, the second day a further *tonneau*. The third day, the buyers came back . . . with a rather better price. Not only Britain but many other countries now purchase the 140 *tonneaux* which Rausan-Ségla produces each year.

A scattered vineyard

Owners come, owners go, but the *régisseur*'s family often goes on forever. The grandfather of the present *régisseur*, Jean-Pierre Joyeux, came to work at Rausan in 1897. His father took over the job in 1937, and Jean-Pierre started in 1960. Before he accepted this important post he already knew the château and its vineyard inside out. He was born at Rausan-Ségla and has been working there since 1944. He is the first to admit that his task is rather simpler than that of his grandfather, at least as far as working the vineyard is concerned. In 1897 the 125 or so acres, as it was then, were scattered over no less than 215 different plots! Through exchange and other means of regrouping, this figure was reduced during the course of the present century to six plots.

Château Rausan-Ségla

The vineyard is now 105 acres, the following percentages of grape varieties being grown: 66% Cabernet Sauvignon, 27% Merlot, 5% Cabernet Franc and 2% Petit Verdot. The wine is allowed to mature for about 20 months in casks. About one-third to a half of the *barriques* are new.

Clear decline

I have exciting memories of earlier vintages of Rausan-Ségla. The vintages of the 1960s were of very high quality, with a perfume redolent of spring scents, blossoming orchards and flowers. The vintages of 1960, 1961 and 1962 were each very attractive, great wines, while the 1964 and 1966 were certainly wines of distinction. During the following decade, however, the quality of Rausan-Ségla declined considerably. The wine became smoother, less exciting, and lost its claim to be considered as a second *grand cru*. Whereas the estate made decent,

correct wines in 1970, 1971, 1975, 1978, 1979 and in 1982, their standard was still disappointing. I even found the 1973 and the 1976 characterless and weak. I have the impression that wine has now become too commercialized and sells mainly on the grounds of its high classification in 1855. One can only hope that Eschenauer will

again start to produce wines of high quality at the château, since its potential for truly great wines has been amply demonstrated in the past.

Château Rauzan-Gassies

Rauzan-Gassies is only a short distance from Rausan-Ségla because the two châteaux are built next to each other. At a certain point, the brown boundary wall of Rausan (with an 's') stops and the white of Rauzan (with a 'z') begins. This of course results directly from the fact that the two châteaux were originally a single property. When it was divided, the château was allotted to Rausan-Ségla, so Rauzan-Gassies has no château of its own. True, there is a house, but you need a lively imagination to see it as an authentic wine château.

There is a natural temptation to lump the Rausan-Segla and Rauzan-Gassies wines together; after all, they both come from different parts of the same vineyard. However, that is a mistake you must never make in Margaux because not only can slight differences in sunlight and soil composition cause appreciable differences in the wine but, what is more, a process of land division has been taking place in this area for generations, so that vineyards which were once similar gradually acquire a different composition. That is also what happened with the vineyards of Ségla and Gassies. That is not the whole story: the human rôle is equally important. It is only thanks to man's devotion, care and skill that the best results are obtained from the existing basic materials.

A rejuvenation cure

It would appear that the human factor has long been the weak link at Rauzan. Most connoisseurs have little good to say about this second *cru*. I was therefore pleased to find that the son of Paul Quié (who purchased the château soon after the Second World War) is devoting much energy to rejuvenating the cellars, the storerooms and indeed the entire wine-making procedure. He is doing so very conscientiously, with a keen eye for detail and without economizing on quality. Jean-Michel Quié is aware that no single factor makes a great wine; here more than anywhere else the whole is surely more than the sum of the parts. Rauzan-Gassies now has a modern *cuvier* with six stainless-

Château Rauzan-Gassies

steel fermentation tanks and a *chai* in which 120,000 bottle can be stored. Both rooms have been carefully insulated. The 80 to 120 *tonneaux* mature in wooden casks for about a year and a half; one-third of the casks are new.

Not impressive

The estate has a 74-acre vineyard planted with 36% Merlot, 30% Cabernet Sauvignon, 30% Cabernet Franc and the balance of 4% mainly Petit Verdot. In terms of quality, I do not consider the wine (at least up to and including the 1979 vintage, the last I tasted) particularly impressive. Although the colour of Rauzan-Gassies is satisfyingly deep and dark, its bouquet often lacks concentration, depth and finesse. It also tends to be short on fruitiness or charm — which is again evident in the taste. The wine nearly always tastes fairly sharp and hard, often with a hint of acidity and a fairly dry aftertaste. The impression is of a rather characterless wine, falling well short of what one might expect from a second *grand cru.* This is recorded time and again in my notes, both for the great vintages such as 1966 and 1970, among others, and for the more variable harvests (including 1976, 1979). The 1974 I found frankly bad. Now that the modern equipment is fully operational, it is to be hoped that Jean-Michel Quié will offer a better product in the years to come, worthy of the status of this estate. Perhaps selection should also be more stringent, and the little-used second label Enclos de Moncabon employed more frequently.

Château Marquis de Terme

4e Grand Cru Classé

Although Château Marquis de Terme is a mere stone's throw from the Rausans and Palmer, it is a relatively obscure name in the international world of wine. The reason for this is that the owners sell much of their wine directly to private customers in France, so that a sad tail-end remains for the rest of the world. What is still available for export goes chiefly to Belgium, the Netherlands and the USA. Nor does the estate seem to be particularly well geared to receiving visitors as I discovered personally — or did I perhaps choose a bad day? Jean-Pierre Hugon is the somewhat laconic *régisseur* who has held the post since 1974. He works for the three Sénéclauze brothers, who in partnership own this 4th growth, the only one at Margaux. Their father, Pierre Sénéclauze, purchased the estate at auction in 1935. It takes its name from Seigneur de Peguilhan, Marquis de Terme, who built up the domaine in 1808-1809. The Feuillerat family later built up its great reputation; and Frédéric Eschenauer was also once joint owner.

Breaking with tradition

The Marquis de Terme's vineyard was for a long time worked only with horses in the traditional manner, but this is now a thing of the past and here, too, the tractor has made its noisy appearance. The vineyard extends for about 74 acres, the vines being 45% Cabernet Sauvignon, 35% Merlot, 15% Cabernet Franc and 5% Petit Verdot. The château itself is a simple house with an overhanging gabled roof. Nobody lives in it. Built on to the house are the modern offices and behind them is the presshouse, with white-tiled concrete tanks on red blocks. After fermentation the wine remains for a relatively brief time in oak casks, for 12 to 18 months. The average yield of 110 *tonneaux* is stored in a long, low cellar located the best part of a mile away on the other side of the village of Margaux.

Château Marquis de Terme

Patience required

I can report only on the recent past of the Marquis de Terme because I have never yet encountered a fully mature vintage. The wine usually has a respectable amount of tannin, so that the Marquis de Terme can be counted an ideal wine for laying down. This was especially true of the 1971 and 1970. The 1971 wine was only bottled in the summer of 1974 and I feel that even in 1994 it will still be relatively fresh. The colour was deep, almost purplish, the bouquet closed, the taste rather less fine than the other great Margaux wines. The 1970 was perhaps even deeper in colour, with an even higher tannin content, sticking hard to the teeth. There was a great deal of fruitiness, which is generally a good omen. I tasted the 1976 several times, finding it a nicely structured wine, but with limited charm, depth and finesse — properties which in later years have been characteristics of the estate. Even the 1982 I found rather lacking in body for that year.

The château had a world-wide reputation earlier in the century, under Armand Feuillerat's management. Nowadays, however, the wine certainly does not reach the level of a fourth growth — at best that of a fifth. To be truthful, I find this estate's most attractive product its second label, Domaine des Gondats. This in fact offers an excellent balance between price and quality.

Château Lascombes

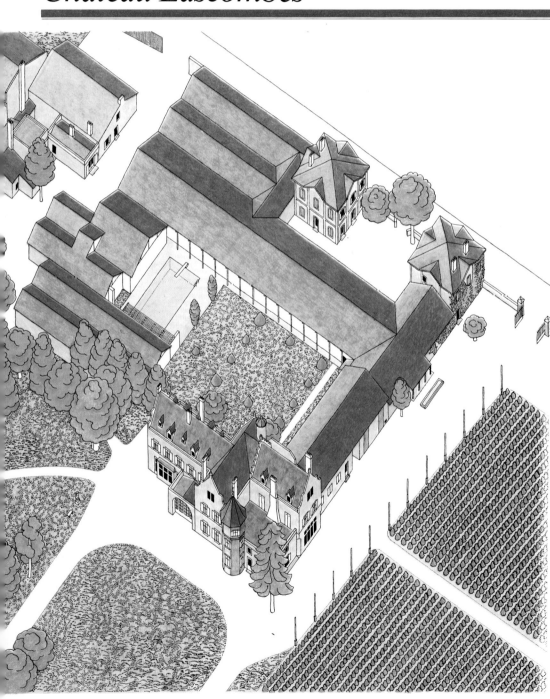

Every great château in the Médoc can look back with pride on a long history. In many cases, the same families have lived in them and tilled the vineyards for generations; in others, the property has changed hands many times over, as has been the case with Château Lascombes.

At the time of the famous classification of 1855, Château Lascombes, according to the original, hand-written deeds, belonged to a certain Mademoiselle Hué. At that time the château's name was written Lascombe (without the final 's') and it was classified fourth in the second *cru* after Châteaux Rausan-Ségla, Rauzan-Gassies and Vivens-Durfort [sic]. Château Margaux was of course classified under the *premiers grand crus*, but Lascombes was then often set on a par with that famous *cru*. The issue for 4 April 1938 of the journal *Le Producteur* states: 'The Lascombes estate lies on valuable land and is planted with the best varieties of old vines. The quality of the wines is such that they match those of Margaux.' This may seem a little exaggerated but it is nevertheless a fact that the Lascombes wine enjoyed very high standing in those days.

Alexis Lichine buys the estate

The importance of Lascombes has increased considerably since the 19th century. The property once formed part of the Durfort, and when in 1844 M. Loraique sold it to M. L. A. Hué for 90,000 francs, the vineyard barely covered 50 acres. The château was for a time called Petit-Lascombes, not because it was intended to emphasize its smallness, but because M. Hué made a gift of the estate to his son-in-law who happened to be called Petit. The latter sold it later to M. Chaix-d'Est-Ange, whose grandson Gustave acquired it in 1867. Gustave Chaix-d'Est-Ange was a famous man in his time. He was the lawyer who won the Suez Canal case for France against Egypt. He was followed in the course of the present century by a series of other *propriétaires*, the best known of whom was undoubtedly the American Alexis

Lascombes receives more and more visitors every year, and is pleased to do so. There is an average of 50 a day from spring to late summer; sometimes they turn up by the busload.

The château has a carpenter, painter and bricklayer on the staff to deal with all extension and maintenance work.

Right:
A tiny part of the Lascombes stock. Anyone who owned this number of bottles of the tremendous Lascombes 1970 would be a fortunate person indeed.

Below:
The impressive main tower of Lascombe, round at the bottom and polygonal at the top. It is clearly visible to anyone driving into Margaux from the north.

Bottom:
A voluptuous lady in the park who finds a headdress of grapes sufficient attire.

Château Lascombes

Lichine. With a few friends he purchased Château Lascombes in the spring of 1952. Thanks to his enthusiasm and his investments Lascombes was soon restored to the ranks of the great wines. Much attention was also paid to the presentation of the château and the cellars and it was Lichine who had the idea of organizing an annual exhibition here of contemporary art on the theme of *Vigne et Vin*. The standard of these exhibitions was high, as may be seen from the paintings hanging at Prieuré-Lichine, Cantenac-Brown and other châteaux. However, this is now past history for in May 1971 Lichine sold Lascombes to Bass Charrington Vintners.

An imposing new building

Rumour has it that the price was in the region of 2 million dollars. According to experts, that would be cheap because the value of a *grand cru* of this kind is somewhere between 6 and 15 million dollars. In any event the new owners began pumping enormous quantities of money into the property so that Lascombes, in terms of appearance alone, already ranks amongst the most imposing châteaux of the Médoc. In the spring of 1973, completely renovated *chais* were brought into use. They are a joy to the eye. On the outside, the walls are of white plaster, dark brown wood and red tiles, while on the inside sophisticated lighting reveals hundreds of casks and a spotlessly clean yet atmospheric cellar. As at Prieuré-Lichine, the *barriques* are varnished along the top, which reinforces the impression of cleanliness. Two large 'no smoking' signs hang in the large *chai* at Lascombes. These are not intended for the staff — because they would never smoke in the cellars — but for the groups of visitors who may be tempted to wander around with cigarettes alight. Quite rightly, at Lascombes they want to keep the air round the young wine absolutely pure. Renovations have not been limited to the *chai*. The fermentation unit, too, is entirely new and consists of concrete vats with dark brown tiles. As for the

Left:
A swimming pool for Château Lascombe's guests. It is interesting to note that half the costs have been covered by tax allowances as the pool can be used as an emergency reservoir in case of fire.

Below:
This cupola has been built as part of the complete restoration of the château hall.

Centre below:
Maître de chai Robert Dupuy, who usually shows visitors around.

Bottom:
View of the spotless cuvier. The apparatus in the foreground cools the must during the first fermentation.

Claude Gobinau not only makes excellent wine at Lascombes, but also at his own small estate called Cap de Haut, in the commune of Moulis. Its annual yield is about 15 tonneaux.

At Lascombes a quarter of the casks are new each year; the wine is matured for about 18 months.

In the Lascombes chai stainless-steel pipes in the floor allow wine to be pumped by means of compressed air from one cask to another.

Château Lascombes

accommodation for the pickers, it is clean and with every comfort, including showers and an ultra-modern kitchen. Last but not least, the château itself was drastically modernized. Seven guest rooms with bathrooms and a number of elegant reception rooms were added.

A world record

The Lascombes vineyard has been appreciably expanded since 1971. It now measures 217 acres which carry the right to the Margaux *appellation*. The problem is only that this area is divided up like no other in the Bordeaux region. A French official once congratulated the *régisseur* Claude Gobinau in having probably set up a new world record — a vineyard consisting of more than a thousand plots! It would be enough to daunt any ordinary mortal, but not M. Gobinau. Not only does he succeed in merging a few plots each year but the patchwork pattern has one advantage — it spreads the risk of hail, night frost and other unwelcome surprises. The vineyard is composed of 46% Cabernet Sauvignon, 32% Merlot, 8% Cabernet Franc, 10% Petit Verdot and 4% Malbec. Although a great deal of replanting has occurred in recent years, a high average age is aimed at for the vines. Half of them are 20 years old or more. Château Lascombes' output generally exceeds 300 *tonneaux* excluding the 20 or so *tonneaux* of rosé made on this estate. A small part of the vineyard lies on flat land near the river and is therefore unsuited to producing a *grand vin*. Chevalier de Lascombes is the name of this fresh, dry, thirst-quenching wine, which is sold in a clear, tall bottle under the *appellation* Bordeaux Supérieur and is named after the nobleman who once gave his name to, or derived it from, the château.

Developing well in the bottle

One characteristic of the Lascombes wines is that they develop very well in the bottle, which gives rise to an odd situation. Patrick Léon, the oenologist responsible for Lascombes, once said; 'I always have the greatest difficulty in understanding Lascombes. It is a wine which changes in time. For example, in the bottle it gains in colour, so that it is difficult to assess the wine properly in its youth.' That Lascombes can mature well was evident at an impressive tasting which I attended in 1982, when 13 different wines were offered, the youngest of 1979, the oldest of 1878. Even the latter wine — noble and soft as butter — was still very drinkable. One of the features of Lascombes is firm elegance. I consider it a highly reliable, sturdy Margaux which deserves its place among the second growths. One of the best years I know is 1966, but other classic vintages have not disappointed either. Among the years of lower standing, 1964, 1967, 1969, 1974 and 1977 and a few others were relatively successful. The bottles are Lascombes' own, bearing the name of the château.

APPELLATION MARGAUX CONTROLÉE

GRAND VIN
CHATEAU FERRIERE
MARGAUX
MÉDOC

ANDRÉ
DURAND

1970

MIS EN BOUTEILLES AU CHATEAU

Château Ferrière

3e Grand Cru Classé

Ferrière is an exceptional château in more ways than one. For many years the wine could be drunk only in France because the *Relais de Campagne* chain of hotels and restaurants had a monopoly of the entire crop. This was possible because Ferrière has the smallest yield of all the *grands crus* — approximately 20 *tonneaux*. It is also worth noting that the vineyard is leased by the owners of the neighbouring Château Lascombes. Under the energetic management of former Lascombes owner Alexis Lichine, the Ferrière vineyard was entirely replanted between 1958 and 1964 so that quantity and quality have been greatly improved. Although Ferrière has a *chai* of its own, the wine is made at Lascombes. In the latter's cellars I noticed a separate row of

casks with the wine from this tiny estate. Another way in which Ferrière is distinguished from the other *crus* in Margaux is the location of the vineyard. In fact, much of it lies at the centre of the village of Margaux, surrounded by a stone wall. Altogether, it covers 10 acres entitled to the Ferrière name and the Margaux *appellation*, and just over half an acre on which rosé is produced for the Chevalier de Lascombes label. When tasting Ferrière, it is natural to compare it with Lascombes. After all, both wines are produced in the same way by the same people in the same cellars. As it happens, Château Lascombes is a second *grand cru*, Château Ferrière a third — and the difference shows. Beside Lascombes, Ferrière is rather more rustic, less fruity and

sometimes more tannic. Five years after being harvested, the Ferrière 1970 had developed less than the same wine at Lascombes. From the viewpoint of finesse, Ferrière was well behind. Even so, it is a well-made, tasty wine which is usually worth its price. Allow Ferrière sufficient time to unfold — assuming you manage to acquire any of this rare Margaux.

GRAND CRU CLASSÉ EN 1855

1971   1971

CHATEAU
MALESCOT St EXUPÉR
MARGAUX

Cette récolte, entièrement mise en bouteilles
au Château a produit 33.500 Magnums,
bouteilles et demi-bouteilles.
Cette bouteille porte le N° 22184

PAUL ZUGER, PROPRIÉTAIRE A MARGAUX-MÉDOC (GIRONDE)
APPELLATION MARGAUX CONTROLÉE
PRODUCE OF FRANCE

Left:
The Malescot Saint-Exupéry
labels are numbered and give
the exact number of magnums,
bottles and half-bottles
produced: there were 33,500 in
1971.

Below:
The livre d'or for Malescot
Saint-Exupéry and Marquis
d'Alesme Becker in which
visitors sign their names. Any
cru worthy of the name has
such a visitors' book.

Below:
The present château dates from
1885 and was built in Louis
Seize style onto an existing,
unpretentious small house. An
illustration of the latter is
preserved in the Album de ma
mère *of 1868 left by Fernand de*
Saint-Exupéry. The château's
oldest cellar was constructed in
1861. It contains a small
private reserve with some very
old bottles, the most venerable
dating from 1878.

The wine matures for two years
in casks, one-third of them new.
There are two subsidiary
brands, Château de Loyac and
Domaine du Balardin.

Château Malescot Saint-Exupéry

3e Grand Cru Classé

Château Malescot Saint-Exupéry lies along the main road of Margaux, and anyone passing by can read something of the estate's history on long notice boards. Two people are responsible for the long, double-barrelled name — Simon Malescot, public prosecutor, and Duke Jean-Baptiste de Saint-Exupéry. The former became the owner in 1697, the latter in 1827. Nowadays, Malescot is not managed by nobility but by the hard-working Zuger family who took over the estate in 1955 from the British Seager Evans group. After Paul Zuger died in September 1981, Roger Zuger became the owner. His brother Jean-Claude then took charge of the Château Marquis d'Alesme-Becker, the other family estate. Roger — president of the *syndicat viticole* at Margaux — and his family live at Malescot Saint-Exupéry. After the Second World War, Malescot was little more than a skeleton, but the Zuger family has been able to make it a comfortable home again.

Wine for people with patience

The Malescot wine comes from 79 acres planted with 50% Cabernet Sauvignon, 35% Merlot, 10% Cabernet Franc and 5% Petit Verdot. The yield is 80 to 180 *tonneaux*, shipped chiefly to Britain, the USA, Switzerland, West Germany, the Netherlands, Belgium and Japan.
A highly characteristic feature of the wine is its austerity, which is most unusual for a Margaux. The fine Margaux bouquet begins to develop only after quite a long time, and the taste becomes rather more friendly. As Paul Zuger says: 'Perhaps I make wines that require some patience from the consumer.' A highly successful year was 1964, immediately followed by 1966. The 1967 was somewhat lighter; it is typical of Malescot that a good seven years after harvesting, this wine still showed no trace of tiredness. The wine acquired true charm only after ten years. Other recommended Malescot vintages are 1969 (good for its year), 1970, 1971 (may be drunk now), 1974 (good for its year), 1975, 1976 (not too deep, but pleasant), 1978, the perhaps even better 1979, 1981 and 1982.

Château Marquis d'Alesme-Becker

3e Grand Cru Classé

Château Marquis d'Alesme-Becker lies in the same street as Malescot Saint-Exupéry. However, you can easily miss it because the avenue is screened off by a park that starts as a narrow strip between two houses but becomes wider and wider the further it gets from the road. The same applies to the château. At first sight, it appears small and insignificant, but that is an illusion because you are looking at it from the side. Marquis d'Alesme is a relatively ornate building, 12 windows wide, which fully deserves to be called a château. The comfortably furnished living rooms look out over the *chais* where the wine has been made and bottled since 1975. In previous years, the process of vinification took place at the Château Malescot Saint-Exupéry. The present owner of Marquis d'Alesme-Becker is Jean-Claude Zuger.

For quite some time the wine from Marquis d'Alesme-Becker was indisputably second to that of Malescot Saint-Exupéry. The wine was less fine, and also very hard. Even a small year such as 1958 produced wine with power and reserve even more than 15 years after harvesting. However, much has changed in the meantime. Jean-Claude Zuger has spared neither time nor expense to introduce improvements both in the vineyard and in the cellars. Since 1979 the château has had a modern *cuvier* with stainless-steel fermentation tanks and an entirely new *chai*. Since that year, the quality of the wine seems to have improved by leaps and bounds. It has become more flexible and also finer. Jean-Claude Zuger has also deliberately reduced the period of storage in the wood to 14 months (one-fifth of the casks being renewed each year). All in all, Marquis d'Alesme-Becker has again become a wine deserving of full attention.

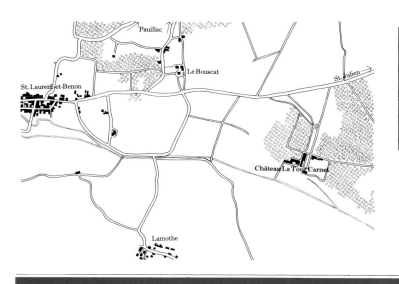

Château La Tour Carnet

4e Grand Cru Classé

I first encountered the wine of La Tour Carnet, one of the *grands crus* of Saint Laurent (entitled to the *appellation* Haut-Médoc) in one of those excellent small restaurants at Bordeaux which only the local merchants seem to know about. There, I drank a six-year-old La Tour Carnet 1966 with an outstanding *escalope bordelaise*. A wine with a far more flexible and friendly mien than most of its contemporaries, in addition to a splendid bouquet, it had a ripe, soft taste, very pleasant but at the same time unusually well developed for such a solid year as 1966. Only much later did I learn the reasons for this when I asked the then owner, the late Louis Lipschitz, about it. He told me that he had purchased the property in a very neglected condition in 1962. The château was a ruin, the vineyard virtually non-existent. So, in the first two years (1963 and 1964) no more than 20 *tonneaux* were harvested, as against 120 in 1974. The fact, however, that the land had lain fallow for years was a great advantage to the new young vines, enabling them to accumulate strength which enabled so successful a wine as the 1966 to be made only four years after the first replanting. Of course this was still a light wine, but thanks to its quiet strength it had acquired sufficient body from the soil to be entirely worthy of the title *grand cru*.

The difference between water and wine

It almost goes without saying that the wines of La Tour Carnet have steadily gained in importance. Proof of this is the 1970, which delights the eye with its clear, deep colour, the tongue with its meaty but appealing taste, and the nose with a fine bouquet, reminiscent of violets. This aroma is very characteristic of La Tour Carnet. The late Madame Lipschitz once told me: 'The nose of our wine reminds me of a very fine scent. I

Château La Tour Carnet

sometimes feel like rubbing just a bit of it between my hands and breathing in the bouquet — just as you do with a perfume.' It is remarkable that the Lipschitz's knew absolutely nothing about wine when they brought La Tour Carnet. Yes, Louis knew how to open a bottle but that was about all. Before this he managed a shipping line; wasn't that a rather drastic change? 'Oh no,' replied Lipschitz, 'I switched from water to wine and aren't they both liquid? Just make sure you have a good staff, good grapes, good equipment and goodwill, because it takes an enormous amount of work. What we have done here would normally take a generation.'

At present the vineyard covers some 76 acres, with 53% Cabernet Sauvignon, 33% Merlot, 10% Cabernet Franc and 4% Petit Verdot. The wine ferments in wooden, metal or concrete *cuves*, and generally matures for 20 to 22 months in oak casks (of which one-third are new). The owner of the estate is Marie-Claire Pelegrin, the daughter of Louis Lipschitz. Her husband, Guy-François, is the general manager.

A walk through the centuries

It is a pity that people who drink La Tour Carnet (living chiefly in the USA, Belgium, the Netherlands, Switzerland and Denmark) cannot see the château at first hand instead of merely as a picture on the label, because this is one of the few genuine castles in the Médoc. The building dates from the 13th century, when it was known as the Château de Saint Laurent. It derives its present name from the lord of the manor of Carnet who took up residence in 1427. He was one of the many noblemen in the district who some 20 years later fell out with the French king, because he fought on the side of the English. Even then, good wine was being made; in 1407, wine from this estate was already being sold for nearly twice as much as red Graves.

If you visit the château now you take a walk, as it were, through the centuries. It starts with the splendid 18th-century ornamental gates, painted blue, after which you see the 17th-century workers' quarters. Then comes the moat and 13th-century tower. After that, you enter the main building whose ground floor dates from the 13th century and the upper floors from the 17th. Downstairs is the reception area where visitors can taste the wine and upstairs are a number of stylish rooms and an impressive hall, where no trouble and expense has been spared on the furnishings. Among other things, it contains an extremely fine, centuries-old chest which was once proof of a master locksmith's skills. Louis Lipschitz never failed to demonstrate to visitors how this hand-made treasure had to be opened via all kinds of secret panels. And what lay in it? Bottles, of course, a magnum and a double magnum of Château La Tour Carnet, the greatest treasures of this exquisite estate.

Recent La Tour Carnet vintages show that this wine has become a fairly flexible, pleasant Haut-Médoc, quite elegant but still firm in the mouth, more often than not with a hint of fruitiness. La Tour Carnet is not a really concentrated or sophisticated wine but decently made. Generally speaking, it does not demand excessive patience, usually 5 to 10 years. Apart from the aforementioned 1970, some of my favourite vintages are 1975, 1976, 1979 and 1981.

Château de Camensac

5e Grand Cru Classé

Château de Camensac, a Haut-Médoc *appellation contrôlée*, is certainly not one of the best known names of the 1855 classification. This is a shame, for the estate has since 1966 been producing excellent wines which are perhaps the best of Saint Laurent. This is thanks to two men, E. H. Forner (who bought Camensac in 1965 together with two other people) and the famous Professor Emile Peynaud, *docteur-ingénieur oenologue* (who gave technical advice). To start with, they were faced with an estate that was wholly impoverished. For years the vineyard, the wine-making equipment and the château had been completely neglected. Of the wine of the time, Forner recalls that 'we bought the château and were obliged to take over the entire 1964 harvest. That was a reasonably successful year in the Médoc but the wine from Camensac was quite undrinkable. We still tried to select the best casks and the wine was even bottled. The bottles are still lying in our cellars. Ten, fifteen years after the harvest, they remain unpalatable. And that from a *grand cru*!'.

Finally, Elisée Forner and Professor Peynaud set to work. They drew up a seven-year plan to raise the quality of the wine to its former status. It was fortunate that the new owner had the necessary funds, because the professor made exacting demands.

An enormous outlay rewarded

In the first place, the vineyard had to be entirely restored. Barely 37 of the present 148 acres were viable. The remainder had to be replanted, with 60% Cabernet Sauvignon, 20% Cabernet Franc and 20% Merlot — according to Professor Peynaud, an ideal mixture of varieties for this soil. All equipment had then to be replaced — fermentation vats, bottling plant and so forth. A third rule was extremely strict selection. Only the best wines could be used which, certainly in the early years, cut the yield drastically. The last rule was the most costly in the long run, because it is an annually recurring expense. Professor Peynaud prescribed the use of entirely new oak casks for every harvest — a luxury that not even many 2nd growths can allow themselves. But the result makes it all worthwhile. On 21 March 1969 Professor Peynaud wrote to Forner that the 1967 had been classified at a blind tasting at the level of 2nd growth. Similarly, the Professor reported in May 1970 that the Camensac 1969 had ended in second place at a professional *dégustation* of 14 different *grands crus*.

Synthesis of St Julien and Pauillac

In my experience, the wines of Camensac are a successful synthesis of St Julien and Pauillac. They are versatile, but with a great

Château de Camensac

deal of body even in the lean years such as 1968. Early in 1975 I tasted Château de Camensac 1968 and was very agreeably surprised by its deep colour, the full bouquet, the generous taste and its still very evident vitality — simply a perfect example of an excellent wine in a very difficult year. The vintages of 1966, 1970 and 1974 were unreservedly good. The first two had a deep dark colour, the taste and aroma of fully ripened fruit, and a tremendous sense of completeness. The 1966 was not without merits, but will still develop further. As to the possible lifetime of the 1970 I can hardly hazard a guess. I also enjoyed the 1975 and

the 1978. The later wine, with its deep, bright colour, a pure, fairly broad scent with traces of wood, and a supple, mouth-filling, meaty taste, was sappy and sound. As to style, this wine is characteristic of what de Camensac is now producing. Only one-third of the casks are now renewed each year. Storage on wood normally lasts for 18 months. The production averages 300 *tonneaux*.

The Spanish connection

When money became available, Elisée Forner had the pale-coloured château — a

former charterhouse — restored. Guests can now also be received there. Elisée is assisted by his nephew Henri Forner. Henri's father has a bodega in the Spanish Rioja area, where he, again with Emile Peynaud, has created an excellent wine, Marques de Cacères. Whatever the Forner family does, it does well. Whenever I visit the Château de Camensac I find not only great craftsmanship but also the owners' unshakeable belief: 'We are *grand cru* and will make sure you know it.' And so they do, to perfection.

Château Belgrave

My first acquaintance with the wine of Belgrave was certainly not the most fortunate. While visiting the Médoc, I saw between the simple table wines in a grocery shop at Margaux a bottle of Château Belgrave A.C. Haut-Médoc. It had no vintage date, and was offered for the sum of 14 francs. That is not much for a *grand cru* and I did not hesitate to buy the bottle. It proved to be an unwise decision because the wine was a great disappointment. It came nowhere near the quality of a *grand cru*. I later heard that the château had in good faith sold the entire 1968 harvest to a dealer, who had then had the Belgrave labels printed himself in order to mark the wine under the name. My second acquaintance with Belgrave occurred at the estate itself — and that was not much better. The cellars were dirty, the equipment soiled, and the wine tasted threadbare.

A major outlay

After Belgrave had been up for sale for years, the estate was purchased in October 1979 by a *groupement foncier agricole*. This consists of an unknown number of shareholders, including Messrs. Dourthe Frères of Moulis. This firm took on a tenancy for 26 years. The new owners renovated the entire domain in a radical and impressive way. The *cuvier* was entirely rebuilt and in addition to the lined concrete vats, stainless steel tanks were installed. A new press was also introduced, and other modern equipment. A start was also made on building two new *chais*, one of 1,000 square metres for cask maturing and one of 300 square metres for bottles. A roomy reception room was installed at the same time. They did not flinch from purchasing new casks — 300 in the first instance. *Gérant* Patrick Atteret intends to replace at least 30% of the casks each year. The wine matures in the cask for about 18 months.

Château Belgrave

Changes in planting

The new owners did not stop at investing in buildings and equipment. The vineyard, too was fully rationalised and also expanded. Ten tons of wire (to bind the twigs) were used to clean up the existing vineyard alone. In 1982, 96 acres were in production, 92 had been replanted, and a further 37 were planned for the future. At the time of the takeover the grape varieties were Merlot 70%, Cabernets 30%. Professor Emile Peynaud advised that the percentage of Merlot should be reduced in favour of the Cabernet. What is now being aimed at is 50% Cabernet Sauvignon, 30% Merlot, and 20% Cabernet Franc, with a little Petit Verdot.

Up to standard again

The new owners' first vintage was 1979. They had in fact asked if they could harvest that year's wine even before the takeover was completed in formal terms. The request was granted and the Dourthe workers set to. As from 1979, I have now tasted all years up to and including 1982. The difference with the past is great. From being a mean, characterless wine, Belgrave is back to the level of a fifth cru. The 1979 was immediately streets ahead of the other wines of that decade, with a dark, deep colour, a clear aroma of wood and a pure taste. The 1980 gave a good impression by comparison with other wines of that vintage, with a clear hint of vanilla (all the wine was then matured in new casks), suppleness, a deep colour and a quality which was certainly good for the year. A sturdy dark-red colour characterized 1981 and 1982. Both were successful wines, the latter seeming rather more generous and broader. These Belgrave wines lacked something in length and depth. One of the causes may have been the young vines of the renovated and new plantings. As time progresses, this problem will disappear of its own accord. I expect Belgrave will in the Eighties and Nineties again find its place amongst the fifth crus; the expertise and integrity of Dourthe Frères is of course a sound guarantee of this.

Since 1979 Belgrave has been put into an improved, stouter-type of bottle, and a cork of better quality has also been used.

Belgrave has its own laboratory where analyses can be made.

Below:
Curios from the reception room at Ducru-Beaucaillou, which is situated directly behind the chai.

Bottom right:
Château Ducru-Beaucaillou in all its glory. There are cellars under the steps up to the terrace. Note the square 19th-century tower. The other tower is not visible, which would please Jean-Eugène Borie, for on it is the TV aerial he so abominates.

Right:
The 19th-century hall of the château. There are paintings of the Breughelian school on the walls.

Far right:
The wine museum, with a goodly number of old bottles, many of them from the 19th century. The cellar where the bottles are stored is the lowest part of the château, and the darkest, as the lighting is minimal.

Château Ducru-Beaucaillou

2e Grand Cru Classé

At first sight Château Ducru-Beaucaillou seems to say: if not here, where else can a great wine be made? It is a majestic, broad building flanked with two solid Victorian towers, seated in all its imposing glory on top of the first hill to rise up from the Gironde. On the ground floor are the tastefully decorated living quarters of the owner Jean-Eugène Borie and his wife Monique. Beneath them lie the lengthy cellars where two years' harvests lie ripening in *barriques.*

A wine of particular charm

Here, in the half-light of a fresh winter's day, I tasted a number of wines in the company of Monsieur Borie and his cellar master, to find my opinion confirmed that Ducru-Beaucaillou is one of my favourite Médoc wines. What attracts me so particularly is its unmistakable charm. Year in, year out, this estate produces perfectly balanced wines which start smiling in the glass while still young. Tannin is of course present in fair quantities, but even when the wine is young it does not taste stone-hard. Fruit is always clearly present, as is a sappy meatiness, roundness and the noble tones of wood. Fine nuances are also to be discovered — even in not fully mature wine. Back in 1975, I drank the Ducru-Beaucaillou 1970, a wine with a dark, almost black colour, a taste like baskets full of fruit, and a closed but very charming aroma. It is one of those wines which should perhaps be drunk around 1985. I tasted various Ducru-Beaucaillou wines from the Sixties. The 1969 demonstrated how the estate was still able to produce a good wine in less successful years, as did, later, the 1972, 1974 and 1977.
It was in the château itself that I first drank the 1961 (with *entrecôte bordelaise* and cheese), a delightful wine which promises to have a long life. I again tasted this 1961 in 1978 at a fantastic blind tasting of wines of

72

Left:
Jean-Eugène Borie on the château steps.

Below:
Figure from the reception room.

The wine matures from 16 to 20 months in casks of which 30% to 60% are new each year. Ducru-Beaucaillou is never filtered.

Ducru-Beaucaillou is not the only château with which Jean-Eugène is associated. He manages Château Haut-Batailley and Château La Couronne in Pauillac (see page 102), and since 1974 he has been the owner of Château Grand-Puy-Lacoste, also in Pauillac (see page 104). In addition he produces the wines of Château Lalande-Borie (Saint-Julien), Clos la Croix (Saint-Julien); the second wine of Ducru-Beaucaillou) and Château Ducluzeau (Listrac).

Château Ducru-Beaucaillou

that glorious year. Of the 19 wines, only the Mouton-Rothschild, Latour and Palmer scored higher. Lafite, Margaux, Haut-Brion and six other *deuxiemes grands crus* were also on the table. Amongst those present were four British Masters of Wine, Serena Sutcliffe, David Peppercorn, Clive Coates and Michael Broadbent. In more recent years, too, from 1974 to 1982, the perfectionist Jean-Eugene Borie has succeeded in making an unbroken series of eminent wines, ranking amongst the finest of Bordeaux.

Much fame early on

In 1800, Monsieur and Madame Ducru were the owners of the vineyard with the '*Beaux Cailloux*', the fine gravel. Just as in other parts of the Médoc, a gravelly soil often produces very good wines and that, too, was the case here. Madame Ducru's father was even so fond of it that when sitting as chairman of the Chamber of Commerce of Bordeaux he had the traditional glass of water replaced by a glass of Ducru-Beaucaillou. Alas, history failed to relate whether he was then inspired to preside with still greater wisdom, but that will undoubtedly have been the case!

Ducru-Beaucaillou changed owners on 3 March 1866 for the tremendous sum of 1,000,000 francs. The purchaser was the prosperous wife of Nathan Johnston Jr, a member of a famous merchant family from Bordeaux. The Johnston's made the wine even better than it already was, and acquired many medals and other tokens of honour. It was they who built the angular towers, perhaps to raise the grandeur of the building to the level of its wine.

Ducru-Beaucaillou eventually passed into the hands of the Borie family in 1942. Of its past fame little was then left. Successive owners had neglected the estate, and the Borie's had to start from the bottom again. That they succeeded is proved by the wines of today. Château Ducru-Beaucaillou is more than worthy of its position among the *deuxiemes grands cru classes*.

The Ducru-Beaucaillou vineyard covers some 124 acres planted with 65% Cabernet Sauvignon, 25% Merlot, 5% Cabernet Franc and 5% Petit Verdot. The yield is between 75 and 220 *tonneaux* a year, which chiefly finds its way to America, Britain, France, Belgium and Switzerland.

Château Beychevelle is not regularly occupied, but its three owners (Aymar, Etienne and Marie-Geneviève Achille Fould) have apartments there which they sometimes use for short visits. Aymar Achille Fould is a well-known figure in France: he has been Secretary of State for both Defence and Transport. His father, Armand, was once Minister of Agriculture.

Besides the wines mentioned in the text, of 1966, 1970 and 1975, there are other very successful vintages: those of 1978, 1979, 1981 and 1982.

The wine matures for 18 months in casks, one-third of which are new each year. Beychevelle is not filtered.

Château Beychevelle

4e Grand Cru Classé

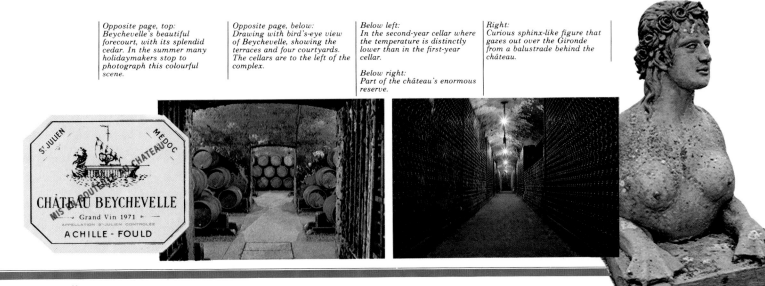

Château Beychevelle

For Jean-Louis de Nogaret de Lavalette, Duc d'Epernon, 1587 was a year to remember. He then acquired three things, the title Admiral of France, a dynamic young wife called Marguerite, and as dowry the Château du Médoc. The estate was quickly nicknamed Beychevelle, because all the ships from and to Bordeaux were ordered to *baisse-voile*, 'strike the sail' (salute), in honour of the Admiral. The name Beychevelle remained, the owner didn't. The château passed through many hands before it was entirely rebuilt in 1757 by the Marquis of Brassier. He replaced the war-like battlements with peaceful balustrades and had an entirely new château built in Louis XV style. This was done with a great deal of taste: Beychevelle was and is one of the finest buildings in the whole of the Bordelais. In 1875 the property was purchased by Armand Heine. His daughter married Charles Achille Fould and his descendants — three in number — are the present owners. As they walk on their pleasant rear terrace they can enjoy a decorative Versailles-style garden with the Gironde in the distance, at the end of a long, green lawn. It is easy to imagine how the Admiral, a good glass at hand, could from this spot observe the ships sailing slowly past with their sails at the salute.

Balanced wines

The vineyard covers 178 acres planted with 58% Cabernet Sauvignon, 28% Merlot, 11% Cabernet Franc and 3% Petit Verdot. The yield is 180 to 380 *tonneaux*, mainly enjoyed in Britain, America, France, Belgium and Switzerland. There is also a second wine, Réserve de l'Amiral — which accounts for some 50 *tonneaux* (of course depending on the year). The Beychevelle wines are nearly always perfectly balanced. One has the feeling that all the elements have been carefully weighed up with a hypersensitive scale. Beychevelle is a wine with breeding, with style. It tastes a little harder than its neighbours and could almost be a Pauillac. A very good year was 1966, while 1970 and 1975 also deserved this tag. The 1975, in particular, which I tasted two years after the vintage, was a highly promising wine. rather tighter than its neighbour Ducru-Beaucaillou, for example, but still rich in finesse. In its youth, Beychevelle often seems to have a rather green aroma, but as the years go by the bouquet develops into a distinguished, fruity perfume. Something similar happens to the taste. The wine must therefore mature for a comparatively long period for a Saint-Julien. The generous dose of tannin which usually characterizes Beychevelle helps to make a success of the wine in lighter years, such as 1968, and the otherwise quite soft 1976 and 1980.

Temperature changes

The man behind the wine at Beychevelle is *régisseur* Maurice Ruelle. He is assisted by the cellar master Lucien Soussette who lays down the law in the extensive (but still too small) *chai*. It is remarkable how the wine changes temperature three times whilst in the cellar. When fermentation is complete, the noble juice travels to the *barriques* in the first-year cellar where the temperature is rather lower. The second year, the wine goes underground, into the cool cellar. And when it goes for bottling, the wine is transferred to the wooden fermentation vats where it is separated from the outside world only by the wooden roof. The advantage of this shifting to larger accommodation is that all wine reaches bottle standard quickly and under equal conditions. M. Ruelle is convinced that the temperature changes are very good for the young wine and in view of the end result one cannot but believe him. The Beychevelle wine is generally sold for the same price as a *deuxieme grand cru*.

Château Branaire-Ducru

4e Grand Cru Classé

I have always had a soft spot for Branaire-Ducru because the 1959 from this château was the first truly great wine that I ever drank. The wine was then undoubtedly still far too young but I can vividly remember how a whole new world was suddenly opened to me. I had never dreamed how good wine could be. This one bottle told me more than everything I had seen, heard and read about wine up till then. It took three glasses — my wife shared the bottle with me — to lift the veil from a series of unknown delights. And from that moment there was no going back, not for our savings, not for our bookcase, not for our holiday travel.

Now, a quarter of a century later, I still find Branaire a particularly attractive wine. It is above all a wine with character, with a taste and perfume entirely of its own. Sometimes I find a hint of violets, or other flowers, the next time around of almonds, now and then of roses. As the co-owner Jean-Michel Tapie rightly told me, 'I have heard many flowers mentioned when people describe our wines.' Branaire-Ducru always comes forward reasonably strongly, but it is never aggressive. In this respect, the wine is a true Saint Julien.
I was greatly impressed by the 1982 which I tasted from the cask. Something of the fine

latent bouquet and strong personality could already be detected, but what was particularly noticeable was the enormously long aftertaste. With a particularly fine chocolate, you always have several minutes' enjoyment of a sublime taste — and that was just as it was here. Earlier, similarly outstanding years were 1981, 1979, 1978 (very fine), 1976, 1975 (much class), 1974 (a success for that harvest), 1973, 1971, 1970, 1966 and 1967. In my notes on the tastings of all these wines I repeatedly find mentions of the characteristic perfume of small flowers.

Right:
*Branaire-Ducru wine is not
bottled until 30 months after
the vintage. Two-thirds of the
chai lies underground and has
an aluminium ceiling giving
perfect insulation. The black,
odourless mould on the walls is
a good sign. Practically all the
wine is matured in wooden
casks. The oak for these comes
largely from Central Europe:
Tapie considers this better
than French wood as it
contains more tannin.*

Below:
*The orangery, used as a
reception area for large groups
of guests. A hundred people
can comfortably lunch or dine
here. The gravel is immaculate.
To the right there is a modern
kitchen where the meals are
prepared.*

Bottom:
*Front view of the château,
which dates from 1794. Behind
the front door is a fine hall
with a number of rooms leading
off it. The white stone staircase
is a splendid piece of interior
architecture, of the same period
as the château itself. The
interior has been kept fairly
restrained, in contrast to many
other châteaux, which often
have too much furniture and
furnishings.*

Château Branaire-Ducru

An inspired grower

When visiting Branaire-Ducru on a sunny morning, don't forget to take a stroll round the park because on top of a small knoll you will find a charming gazebo which offers a view over the vineyards of Saint Julien. Those of Branaire cover 111 acres, and are planted with 60% Cabernet Sauvignon, 25% Merlot, 10% Cabernet Franc and 5% Petit Verdot.

The château itself lies immediately opposite Beychevelle and dates from 1794. The Tapie family inhabit it occasionally, chiefly during the school holidays. The children are at school in Bordeaux, which is why the parents mainly live in the city. This does not mean that Jean-Michel Tapie is not personally involved with his wine. On the contrary, his business, his château and his parish receive his full attention. He regards the *commune* of Saint Julien-Beychevelle as the Pomerol of the Médoc — the surface area is small, the quality high; the number of properties is small but those that are there are very well maintained.

Non-vintage wine

Like the several other châteaux, Branaire-Ducru produced a non-vintage wine during the Sixties. Jean-Michel Tapie thought it pointless simply to sell off a wine from a poor year either anonymously or with the vintage attached. Poor wine is poor wine, whatever the label. He thought it was better to improve wine from a poor year with wine from a better year. The consumer would then still have a good wine while the château maintained its reputation. A decent price could still be asked. However, M. Tapie, like other proprietors, has abandoned the non-vintage idea. Demand for such a wine has become less now that the chance of really bad harvests has been virtually eliminated with the aid of chemical controls and other technical advances.

No change of name

On occasion you hear it said that Branaire-Ducru would like to simplify its name to straightforward Château Branaire. The addition Duluc-Ducru appearing between brackets on the label would then be dropped. M. Tapie has assured me, however, that he has no intention whatever of changing the Château's original name. The two former owners, Messrs. Louis du Luc, oenologist, and Ducru did so much good work that their names should continue to live on in honour on the label. It is probably also thanks to the efforts of these two gentlemen that Branaire had assigned to it the status of fourth growth. Nowadays, Branaire-Ducru has clearly grown above this status. I personally would award the wine a place amongst the third growths.

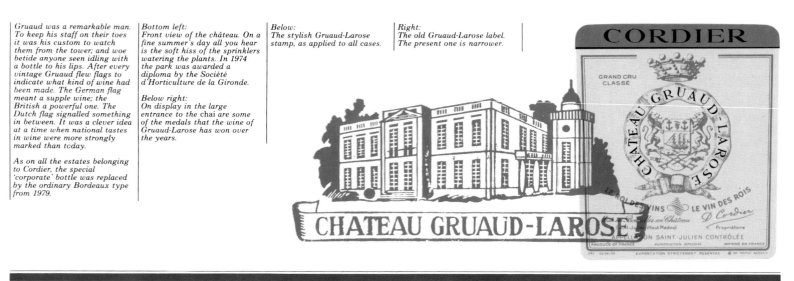

Château Gruaud-Larose

Gruaud-Larose is certainly not the easiest name for a Château which is sold chiefly in non-French speaking countries. How did it acquire such a name? In 1757, M. Gruaud joined up a number of small vineyards into one large one, hence the name Gruaud. Years passed and a descendant of the first owner took possession of the estate. His name was Larose and he had no hesitation in adding it to that of the property; thus why Gruaud-Larose. In the 19th century the estate was split up into two parts, which both again bore the name of their *proprietaire*. For quite a time, therefore, there were two Châteaux Gruaud-Larose, the one being called Gruaud-Larose-Sarget, the other Gruaud-Larose-Faure. Eventually, in 1936, the divided-up vineyard was reunited by M. Désiré Cordier. Since that year this estate has only risen in esteem. Désiré Cordier did not add his name to that of the Château, but a tiny portrait has ever since remained stuck to the bottle. It was intended more as a distinctive sign for all great wines of the house of Cordier than as personal affectation. The little man with the moustache also graced the bottles of Talbot, Meyney and other châteaux at least until 1970.

An exemplary vineyard

Georges Pauli, the technical director of all the Cordier estates, is still a young man. But he has not hesitated to reintroduce methods of working which were common at the beginning of the present century. He has a perfectionist approach to the care of the vineyard, aimed at enabling the grapes to ripen under optimum conditions. Three weeks before the harvest at Gruaud-Larose and Talbot, a group of workers go through the entire vineyard to remove the leaves which shield the grapes. Consequently, the sun can shine unhindered on the fruit during those last, often crucial weeks of ripening. In those years when the harvest looks like being too large, an early, selective picking takes place in July, sacrificing quantity for quality. Some of the immature grapes from each vine are pruned away. Those that remain can then grow and ripen to their full extent. Nature is therefore forced a little in the vineyard, in order to make not just a good wine but a superior one. That this work is certainly no sinecure is demonstrated by the extent of the vineyards. Those of Gruaud-Larose alone cover 200 acres, planted with 62% Cabernet Sauvignon, 25% Merlot, 9% Cabernet Franc and 4% Petit Verdot.

Château Gruaud-Larose

'King of wines, Wine of kings.'

It was M. Larose in the last century who gave the wine of Gruaud-Larose its great reputation. He familiarized the French aristocracy with his noble product and launched a slogan which was entirely in line with the status of his wine, '*Le roi des vins, le vin des rois.*' Château Gruaud-Larose still keeps this motto on the label. I find it rather confusing. Not because I don't allow the wine a royal allure, but because it gives the impression that Grauaud-Larose is a powerful, masculine wine. It is in fact one of the finest, most elegant wines of the commune of Saint Julien. I have tasted a good many vintages of Gruaud-Larose, partly thanks to an auction which the Cordier house organized through Christie's in 1976. At the tasting, the wines went back to the beginning of this century, with the 1971, 1970, 1967, 1961, 1937 and 1921 proving quite exceptional. A good Gruaud-Larose catches the imagination with its civilized aroma and taste. Someone once said that this wine made him think of the music of Vivaldi and it is easy to understand why. A good Gruaud-Larose (such as the 1967) is, moreover, a wine with power, depth and fruit. Eleven years after the vintage, this wine was still lively and was not yet fully developed — something which certainly could not be said of all 1967s. Its colour was good, the perfume fine and complex, the taste pleasing and mouth-filling, the aftertaste pronounced. An excellent wine from a mediocre year. The 1973 also appealed to me — a full colour, fine bouquet, civilized taste. The 1975 is a powerful, concentrated, great wine. My notes on the 1978 are also highly positive. This highly nuanced, fine, deep-coloured wine has a rich quality. The 1979, too, tasted excellent, while the 1981 and 1982 will also enter history as very great vintages. But the property also produces very successful wines in lighter years, such as the 1974 and 1977. The 1980 harvest was used to launch a second wine, Sarget de Gruaud-Larose. I found it an attractive wine, with style, refinement and a silky taste.

Château Lagrange

3e Grand Cru Classé

Lagrange is perhaps the only property in Médoc that has ever belonged to two different Ministers. In 1790, it was the Comte de Cabarrus, who governed Spain for Napoleon I, and from 1842, Comte Duchâtel, a Minister under Napoleon III. But then the estate has an allure which is certainly worthy of men of state. It lies almost on the dividing line between the communes of Saint Julien and Saint Laurent, at the centre of a park with centuries-old, towering trees amid which a man certainly feels very small.
The estate covers a fraction over 400 acres.

At one time it was even larger. I have seen a map dating back to 1843 showing 697 acres. The Château was the property of Louis Mouicy between 1875 and 1919, and then pasted to the Société des Grands Crus. This group sold it again in 1925 to the Spaniard Manuel Cendoya (from the Basque region) and his family still controls Lagrange. The likeable Ignacio Cendoya acted as manager for many years. He died on 1 March 1975, on exactly the same date on which his family had purchased the château 50 years earlier. Management is now in the hands of Jesus Cendoya who lives in a small house near the

Château. The family lives only occasionally in the main building with its roomy salons, generally in the summer. The oldest part of the Château unfortunately burned down in 1960.

Much unused space

Because Lagrange once made more wine than it does now, it has none of the problems of space which some *grands crus* have been faced with on changing over to château-bottling. Everything at Lagrange is outsize. Between the two largest of the long *chais* a

Château Lagrange

reasonable game of football could be played, and there is all kinds of other storage space which is only partly used. The vineyard, too, is still far from maximum capacity. At present, some 121 acres are planted, with 65% Cabernet Sauvignon and 35% Merlot, but early in 1982 Jesus Cendoya told me that they hoped to double this area. The fact that they are thinking about expanding in this way is undoubtedly connected with the improved quality of Lagrange. The wine is now more appreciated — and honoured — than it has been in the past. In terms of quality, Lagrange has recently passed through a difficult period.

There are few *grands crus* which enjoy such favourable circumstances. It seems to me, however, that expansion projects should be the least of Lagrange's concerns. Before thinking of boosting quantity (now an average of 200 *tonneaux*). It is worth giving some serious thought to quality.

On course for quality

In the years up to 1970, in particular, the wine repeatedly proved a disappointment. This applied both to the moderate years (including 1973) and the great ones (including 1970). The wines tasted thin, lacked charm, and in no respect reached the level of a third growth. Fortunately, however, the tide has turned. The Cendoya family employed an expert oenologist who now advises the estate. From 1979 there has been a clear upturn in quality. The wine of that vintage took on a virtually opaque colour, a good, noble perfume with an aroma of wood and fruit, and a firm, not too rounded, taste which lingered harmoniously in the mouth. The 1980 tasted rather tighter and lighter, but was still quite up to standard. The colour of the late-harvested 1981 was almost black, with a meaty, relatively concentrated taste with a dash of fruit. The signs are that this quality will be maintained. Lagrange is set on course for quality. The wine now matures in casks, one-third of which are new each year. The period of storage varies from 18 to 24 months. It is clarified with fresh white of egg and lightly filtered before bottling.

PRODUCE OF FRANCE

Château Saint Pierre

SEVAISTRE

S. Julien-Beychevelle

GRAND CRU CLASSÉ EN 1855

M.M. Van den Bussche Propres

1969

MÉDOC

Appellation Saint-Julien contrôlée

Château Saint Pierre

4e Grand Cru Classé

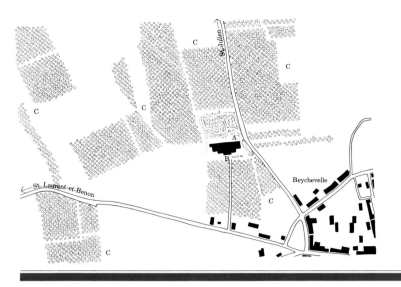

Château Saint Pierre

Château St Pierre takes its name from the Baron of St Pierre who purchased the estate, then called Château Serancan, from the Cheverry family in 1767. The story goes that the Baron was convinced that his patronage would give him access to Paradise because his wine 'pleased the Eternal Father for dessert'. The estate was split up after the death of the Baron in 1832. Part went to Colonel Bontemps-Dubarry another to Madame O. De Luetkens. The latter in turn sold her property at the end of the last century to Léon Sevaistre. In this way two Châteaux St Pierre arose, St Pierre Bontemps Dubarry and St Pierre Sevaistre. The two were again united in 1922, by the Antwerp family of van den Bussche.

The Martin takeover

The Belgian administration lasted exactly 60 years. At that time, the hospitable homestead that stood against the *cuvier* served as château. The actual château — which in fact retained the name Château St Pierre as its postal address — remained in the hands of the Bontemps Dubarry heirs for decades. It lies by the northern entrance to Saint Julien-Beychevelle, opposite the large metal bottle and Château Gloria. The vineyard during the Belgian era comprised 42 acres spread over various plots. In September 1982, St Pierre was taken over from the Fleming Paul Catelijn (related to the van den Bussche family) by Henri Martin, the owner of, amongst other things, Château Gloria. He in turn had already approached other proprietors with a view to dividing up the estate. Martin himself retained 25 acres, and the name St Pierre. The rest of the land went to Gruaud Larose and Ducru Beaucaillou. The latter estate also purchased the former château's cellars.

All one again

With the purchase of St Pierre, Henri Martin realized the wish of a lifetime — to be the owner of a *Grand Cru Classé*. Links had long existed with St Pierre. After all, his father

Alfred had already purchased part of the *chai* and the vineyard in 1922, while Henri himself was able to acquire a number of split-off parts of St Pierre in the course of 20 years. Martin's daughter Françoise Triaud became the owner of the original Château in May 1982; this 17th-century building is to be entirely renovated. St Pierre, in brief, became all one again, as it had been many, many years ago.

Enlarged vineyard

At present, the St Pierre vineyard covers 74 acres. Twenty-five acres were purchased by Martin in 1982, while he had already acquired the other 49 earlier. The latter parcel formed part of Château Gloria for many years but is now regained for St Pierre. The planting consists of 70% Cabernet Sauvignon, 20% Merlot and 10% Cabernet Franc.

Almost a Pomerol

I have not yet come to a satisfactory conclusion about the wine from the new St Pierre, but it is certainly a fact that great care is taken in its making. The 1982 was vinified at Gloria, and matured in casks, about one-third of which were new. The first harvest was around 50 *tonneaux*. I have frequently tasted wines from the former St Pierre. They were not noticeable either for breeding or fine nuances but still tasted delicious because of their round, sometimes almost Pomerol taste, their generous aroma of fruit, and their healthy colour. The 1970, 1975 and 1978 vintages produced undeniably great wines but I have also served and drunk years like 1971, 1974 and 1976 with full satisfaction.

Left:
Hoisting the grapes.

CHATEAU
LANGOA BARTON
APPELLATION ST.JULIEN CONTRÔLÉE

PROPRIETAIRE / SOCIÉTÉ CIVILE AGRICOLE
DES CHATEAUX LANGOA ET LÉOVILLE BARTON

MIS EN BOUTEILLE AU CHÂTEAU
1970

Bottom:
Château Langoa-Barton seen
from the St Julien road. Ronald
Barton lives in the right-hand
wing.

In this cellar Ronald Barton
has a collection of about 30
wine carafes. They stand
upside-down on wooden slats
so that they drain thoroughly
and do not collect dust.

In the Lebanon during the
Second World War Ronald
Barton was surprised to find a
white wine called Château
Léoville-Barton that had been
imported into Beirut from
Greece. The ensuing legal
battles, proving that he was
the owner of the French
château in question, caused
him a great deal of trouble and
effort. He won the case
eventually and the offending
importer was fined in 1941.

Château Langoa-Barton

3e Grand Cru Classé

In a dip in the road between the hamlet of Beychevelle and the village of Saint Julien lies Château Langoa-Barton. Drivers are advised not to exceed the 60 kilometres per hour speed limit for the property lies on either side of the road, and people and vehicles cross over regularly. But not for that reason alone are you advised to drive somewhat slower: the view of Langoa is well worth pausing for. The Château was built around 1750 and has weathered the ravages of time well. It is long and low in shape, with squat towers at each end, and stands above its grounds because it is built on top of a semi-basement. The great grandfather of Ronald Barton, owner of Langoa, purchased the property in 1821. In the Langoa cellars is also made the wine of Léoville-Barton, an estate for which the same ancestor, Hugh Barton, made the first down payment in 1822. Léoville-Barton, like Léoville-Las-Cases and Léoville-Poyferré, descends from the once extensive Léoville property. Although the other two Châteaux retain cellars and buildings from the division, Léoville-Barton had to do without.

'Religiously kept apart'

Because they have the same accommodation and the same owner, Léoville-Barton and Langoa-Barton are always mentioned in the same breath. However, this does not mean that the two wines should be confused. 'On the contrary,' Ronald Barton told me as we drank a glass of Roederer 1955, 'the two wines are religiously kept apart.' And that with good reason, because they come from different soils and each have their own personality.
The Langoa vineyard lies chiefly to the south of the Château at Beychevelle, and that of Léoville to the north, around the churchyard of Saint Julien. Of the two, Léoville produces the higher yield, approximately 100 tonneaux as against some 50 from Langoa. A happy circumstance is that the Léoville-Barton wine also reaches higher standards. Although there is a clear family relationship with Langoa, Léoville-Barton is just that much finer, more complex and more concentrated. But that is not always the case. Ronald Barton remembers how at a blind tasting of six grands crus from Saint Julien, the Léoville 1967 scored higher than Langoa, but for 1966 Langoa came second and Léoville sixth. How educational blind tastings can be Ronald Barton experienced at a luncheon which brought together the owners and the wines of the three Léovilles. The wines were served, everyone made notes, and the outcome? No-one had recognized his own wine!

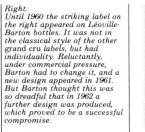

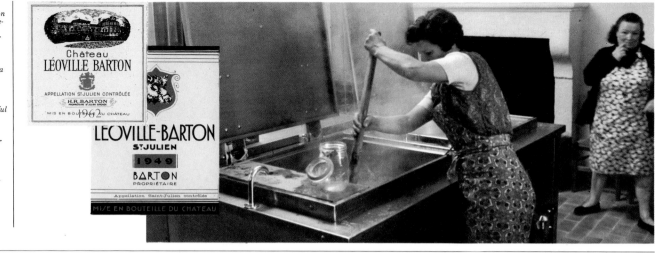

Château Léoville-Barton

2e Grand Cru Classé

Ronald Barton regards himself as a wine maker in the traditional mould. His wines still ferment in oak vats and then spend the best part of two years maturing in partly new casks. The Barton wines can generally do with their fair share of cellar life before they have fully developed. One factor contributing to this is the relatively high percentage of the two Cabernet varieties (77%, with 15% Merlot and Malbec, and 8% Petit Verdot). Perhaps that is why I have drunk more of the old than young vintages of the two Châteaux, particularly those of the Fifties. Léoville-Barton is consistently the better wine of the two. The estate produces excellent wines in good years and good wines in moderate years. Examples of successful wines in weak or average years have been the 1950, 1954, 1962, 1964, 1967, 1973 and 1970. The acknowledged great years of Léoville-Barton include 1953, 1959 (perhaps the best wine that was made in Saint Julien that year), 1966, 1971, 1975, 1978, 1979, 1981 and 1982.

Two years in cask

The wine of both the 99-acre Léoville-Barton estate and the 49-acre Langoa-Barton mature a full two years in oak casks. In principle, half the casks are renewed before each harvest. In view of the traditional way of working, it goes almost without saying that the wines are fined with fresh egg-white and never filtered. Both wines offer the elegance and flexibility of Saint Julien combined with the tannin and backbone of Pauillac, Langoa-Barton appearing the more accessible. The best Langoa wine of the Seventies is probably the 1975, followed immediately by the 1970, 1978 and 1979. For many years Léoville-Barton and Langoa-Barton were sold exclusively by Barton and Guestier, but since the 1975 harvest Anthony Barton at Saint-Loubes has had exclusive rights.

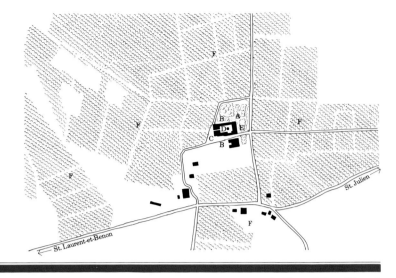

Château Talbot

4e Grand Cru Classé

It is a fact that the English Marshal Talbot gave his name to this château but it is not clear whether it was ever his property. He probably only used it as his headquarters before he left for Castillon in 1453 to lose the decisive battle which was to put an end to British hegemony in this part of France.

The Talbot treasure

Talbot cannot have been too optimistic before he went off to the field of battle: there is a persistent rumour that he buried his treasure at Talbot in one of the many underground passages which have been traced all the way to Cos d'Estournel and further north. The Marshal's premonitions appeared correct. He lost the battle and his life. The treasure — if it ever existed — still lies on the grounds of Talbot and optimistic people now and then dig deep holes in the hope of finding a hoard of centuries-old valuables. But even if the Marshal's treasure is never found, Talbot still has grounds which are worth any amount of gold, in the form of an outstanding 242-acre vineyard. It surrounds the Château and is ideally oriented to the south-west. As at Gruaud-Larose the estate is tended as carefully as a garden. The grapes reach their full growth under super-hygienic conditions, so that rot is a rare occurrence and the harvest is often a week later than at the other Saint Julien châteaux. Artificial fertilizer is taboo: a herd of 80 cows spends its time producing organic fertilizer for Talbot and Gruaud-Larose. They graze on part of the remaining 153 acres of the estate.

Working areas as bright as day

The owner, Jean Cordier, lives in the Château and he no doubt enjoys being able to look from his back garden across to the

Château Talbot

spotlessly maintained cellars where the wine is made, stored and bottled. I was very impressed by the *cuvier,* a room as bright as daylight with 25 stainless-steel fermentation tanks, each holding 3,500 gallons. They are tiled on the underside with sea-blue floor-tiles. Because production is pretty extensive at Talbot — 350 to 500 *tonneaux* — shortage of space can be a problem in abundant years. As at Gruaud-Larose, some of the wine does not then go to the casks but into large wooden *foudres* each holding 880 gallons. Generally speaking, all the wine matures in ordinary casks for between 18 and 22 months. About one-third of the casks are new each year.

Overwhelming bouquet

When I tasted the Talbot 1970 with the cellarmaster Michel Potier, even he exclaimed on sniffing the wine, so tremendous was the bouquet. Nor did the wine then disappoint in the mouth. It was very complete, very balanced and fine on the palate. By 1985, it will be a delicious wine. The wine which can be drunk now is the 1966, which has an exciting perfume and a pleasant, long aftertaste. The 1967 was similarly a fine wine. I have also appreciated the 1962, 1961, 1958 and 1955. I have particularly good memories of the 1962. It was served in 1977 to a company which included the French master chef Jean Troisgros. The wine followed the 1966 and 1964, and was at that point already clearly the finest of the three. Could the rumour really be true that three châteaux added some 1961 to their 1962? They are said to be Latour, Ducru-Beaucaillou and Talbot. Some more recent vintages of high quality were 1975, 1976 (perhaps even better than the Gruaud-Larose of that year), 1977 (far from bad for that harvest), 1978 and 1979.

The 1971 wine, on the other hand, was a great disappointment. As from the 1980 harvest, Talbot have marketed a second brand, called Connetable de Talbot. The wine is very acceptable.

Château Léoville-Poyferré

2e Grand Cru Classé

As at Léoville-Barton and Léoville-Las-Cases, Léoville-Poyferré is a section of the once powerful domaine of the Marquis of Léoville. The proud estate was confiscated at the time of the French Revolution and put up for auction. The sale led to a division into three parts. Half went to the Marquis de Las Cases, and the rest was divided between M. Barton and M. Poyferré. Around the middle of the last century, Château Léoville-Poyferré changed owners. Armand Lalande, who is also involved with Cantenac-Brown, then took over the property from the Baron Poyferré de Céras. The present owners are combined in the Société Civile des Domaines de Saint Julien, set up by members of the Cuvelier family. The manager is Didier Cuvelier.

Château Léoville-Poyferré

While Léoville-Barton is really domiciled at Langoa-Barton, Poyferré and Las-Cases lie side by side in the village of Saint Julien. The border is not always all that clear. My first visit to Poyferré took a very curious turn as a result. I had an appointment with M. Delon, but did not know exactly where I was to meet him. When I drove into Saint Julien, I saw a large metal gate with a sign 'Léoville-Poyferré' and an entry to a courtyard. I concluded from this that I had arrived at the right spot and entered the office. I announced myself and told a friendly girl that I had an appointment with M. Delon. Her reaction was one of surprise, as neither she nor M. Delon knew of my visit. She would. however, quickly find out whether M. Delon could spare the time. Fifty minutes later the report came that M. Delon could not disengage himself. As I did not want to give up straight away, a polite but somewhat agitated discussion ensued when suddenly the truth dawned. I was not at Léoville-Poyferré but at Léoville-Las-Cases! The sign on the gate was in fact rather misleading, because on the other side of the same gate hung one saying Léoville-Las-Cases. The first one you see is Poyferré or Las-Cases, depending on the direction from which you come. This was done to indicate that the dividing line between the two properties runs straight through the territory, here and there I think through the buildings themselves. The fact that my mistake was not clear earlier was due to both Poyferré and Las-Cases being managed by a M. Delon, two brothers. The entrance to the two châteaux is now rather better indicated.

The legendary 1929

The Léoville-Poyferré vineyard will be expanded in the coming years from 148 acres to about 200. The yield — now 235 *tonneaux* in generous years — will therefore rise appreciably. They have opted for a planting comprising two-thirds Cabernet Sauvignon and one-third Merlot. The most legendary of Léoville-Poyferré's wines was undoubtedly the 1929. You can hardly open any book on wine without the Léoville-Poyferré being praised as perhaps the best of that phenomenal long-gone year.

Positive development

During and after the Second World War, the quality of Léoville-Poyferré was not always that praiseworthy — at least not for a second growth. With the exception of such years as 1961, 1966 and 1970 the wine was clearly inferior to Léoville-Las-Cases. True refinement, finesse, were missing. However, since 1979 a good deal has changed. The Cuvelier family have invested a great deal of money in the total renovation of the cellars, fermentation tanks and equipment, while the advice of professor Peynaud has also been obtained. As from the 1979 harvest, more new casks were purchased than in the past, the average now being about a third of the stock. The maturing period is 18 months. The 1979 showed that the renovations were worthwhile. The wine had a new colour and a meaty taste with breeding, fruitiness, breadth and a good structure. I also tasted more tannin than in the past. There can be no doubt that this positive development will continue into the Eighties and beyond. In their callow youth, the wines of 1981 and 1982 already gave an indication of this.

Château Léoville-Las-Cases

2e Grand Cru Classé

On a slight bend in the road between St Julien and Pauillac lies one of the most memorable landmarks of the Médoc, the gate to Château Léoville-Las-Cases. The vaulted passageway forms the entry to the *enclos*, the largest part of the Las-Cases vineyard, which is entirely walled about. From beneath the gate you gain a fine view over the vineyard, the river and the adjoining Château Latour — but you will look for the Château of Léoville-Las-Cases in vain. In fact it lies at Saint Julien, partly surrounded by another piece of the vineyard. No-one lives in the grey building with the white shutters and for that reason Michel Delon's great grandfather turned part of the park into a vineyard at the start of the 20th century.

The *cuvier* lies in an extension of one of the wings of the Château. It is fitted out in extremely traditional fashion, with large oak fermentation vats. The size of these is based on the quantity of grapes that can be picked in one day. Maturation in the wood — which takes at least 20 months — starts in the *chai* next to the *cuvier*. In mid-summer, the wine is transported to the large *chai* at the other side of the street. This was built in 1910, expanded in 1913 and 1973, and also served as a reception area for groups of guests. The building is called Le Chai du Lion. Visitors can admire not only the long rows of *barriques* (a good third being renewed each year) but also examine the fine equipment, all still in working order, formerly used for filling and labelling the bottles.

A well-organized family business

The property has been run by the family in an efficient fashion for an uninterrupted 270 years. The members of the present Société du Château Léoville-Las-Cases are in fact all descendants of the Marquis of Léoville, who purchased the property in 1912. Only Michel Delon is not related to the family. Each of the branches of the family has appointed a representative who looks after their interests. The family take no part in day-to-day management of the estate; Michel Delon

is in total charge. They meet only once a year, at the general meeting of shareholders.

Now one of the best Médocs

Altogether Château Léoville-Las-Cases has 205 acres of productive vineyard. The yield is appreciable, an average of about 280 *tonneaux*. This has undoubtedly contributed to the Léoville-Las-Cases wines being so well known in Britain, America, Scandinavia, Belgium, the Netherlands, Switzerland and France, and really all the countries where *grands vins du Médoc* have a fixed clientele. But the Las-Cases fame rests not only on the large yield but also on high quality. More often than not, the wines are among the best in the Médoc. That has been the case since 1959, because before that date the Château seems to have had a difficult period.

Aristocratic nature

The wines of Léoville-Las-Cases are very distinguished, with a certain reservedness early on. The reasons for this are the traditional maturation methods and the high percentage of Cabernet Sauvignon, 65% (with 14% Cabernet Franc, 18% Merlot and 3% Petit Verdot). The high class of Léoville-Las-Cases is clearly manifested in recent vintages. Although the 1982 is a fine, memorable wine, the 1981 also certainly deserves attention — intense, colourful, stylish and rich. Rather less concentrated but also outstanding was the elegant, fruity 1979. The 1978 is impressive, with a very fine tannic structure, masses of fruit, and its fair share of subtlety. The 1976 tastes attractive and supple, while the 1975 will perhaps be one of the best Médocs of this already outstanding harvest.

Older vintages

The 1959 was a decent, well-made wine, with a highly defined nose. To my taste, it is rather less finely strung than the Léoville-Barton of the same year, but still certainly a bottle to appreciate with a few good friends.

Château Léoville-Las-Cases

The 1960 was on the light side but that was typical of that harvest. The 1961 had a solid colour and a bouquet which gave undeniable witness of a noble origin. A wine which will develop only slowly, but which will amply reward anyone with the necessary patience. The 1964 has developed favourably. It is now quite ripe; nose and taste are at their best; delicious. In 1966 Léoville-Las-Cases also produced a wine which requires every attention on account of its noble bouquet and lasting taste. The 1967 was something of a disappointment — or had I expected too much after the '66?

The 1970 is one of the traditionally great wines, with plenty of power, overtones of ripe fruit, and a long aftertaste. In 1971 the estate produced a smooth, elegant wine, chiefly from Cabernet grapes; a little lacking in depth and complexity. Very successful for their years were the 1973 and 1974, charming, harmonious wines, which gave me much pleasure.

GRAND VIN DE CHATEAU LATOUR

Château Latour

'Château Latour has based its activities on the fact that today's tradition was yesterday's progress, and that today's progress will be the tradition of tomorrow.' This was how director Jean-Paul Gardère outlined the philosophy underlying the radical technical changes at Latour since 1963. In that year the estate acquired a new management when 51% of the shares were purchased by the Pearson group of London, with Viscount Cowdray at its head. Harveys of Bristol (Allied Breweries) also took 25%. The remainder stayed in the hands of a number of Frenchmen, some of them descendants of Alexandre de Ségur who acquired Latour in the 18th century. The price paid by the British lay in the region of three million dollars; in addition, an estimated $750,000 were invested within six years in new buildings, the cellars, the fermentation unit and the vineyard.

Bungalows for the employees

The largest single item, two million francs, was spent on housing for the workers. On the initiative of Lord Cowdray, a start was made in 1964 on renovating the existing workers' cottages and building new ones. These bungalows (25 were planned) have every comfort, including a garage, television aerial, cellar, garden etc. Social benefits like these are unique, at least in such a relatively conservative area as the Médoc. In fact, the human factor was predominant when the decisions concerning nearly every aspect of this extensive renovation programme were made. No-one benefits, so the new owners reasoned, if work is done by hand simply because of tradition, when in fact modern technology can do the same work faster and more efficiently. As a result, work in the vineyards has been highly mechanized, and *égrappage à la main* abandoned. This task — removing the stalks and lightly bruising the grapes — employed a team of 12 men, where now one machine does the same work more hygienically and faster.

Stainless-steel fermentation tanks

De-stalking and bruising the grapes is followed by fermentation, and here, too, things have changed drastically. The antique oak casks had reached the end of their useful lives by 1963, and one was already splitting. They needed to be replaced — but in what

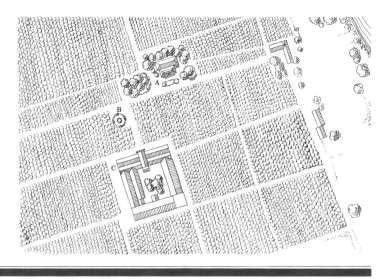

In 1968 the Gratadour estate in the hamlet of St Lambert was bought for the production of the château's extraordinarily successful second wine, Les Forts de Latour. Two buildings with living quarters have been put up and also a storage area for bottles. It has been officially decided to call this cluster of buildings the Château Les Forts de Latour.

The Latour managers are not sure which countries represent the biggest markets for their wine: they lose track of it once it has left the estate. They assume, however, that Britain, the United States, Belgium, Switzerland and West Germany are the main customers.

Below (both pages):
Latour's remarkable tower, with the château across the road to the right. It is said to have been built with stones from the fort that once stood on this spot. A few years ago it was completely restored and the fabric cleaned. The château is only occasionally occupied, by special guests such as Viscount Cowdray, or David L. Pollock, chairman of the board of directors, who lives in London. Another regular visitor is Harry Waugh, a director of Latour and a celebrated wine writer.

Opposite page, left:
Hand-wrapped bottles ready for putting into cases.

Right:
Map of Latour amid its vineyards; the Gironde is in the top right-hand corner. A château, B the tower, C chais, cuvier and offices.

Château Latour

material? It was to be stainless steel. First, because this non-corroding metal guarantees cleanliness. Second, its toughness allows the walls to be very thin, and this in turn ensures efficient cooling of the fermenting must when necessary — cold water can be run over the outside of the tanks. Third, stainless steel was adopted because this material lasts a long time. Fermentation vats are used for only three weeks each year and in view of the heavy investment, it is particularly important that a new *cuvier* should serve for as long as possible. And one of the basic considerations was that the new tanks should produce at least as good a result as the old vats. The new *cuves* were brought into use with the vintage of 1964: twelve 4,400-gallon and five 3,000-gallon tanks. The cooling process is automatically operated via a thermostat which measures the temperature within the fermenting must. Thanks to this installation, vinification can proceed at Château Latour under the conditions that are the most suited to the vintage concerned. Nature is then helped without being upset.

A gentle pump

After the first fermentation, the wine is transferred to new oak casks in which it spends the first two years of its life. At Latour they believe that the wine should be disturbed as little as possible during this critical initial period because of possible harmful effects later. Particular care was therefore taken when choosing a pump for transferring the wine to the casks. The apparatus is calibrated on the same principle as the pumps used in heart surgery: it produces a steady but gentle pulse instead of the traditional, more violent action. For the same reason, Latour is the only *premier grand cru classé* still bottled by hand and not on a fully automated bottling machine. At Latour the wine is poured gently into the bottle, while elsewhere it is injected under some pressure. Even the presses for the less important *vin de presse* are modern machines with the advantage of working with the minimum pressure. As a result, the Latour *vin de presse* is always of superior quality.

The vineyard enlarged

Despite the extensive mechanization of work in the vineyard, views on its planting are still traditional. The strict rule adopted is that of Latour's 148 acres, at least 118 should be

Château Latour

planted with old vines: 'You need old vines to make a great wine.' Since the takeover by the British, the vineyard area has been greatly expanded. The new directors — the *négociant* Jean-Paul Gardère already mentioned, and Henri Martin — discovered that a couple of miles from the main vineyard they had two unproductive plots that had formerly been planted with vines. One plot was called 'La Pinada' and was barely 6 acres in size; the other was Petit-Batailley, of 25 acres. Both were replanted in 1965. The main vineyard, too, was given a careful going over but here the discoveries were less pleasant. There were a fair number of bare spots up to 65 feet across where the vines did very poorly. Everyone was very puzzled, until on consulting some old maps it was found that these patches corresponded

precisely with the drains laid down at the end of the 19th century. So they started digging and found that the pipes had become blocked. The only answer was to dig up all the pipes in the vineyard, and clean and repair them: very labour-intensive work and extraordinarily expensive, requiring years to complete.

In the vineyard, the Cabernet Sauvignon (75%) predominates. The remainder consists of 10% Cabernet Franc, 10% Merlot and 5% Petit Verdot. Output — including that of the second wine — varies from 190 *tonneaux* to over 330. There are no plans to expand the vineyard beyond what has already been undertaken.

The manliest of them all

The appreciable percentage of Cabernet and, of course, the subsoil from which the vines derive their nourishment, determine much of the character of the Latour wine. But the method of vinification is also important; at this château, the wine is left in contact with the grape skins for a further week or two after fermentation, so that it acquires more colour and tannin. Latour is one of the manliest of the first *crus*; a wine that in its youth is often rather inaccessible and needs very many years to develop fully. Should you ever accompany a meal with the four *premiers crus* of the Médoc, the order would normally be Lafite first, then Margaux, then Mouton and finally Latour. In good years, Latour is a wine for laying down for your

Château Latour

children, and in excellent years for your grandchildren. It is a very intense wine, full of compact power. Its bouquet is overwhelming and the taste has great depth in which more and more nuances are encountered the longer you savour it. Latour is like a fine thoroughbred with the strength and wind to outlast all others — you rarely come across a bottle of Latour that is really *passé*.

Latour has a reputation for producing relatively good wines in lean years. I can remember the 1954 whose vitality was still impressive 20 years after it had been bottled. The colour had turned only slightly brown, the bouquet still not fully revealed, the taste mild but at the same time firm and lasting. You would let your food get cold for it (fortunately I drank it only with cheese). The 1963 was also a success. In that difficult year, Latour undeniably made the best wine in the Médoc. I have also tasted the 1965. This was rather less successful than the 1963 — the 'middle' taste seemed somewhat dry — but still gave much pleasure. And thanks to stringent selection, the château was able to produce in 1968 a wine that was still very lively in 1983.

Thanks to this ability to produce a good wine in poor years, the list of worthwhile Latour vintages is virtually unending. Latour is reliable through and through. For the sake of completeness, I list the best vintages since 1945, all wines that will hold their own for many a year: the 1945, 1947, 1948, 1949, 1950, 1952, 1955, 1957, 1958, 1959, 1960, 1961, 1962, 1964, 1966, 1967, 1970, 1971, 1974, 1975, 1977, 1978, 1979, 1981 and 1982.

The château also deserves praise for its really quite outstanding second wine, Les Forts de Latour.

Château Pichon-Lalande

The 20-year-old Louis XIV was on his rather disconsolate way to his future bride Marie-Thérèse, the Spanish Infanta, whom he was to marry purely for political and diplomatic reasons, and readily agreed when Jacques de Pichon, Baron de Longueville, invited him to the hunt. Any diversion was more than welcome. During his short stay on the baron's estate the young king was charmed by the soft colours of the woods and vineyards, and the delicate bouquet of the wines allowed him briefly to forget his regal duties — according to archives of Château Pichon-Longueville Comtesse de Lalande at Pauillac.

The division of Pichon

During the 17th century, the Médoc woods began gradually to make way for vineyards. Pierre Mazure de Rauzan was one of the greatest magnates who besides his lands in Margaux also owned the large estate of Saint-Lambert-Pauillac. This was earmarked as the dowry for his daughter Thérèse when in 1700 she married Jacques Pichon de Longueville, the first Speaker of the Bordeaux *parlement*. The estate remained in the family until 1850, when it was divided up among the heirs. The Baron de Pichon retained two-fifths and the remainder went to his three sisters, the Comtesse de Lalande, the Vicomtesse de Lavaur and the Comtesse

de la Croix. In 1926, the sisters' vineyards were combined in the Société Civile du Château Pichon-Longueville Comtesse de Lalande. Later, the estate passed into the hands of the Miailhe family. Since 1978, the owner has been Madame May-Elaine de Lencquesaign, the youngest daughter of Edouard Miailhe, who died in December 1959. She and her husband, General Herve dé Lencquesaign, have invested a great deal in the property.

Half the casks renewed

Pichon-Longueville Comtesse de Lalande has had a new *cuvier* with stainless-steel tanks since the 1980 harvest. It is a copy of the one at the neighbouring Château Latour, albeit half the size. The cellar was also extended by one-third. It is now 295 feet long, 33 feet less than that at Mouton-Rothschild. Normally, half of the casks are renewed for each vintage. The wine is fined in the casks with fresh egg white. Much of the equipment was also replaced. The enormous outlay — made in consultation with Professor Emile Peynaud — has clearly borne fruit. Whereas during the period from 1972 to 1974 the Pichon-Lalande wines were a downright disappointment, quality has been continuously excellent since 1975.

Imposing quality

The 1975 is indisputably an excellent wine, and the 1976 I would put among the best of all that year. In 1977, the estate produced a very good, attractive wine in the circumstances, and the 1978 can be regarded as outstanding. The wine has an almost luxurious elegance with much fruit, a lot of tannin and a fine balance. I also enjoyed the 1979 tremendously. The taste, like its bouquet, had a great deal of wood, and I also had impressions of ripe, almost sweet fruit. It will no doubt be possible to drink this wine much earlier than the 1978. The first wine from the new *cuvier*, the 1980, was a sparkling success. In this relatively poor year, the château produced an almost black

Château Pichon-Lalande

wine, highly concentrated, rich with fruit, and with a long aftertaste. You could almost chew the 1981, a formidable wine combining the power of the 1978 and the charm of the 1979. This imposing series was continued with the monumental 1982. In less than 10 years, Pichon-Longueville Comtesse de Lalande has reached a level which I feel can equal that of any *premier grand cru classé*.

Partly Saint Julien

The Pichon-Longueville Comtesse de Lalande vineyard covers 148 acres, planted with 45% Cabernet Sauvignon, 35% Merlot, 12% Cabernet Franc and 8% Petit Verdot. Part of the vineyard — 32 acres — lies in Saint Julien. It was formerly larger and the estate marketed a Saint Julien as well as a Pauillac. The two wines were separately vinified, bottled and labelled. Thanks to an exchange of land with Léoville-Las-Cases and others, since the early 1970s the estate has had more of its land in Pauillac than in Saint Julien, and all the wine can now be sold as Pauillac. The Pauillac *appellation* is also carried by the second brand, Réserve de la Comtesse.

Château Pichon-Longueville

2e Grand Cru Classé

As wine estates go, Pichon-Longueville (which is often prefixed 'Baron' to distinguish it from Pichon-Lalande) is small. The property covers 124 acres in all, of which 74 are planted with vines. Another 54 acres that used to be cultivated now lie fallow as the soil there is rather less suitable for producing a great wine.

This is quite characteristic of Pichon-Longueville, proving that people there prefer quality to quantity. In 1982 the manager, Bertrand Bouteiller, told me 'the best land is now planted. We shall not sacrifice quality for greater output.' So there are no plans to expand. Annual production varies from 80 to 178 *tonneaux*.

The vineyard is in one large piece with a few small plots and is almost entirely enclosed by that of Château Latour. There has been an exchange of land with the latter château, which certainly cannot have been to Pichon-Longueville's detriment. The vines have reached a respectable average age of 30 years, which greatly benefits the quality of the wines. The break-down of varieties is 60% Cabernet Sauvignon, 30% Merlot and the remainder a mix of Cabernet Franc, Petit Verdot and Malbec.

Cool fermentation

The soil and the grapes produce a gossamer, delicate bouquet, reminiscent of the perfume of violets. It goes without saying that at Pichon-Longueville they do all they can to keep this tender element in the wine. That is why the first fermentation is allowed to proceed at a very low temperature. Normally, this would be 30°C (86°F), but at Pichon-Longueville they do everything they can to keep the fermenting juice below 28°C (82°F), preferably at 25° to 26°C (77-79°F).

Château Pichon-Longueville

Below left:
Bertrand Bouteiller, the gérant of Pichon-Longueville, whose family owns the château.

Below right:
The pickers obviously like their work. Many Spanish gypsies come to the Médoc vintage as well as French families.

Pichon-Longueville wine is exported mainly to the United States, Britain and Switzerland.

Every year a third of the wine goes into new casks, except when there is a particularly good harvest and then all of it is matured in new ones — as, for example, in 1961, 1966 and 1970.

The people responsible are the *maître de chai*, Francis Souquet, and Bertrand Bouteiller (who is also manager at Château Palmer). The Bouteiller family are the owners of Pichon-Longueville, having bought the estate in 1935 — from the Baron de Pichon-Longueville.

Cellars beneath the château

Pichon-Longueville is faced with a serious shortage of space. Before the era of *mise en bouteilles au château* for the whole vintage they could still just manage, but since château-bottling has been established, the *chais* have become too small. They accordingly decided to store the bottles in the cellars below the residential part: thus wine became the château's only inhabitant. This splendid little château with its pointed turrets and steep roofs has been empty for

many years — the more the pity, because it is a graceful example of mid-19th-century architecture in the Médoc. With a little capital, it could be conjured into a first-class hotel — something that is still lacking in the area, as every visitor to the Médoc will confirm.

Recovery after a period of weakness

Towards the end of the 1960s and in the early 1970s, Pichon-Longueville Baron went through a difficult period. Even wines of such great years as 1966 to 1970 were below the standard of a *deuxième grand cru classé*, although they were of course far from bad. Serious work began again on the estate from 1974-5. The 1975 was very good, but the 1976 was lacking concentration and standard. The 1978 vintage was the first for a long time to produce a truly great wine,

with a lot of depth, length and tannin. In terms of quality, 1979 could hardly compete, although this wine had more fruit, charm and elegance. The 1980 was very acceptable for that year. Wines of allure were produced in 1981 and 1982. As to style, Pichon-Baron is rather more elegant, svelte and less concentrated than Pichon-Comtesse; at table, the Lord should precede the Lady.

Château Batailley

5e Grand Cru Classé

The peaceful setting of Château Batailley hardly suggests that a few centuries ago it was the scene of a bloody battle. Thousands of soldiers fought each other where the vines now stand in serried ranks. They were the men of the French commander Duguesclin, who here defeated a large English army; a victory that enabled the French first to lay siege to and then raze the fortifications of nearby Château Latour. To this encounter Batailley owes its name: *bataille* is French for 'battle'. However, even older than the history of this estate is that of its present owners.

Old wine family

The château with its 124 acres belongs to Madame Denise Castéja, who inherited it in 1961 from her father Marcel Borie, who had in turn acquired it in 1929. Madame Denise's husband is Emile Castéja, a descendant of a very ancient wine family whose roots go back to the 14th century. By a happy coincidence, Batailley had already briefly belonged through marriage to the Castéja family in the 17th century, but they had subsequently then lost it again. Ancestors of Emile Castéja, an engaging man with a dominating personality, were mayors of Bordeaux and Pauillac. He himself is fully occupied with Batailley and other estates, and is a director of the well-known wine firm

In addition to its antiques and art treasures Batailley has a large collection of trees. In the splendid garden behind the château many generations of owners have planted trees from all parts of the world, including India, Mexico, China and the United States. Wild strawberries also grow here and cyclamens bloom. They are seen in their full pink-and-white glory just when the air is heavy with the scent of newly pressed juice about to start fermenting in the cellars.

Right:
Part of the sumptuous interior.

Far right:
The rear of the château.

Below:
A view of the beautiful park.

Bottom:
One of the long, low cellar buildings. The 15 families that work at Batailley live in rather similar buildings.

Château Batailley

of Borie-Manoux.

The Castéjas live at Batailley the whole year through. They have transformed the interior of the fine château (built between 1750 and 1810 in 17th-century style) into a splendid private museum of antiques. Virtually every room contains previous items that Emile Castéja has collected in the course of the years: good salon furniture, Chinese porcelain, Flemish masters and an impressive collection of books. Despite all these treasures, the château is still extremely habitable.

Aromatic and constant

In some books the Batailley wines do not rank too highly. They speak in terms of 'not one of the more outstanding', or, 'a respectable but not exciting wine'. However, I have come across many good bottles at Batailley, such as the 1955 served by Emile Castéja at an exquisite lunch at his château. The wine was already brownish in colour and really quite beautiful — a powerful bouquet and much finesse. The 1953 was if anything even better than the 1955. In that year, Batailley made one of the best of the Pauillacs. I was also impressed by the Batailley 1966, which I drank on several occasions, and I have pleasant memories of the 1970, 1971, 1973, 1975 (to be drunk only around 1990), 1976 (very successful for that year), 1978 and 1979. Batailley is never a particularly dark, powerful or highly refined wine, but a reliable fifth *cru* with a firm structure, good fruit and a pleasant personality. The wine is normally matured in casks for 16 to 18 months; a quarter to a third of them are new.

Château Haut-Batailley

5e Grand Cru Classé

Haut-Batailley was separated from Batailley in 1942, and naturally the wines of the two estates have very much in common. This does not mean, however, that the two wines do not have their own personalities: to suggest otherwise would be doing the makers a great wrong. What I find typical of the wine of Haut-Batailley is that it has clearly been made by Saint-Julien people, namely Jean-Eugène Borie (owner of Ducru-Beaucaillou), and his cellar master André Prévôt. You just feel that someone is trying to produce a wine in Pauillac that is as amiable as the Saint-Julien wines. And with great success. Even young wines take on an extremely friendly air. They are of course still purple in colour, the bouquet not yet released, the taste full of tannin. But strong acids are lacking and a pleasant suppleness prevails, together with what I can best describe as 'red fruit'. There are Pauillac wines that are hard as nails in their youth, but Haut-Batailley tries to charm at a very early age.

However, it is still a wine that is worth laying down. I drank an Haut-Batailley 1964 when it was ten years old and it was particularly successful, firm and vital; 1966 and 1970 were of even higher standard. More recent successes of this seductive, charming Pauillac include the 1975, 1976, 1978, 1979, 1981 and 1982 (a deep-coloured, sappy wine, pleasantly rounded). Even in the less great years, Haut-Batailley seldom disappoints. I can recall good bottles from 1968, 1972 and 1977 — not strong, long-lived wines, but still very agreeable.

No château of its own

In 1849, the poet Biarnez wrote 'we must make great wines not great buildings'. This dictum is tailor-made for Haut-Batailley, because there is only a vineyard, no château.

The wine is made at the adjoining château La Couronne (a *cru exceptionnel*). Its *chai* looks relatively neglected but appearances are deceptive. In fact, Jean-Eugène Borie had brand-new vinification plant installed in 1974.

Yield at Haut-Batailley fluctuates between 60 and 120 *tonneaux*. It is produced from a vineyard of about 25 acres, two-thirds of which is planted with Cabernet Sauvignon. It is divided into two parts, one of 15 acres next to La Couronne and one of 35 acres 1½ miles further on. The latter is situated very favourably on a plateau where the grapes ripen up to four days earlier than elsewhere — which in a rainy autumn can mean all the difference between failure and success.

1970

GRAND CRU CLASSÉ

CHATEAU
LYNCH- MOUSSAS

APPELLATION PAUILLAC CONTROLÉE

CASTÉJA
PROPRIÉTAIRE A PAUILLAC (GIRONDE)

PRODUCE OF FRANCE

MIS EN BOUTEILLE AU CHATEAU

Château Lynch-Moussas

Château Lynch-Moussas is an example of a *cru* that has regained its reputation. When Emile Castéja, the owner of neighbouring Batailley, took over the property in 1969 from other members of the family it was little more than a ruin. The work areas, the fermentation cellars, the vineyard, everything had to be replaced or drastically repaired. And that was done, little by little. Steel fermentation vats painted red were introduced, so were underground blending tanks, a roomy cellar, and new planting on a generous scale (with 75% Cabernets and 25% Merlot). As a direct consequence output rose, as did quality. Production is now between 75 *tonneaux* (as in 1980) and 125 (as in 1982), and the vineyard covers 64 acres. The Lynch-Moussas château has been let out to some hunting enthusiasts who have rented its 247 acres of woods for pheasant shoots.

Initially quite light

The older vines become, the deeper their roots penetrate the ground, and the more the wine gains in nuance. As the roots obtain their nourishment from more layers of soil, so more elements of aroma and taste will be added to the grapes and, subsequently, to the wine. That is why the years 1969 to 1974 were fairly light at Lynch-Moussas, and offered relatively little depth of taste — although they had a certain quality. The best years in my view were 1970 and 1971 — with a slight preference for the latter. It was not a full or deep-coloured wine, but had a fine balance and fruit. The 1971 was a good wine for its year, while the 1970 lacked somewhat in weight compared with other wines.

Not a heavyweight

Since the 1975 harvest, the wines seem to have gained something in body. Except for 1977 and 1980, reasonable wines have been produced up to and including 1982. Even the most powerful of these (such as the 1978) were not true heavyweights, nor particularly rich, concentrated or subtly shaded in taste. But they were far from unpleasant in taste. To my mind, Lynch-Moussas has still not fully achieved the quality of a fifth *cru* but I expect it to do so in the long run, as the vines increase in age and as the effort and expertise of the Castéja family begin to tell.

Château Grand-Puy-Lacoste

5e Grand Cru Classé

It always does a château good to have a gourmet as its owner: anyone who can appreciate good food will try and make as good a wine as possible simply out of self-interest. That this is true was proved years ago by Grand-Puy-Lacoste's Raymond Dupin, who sold his château in 1978 to Jean-Eugène Borie of Ducru-Beaucaillou, having no heirs; he died in August 1980. Visitors are usually asked on arrival whether they have had a good good journey, but the first time I arrived at Grand-Puy-Lacoste M. Dupin asked where I had eaten that afternoon. I replied 'Somewhere in Pauillac'; whereupon he said 'then it can't have been too good'. When I concurred I received an elaborate explanation as to where I should in future betake myself and what dishes I should order where. This incident was characteristic of Raymond Dupin. I was later to learn that he was also the owner of Pauillac's only flock of sheep. And anyone who has eaten *agneau de Pauillac* knows what a precious possession this flock represents.

Chaotic private collection

When it came to wines, Dupin's sights were also set high. His favourite white wine was Domaine de Chevalier, and he had built up a unique private collection of red wines. However, this was not accommodated in an underground cellar, according to the rules, but simply housed in a secure junk room in the unoccupied château. On the dusty floor, case after case of precious treasures lay stacked at random, some closed, some half-open. Cautiously stepping over the boxes and cases I saw Cos d'Estournel 1895, Pétrus 1947, Palmer 1924 and many, many other greats from the distant past.

The property in figures

The Grand-Puy-Lacoste vineyard consists of one large piece of land, with a further 2½ acres near Mouton, and like that of Croizet-Bages lies on the Bages plateau. The estate derives its name from its lofty situation: *puy* means hilltop. A certain Lacoste was once an owner. Altogether, the *vignoble* consists of 86 productive acres planted with 70% Cabernet Sauvignon, 5% Cabernet Franc and 25% Merlot. After the grapes have been picked, de-stalked and bruised they are allowed to ferment in fairly small wooden *cuves*. The wine is then transferred to oak

Château Grand-Puy-Lacoste

casks where it matures for 16 to 20 months. The average annual yield is 100 *tonneaux*, sold chiefly to the United States, Britain, Switzerland and Belgium. It is characteristic of Grand-Puy-Lacoste that its people know how to produce fine quality with great regularity.

The best wine in 40 years

Raymond Dupin bought the estate in 1932, and he knew precisely all the attributes of each year. He told me about the cold spell of 1938-9 which was much worse than in 1956; about 1964, when his last grapes were gathered in by 12 noon on Wednesday 8 October, and the rain started at 2 o'clock and lasted for three weeks; and about his 1961, which he regarded as the best wine that Grand-Puy-Lacoste had made under his

aegis. The yield in that year was only 35 *tonneaux*.

In itself this would not have been such a problem because nearly all the wines of 1961 were sold for high prices. But Raymond Dupin had sold one-third of his normal crop *sur souche*, which means well beforehand when the grapes were still on the vine, and for an agreed, fixed price. This practice is often advantageous, but in this case it proved a disaster: one-third of his normal production was 33 *tonneaux*, which now changed hands at the ridiculously low price of 2,750 francs. Dupin retained barely 2 *tonneaux* for public sale and this brought him no less than 7,500 francs, a record sum for those times.

I was lucky enough to drink this 1961 with a good meal. It was a tremendous experience. The wine had a deep colour and an

enchanting bouquet, full of soft fruit, and the more you sniffed at it the more new subtle fragrances you discovered. The taste was supple, full and powerful. A greatness was present here that reproduced the essence of what a Pauillac should be, *corps et parfum*. Raymond Dupin also produced excellent wines in 1959, 1962, 1966, 1970, 1975 and 1978. Under the management of the Borie family (with François-Xavier Borie as *régisseur*) the average quality has risen further. The wines have gained in colour, strength, depth and length, as witness the 1978 and later vintages.

Château Lynch-Bages

5e Grand Cru Classé

From Lynch-Bages there is a fine view of the Gironde and the small town of Pauillac some half a mile away. The château is on the outer edge of the plateau of Bages where much of the 185-acre vineyard lies. The château itself is a light-coloured, fairly angular building which was completely renovated in 1982. The present occupants are Jean-Michel Cazes, his wife Maria-Thereza and family. Jean-Michel's grandfather Jean-Charles bought Lynch-Bages in 1939 and the property has since remained in the family. André Cazes, Jean-Michel's father, has done much for the wine's reputation. André, who was Mayor of Pauillac for 37 years, has managed the estate since 1966, assisted increasingly by Jean-Michel. Together they are also Médoc's leading insurers; their computerized office is located in the centre of Pauillac.

Metal fermentation tanks

The Lynch-Bages *chais* lie directly behind the château and are much larger than you might suppose from the outside. They are entered via a long *cuvier* where 18 red metal fermentation tanks have been standing since 1975. That was the year when the château finally gave up wood for fermentation purposes. The wine is of course still matured in the wood. It normally stays in oak *barriques* for 15 months; a third of them are replaced each year. The wine is clarified with fresh egg white and generally only the *vin de presse* is filtered (10% of it is added to the *grand vin*). The average output at Lynch-Bages fluctuates between 250 and 280 *tonneaux*.

Cabernets predominate

Cabernet predominates on this estate. Some 70% of the planting is of Cabernet Sauvignon, 10% of Cabernet Franc, and 18% of Merlot and 2% of Petit Verdot. That is why most of the Lynch-Bages vintages require a long time to develop. I had the privilege of visiting the château several times and tasting some of the older vintages. All the wines were still very drinkable — the 30-year-old 1952, for example, served from a half-bottle. The wine had a mature, attractive taste, with softness and

Château Lynch-Bages

roundness. An almost legendary wine at Lynch-Bages was the 1953, rich with nuances of taste and with a long aftertaste. I have pleasant recollections of the almost sweet, full 1959, and highly successful wines were also produced in 1954, 1955, 1957 and 1960. The 1961, 20 years after its vintage, offered fruit combined with charm and strength. The light, minty tone was still present in the bouquet, which is characteristic of many wines from this château.

Ripe cherries and strawberries

Although this estate produced an unsuccessful, thin wine in 1964, and in 1966 fell somewhat short of the standard of that year's class, the 1962 was a splendid wine, and I have enjoyed the 1967 many times, a harmonious wine whose taste, from some bottles, reminded me of ripe cherries. The best wines of the 1970s are the 1970, 1975 and 1979. I would not venture to say when the 1970 will be ready for drinking. The concentrated, dark 1975 with its fine tannin will be drinkable only somewhere between 1985 and 1990. The 1979 appeared almost black and possessed not only strength but fruit and subtlety. I prefer it to the 1978, a very correct wine in itself, but rather less great and intense than might have been expected from that vintage. The 1976 has much charm and fruit (strawberries) and will develop relatively quickly. This estate's 1977 was very successful, as was the 1980.

Complete Pauillac

Both 1981 and 1982 will be regarded as classic, great years for Lynch-Bages. These are wines which in their youth had tones of wood and plenty of fruit (blackcurrants), a rich taste, a long aftertaste and an opaque colour. Of the two, the 1982 was the broader, the fatter. From all these tasting notes, Lynch-Bages emerges as a reliable, sturdy, complete Pauillac, often with fruit in its taste and a good balance. In terms of quality the wine is well above fifth *cru* level and would be more at home among the third *grands crus classés*.

Château Croizet-Bages

Like Rauzan-Gassies, Château Croizet-Bages belongs to the heirs of Paul Quié and here, too, improvements have been made to the *chais*. Jean-Michel Quié has also built a new storage area for 120,000 bottles, opposite the present château. Much work has also been done in the vineyard. And it was necessary. Quite a few vines had to be replaced. The work became very urgent after the frost of 1977 which did a great deal of damage to the Croizet-Bages vineyard.

Altogether there are 74 plantable acres of which at present some 54 are in use. These produce 80 to 100 *tonneaux* of wine and are planted with about 37% Cabernet Sauvignon, 30% Cabernet Franc (a relatively high percentage for Pauillac), 30% Merlot and 3% Petit Verdot, plus Malbec. There is no actual château at Croizet-Bages just cellars and a *cuvier* in the hamlet of Bages, with hardly any suitable space for receiving visitors. This fact undoubtedly contributes

Château Croizet-Bages

to Croizet-Bages being one of the less-known *grands crus* in Médoc. The original château of Croizet-Bages nowadays answers to the name of Château La Tourelle and stands in Pauillac. It serves as a youth centre. Jean-Michel Quié ferments his wine in lined concrete fermentation vats. The wine is lightly filtered through screens before bottling. The vineyard is exceptionally well sited on the Bages plateau; the first vines start a few yards from the *chai*. There are 49 productive acres, planted in the traditional Pauillac fashion with 60% Cabernet Sauvignon and Cabernet Franc, about 30% Merlot and the rest Malbec and Petit Verdot. The wine is mainly exported to Britain, Switzerland, the United States and Belgium.

Attention to detail

A typical example of the Quié policy (Paul Quié died on 17 December 1968) can be found in the *fouloir*, which was installed in the 1970s. In itself, an apparatus of this kind is nothing special — it removes the stalks and slightly crushes the grapes — but the one at Croizet-Bages has been very carefully thought through. To maintain the utmost in hygiene, a machine of this kind must be cleaned regularly during the vintage, but there must be no protracted interruption during that period. This means it must be possible to clean the *fouloir* quickly and thoroughly, and also to put right any defects on the spot and promptly. These two criteria pose a problem everywhere (albeit not an insuperable one) except at Croizet-Bages. Here, they have made a special access with steps down into the apparatus, allowing the mechanics to enter and leave the hopper without any loss of time. In itself a *fouloir* respresents a considerable investment, and an additional access of this kind adds to it. Croizet-Bages deserves credit for not shrinking from this extra cost. They pay attention to detail at this château.
After the *fermentation tumultueuse* has taken place in the concrete vats, the wine is transferred to oak casks to mature for 18 to 20 months. A selection is made each year with the assistance of an oenologist; anything that does not meet the required standards is sold anonymously. It should be noted that two versions of the Château Croizet-Bages label are in circulation on the older vintages — one with a red band at the bottom (the usual one) and one with a blue band (for wine not bottled on the estate). Another tip: good years of Croizet-Bages can sometimes be recognized by the size of the bottle. Magnums and the other large sizes are only used for the *très bons millésimes*.

Not reserved

The ideal way in which to drink a wine is at the château itself; nowhere does the bottle taste better. However, at Croizet-Bages this is difficult and when the Quié family invited me to lunch, it was arranged at the Château Bel-Orme-Tronquoy de Lalande, another of their properties. It lies to the north of Saint Estèphe, but the Croizet-Bages tasted wonderful there. I drank the 1964 with a really delicious entrecôte, and the two went very agreeably together. The 1964 had a fine colour, a praiseworthy nose and a full, velvety taste with generous fruit. Clearly a wine that was harvested before the famous rainy period of that vintage.
At home I have had much pleasure with the 1962, with its fruity bouquet and taste to match. Croizet-Bages is, generally speaking, a relatively friendly wine for its locality. The reserve and hardness for which Pauillacs are known is much less in evidence with this wine. Even so I feel that the Croizet-Bages wines could still be improved. They can in fact lack roundness and fruit, even in such outstanding years as 1970 and 1975. Both of these came across as rather thin, and the 1975 even seemed somewhat oxidized (or was it just that one bottle?). I found the 1973 a disappointment. Five years after it had been harvested it still tasted acid and lacking in charm. There are still a few important tasks in store for Quié Junior.

Pauillac's Maison du Vin is at Château Grand-Puy-Ducasse, and also the headquarters of the Commanderie du Bontemps de Médoc et des Graves. This wine fraternity held its first official ceremony in 1950, under the splendid cedar trees at Lafite-Rothschild. Among its numerous activities in and around Bordeaux the Commanderie organizes three big annual events: the Fête de Saint-Vincent towards the end of January; the Fête de la Fleur in June; and the Ban des Vendanges immediately before the start of the grape harvest. The wines of the two districts always flow freely and so these occasions end less solemnly than they begin. The fraternity has a cuvée of its own.

Right:
A member of the Commanderie du Bontemps de Médoc et des Graves at an inaugural ceremony. Wearing the thick purple robes on a hot day is no fun.

Below:
Rear view of the 18th-century château. Part of the garden went to make room for an enlargement of the cellars.

Château Grand-Puy-Ducasse

5e Grand Cru Classé

In the 1969 *Bordeaux et Ses Vins* it says that Château Grand-Puy-Ducasse has only 25 acres of vineyard, with an average yield of 40 *tonneaux*. New developments have now overtaken these figures. In fact, the property changed owners in 1971, coming into the possession of people closely linked with Mestrezat-Preller, a wine firm dating from 1815. They appointed a highly expert team both in the cellars and the vineyard (the present *régisseur* is Patrice Bandiera) and immediately set in motion a number of ambitious projects.

For example, the vineyard area was greatly expanded, to 89 acres, planted with 70% Cabernet Sauvignon, 25% Merlot and 5% Petit Verdot. The vineyard is scattered around the commune of Pauillac. Part of it (the oldest) adjoins Mouton-Rothschild and Pontet Canet, another part Batailley and Grand-Puy-Lacoste, and a third has Pichon-

Château Grand-Puy-Ducasse

Lalande and Pichon-Longueville as neighbours. It is therefore in good company. While the vineyard was being expanded, the urgently necessary improvements were being made in the cellars, both to the equipment and the method of working. Stainless-steel fermentation vats were installed; it was decided to use 15% new casks for maturing; the wine was henceforth to be transferred according to the best practice; strict standards of cleanliness were laid down: the wines were rigorously selected — and the result has been a much better product than in the past. Naturally, the annual production gradually increased. The 1974 harvest raised it to 133 *tonneaux*, a record at the time. Nowadays, the château generally produces more than that: 150 to 190 *tonneaux* (188 in 1982). The increased output obliged the château to expand its *chais* quite appreciably, and part of the garden was sacrificed to this end. Now, the bottles need no longer be transported to Bordeaux for storage in Mestrezat-Preller's capacious warehouses.

A wine reborn

Château Grand-Puy-Ducasse wine can be said to have been reborn in 1971. This can be tasted quite clearly, which shows once again that the human factor should never be underestimated. In the final analysis, the owner's outlook is decisive. Even the ripest grapes from the best soil can be turned into a disappointing wine — as plenty of examples show. All too often we read in the histories of the *grands crus classés* that the wine deteriorated badly in quality over a certain period. This can never be attributed to a sudden worsening of soil or climate, but only to the owner. Developments in vinification techniques and the occurrence of grape disease apart, the attitude of the owner is the only truly variable factor for the quality of a *cru*. It is therefore a risky business buying a wine solely by its label. In fact, it is better to buy on the reputation of the owner than by the wine's allotted place in a classification; and that perhaps is the message of this book.

But back to Grand-Puy-Ducasse. The recent vintages from this château are obviously the most worthwhile. I found the 1972 very successful, and the 1973 could also hold its own. However, they were overshadowed by the 1975, which seven years after harvesting proved to be a highly balanced though still young wine. Its colour was dark red, its bouquet (still latent) offered concentrated blackcurrants. Fruit could be detected in the pliant, firm taste. Excellent, too, are the 1978, 1979, 1981 and 1982.

Fraternity headquarters

The château of Grand-Puy-Ducasse is at some distance from its vineyards, at the heart of Pauillac along the great Gironde quay. The building serves as Pauillac's *Maison du Vin* and is also the headquarters of the illustrious Commanderie du Bontemps de Médoc et des Graves. This wine fraternity derives its name from the *bontemps*, the wooden box in which the egg white is beaten for clarifying the wine. This lowly, unpretentious aid is indispensable to the making of an honest, pleasurable wine. Or as they shout during the investiture ceremony of the Confrérie, '*Par le bon temps, pour le bon temps, Graves et Médoc*'.

Château Pédesclaux

As you drive from Pauillac in the direction of Lafite-Rothschild, just beyond a T-junction marked by a wayside calvary, an angular little building can be seen standing among the rows of vines, with *Vignoble Pédesclaux* written on it. The château is just a little further on and the eye-catching pointed roof can already be seen outlined against the broad ribbon of the Gironde. The building dates from the 19th century. What surprised me is that earlier labels (see below) showed a building that in no way resembled the present château. The Pédesclaux vineyard has covered 49 acres for a long time now, and there are no plans for expansion. The grape varieties are Cabernet Sauvignon (70%), Merlot (20%), Cabernet Franc (5%) and Petit Verdot (5%). Output can vary widely. In 1977, only 35 *tonneaux* were harvested, but 80 two years later.

A pleasant reception for visitors

The Pédesclaux château has been divided up by its owners into several flats for rent. Visitors can therefore only see the *chais*, and that is why the owners have done a great deal in recent years to improve their appearance. A pleasant reception room has been created behind the *cuvier* with its enamelled steel vats and bottling area. The small room has been plastered in a quite distinctive way. It looks as if sprigs of chicory were first glued to the wall and then painted over white. The friendly, enthusiastic joint owner and administrator, Bernard Jugla, has already assembled a number of interesting wine exhibits in his reception room. That their number is still limited is due to his family being spread all over the world, and getting their curios to

Pauillac is no easy matter. In any event, there is an adequate supply of sawdust boxes and I made plenty of use of these during an interesting wine tasting that Jugla organized on the occasion of my first visit.

Four recent years

We restricted ourselves to four recent years at Pédesclaux. The first wine was the 1973. Surprisingly, the colour of this still immature wine was already on the brown side! Hardly a hopeful sign for a wine in cask. However, three years later I again tasted the same wine — and the result was even more surprising. The wine had gained rather than lost in colour, possessed pleasant nuances of aroma and taste (the latter suggested strawberry), and lingered nicely in the mouth. It also had a great deal of zest. In

Château Pédesclaux

his cellar, Bernard Jugla told me that he himself was not altogether satisfied with the 1973, but as far as I am concerned he's got nothing to be ashamed of.

The 1972 had a fine, dark-purple colour and a very characteristic Pédesclaux bouquet: piquant, even somewhat peppery. The taste had a lot of fruit, but was otherwise a little on the light side — a particular feature of this year. It is a wine that should have been drunk by that time, like the 1967 and 1969. The 1971 was an oddity. That year, the Merlot grape completely failed at Pédesclaux, with as a result a wine of perhaps 90 to 95% Cabernet, against the normal 80%. This absence of Merlot was immediately noticeable from the colour, which was unusually dark. The bouquet and taste made a striking contrast with the

previous two wines, because every trace of suppleness or cheerfulness was suddenly gone. The wine was sturdy, strong and hard; a true wine for laying down. I have a few bottles of it laid down at home but I do not intend to open them before the mid-1980s. Although the 1971 was a very balanced wine, it was the 1970 that stole the show. An opaque colour was followed by a rather reserved but fruity taste, a rounded bouquet which also had its hint of fruit, and a formidable aftertaste.

Since that first visit, I have been able to

taste a number of later and earlier Pédesclaux vintages. Particularly successful for its year was the 1962, a still very vital wine; 1964 and 1966, too, produced superior wines here. In 1975, the estate made a concentrated, mouth-filling wine that will need to mature for some time yet, but the 1978 was even better. The 1979, however, was rather disappointing, although the quality may still be regarded as very acceptable. All in all, the Jugla family, owners since 1950, are doing good work here, at fifth *cru* level.

Château Pontet Canet

The history of Pontet Canet takes us back to 1720, when the estate was created by a certain M. Pontet, a rich gentleman with the imposing title of Master of the Horse of the Ancient Order of the Keepers of the Seal, attached to the *Cour des Aides de Guyenne*. Where can you find such flowery honorifics these days? M. Pontet owned not only Pontet Canet but also Pontet St Julien. Both estates remained in the family for a long time, but were eventually sold. Pontet Canet was acquired by Herman Cruse in 1865 after the then Madame de Pontet died, and Pontet St Julien was sold earlier, in 1821, to Hugh Barton who rechristened it Langoa-Barton. From 1865 to 1975, the Cruse family held sway over Pontet Canet. After that, it was sold to a group led by Guy Tesseron of Lafon-Rochet. He is married to a Cruse daughter, so that the estate is still almost 'in the family'. Excellent wine was made throughout the Cruse regime; and it was frequently sold at second *cru* prices. Many reference works rightly state that Pontet Canet deserves far more than its official status of fifth *cru*. It may certainly be wondered why neighbouring Mouton-Rothschild was — quite rightly — promoted,

Château Pontet Canet

but not Pontet Canet.

The dissatisfaction on this point is perhaps best expressed by Maurice Healy in his *Stay me with Flagons*, published as long ago as 1940. He writes, 'But how Pontet Canet has been content to remain a fifth growth I cannot understand. I have always found this wine elegant and full of breed; and in a "blind" guessing I have invariably named it as a second, if not, as I did once or twice, a first.'

Everything for the guest

The château dates from the 18th century but no member of the Cruse family lives there. It does not stand empty, however, nor is it in a dilapidated state. Pontet Canet is fully furnished and is at the entire disposal of guests of the estate. The small salons, the brown dining room, the striking bedrooms and the blue-green billiard room; all these point to hospitality on a generous scale. And so it regularly happens that large groups of visitors arrive to taste the wine and sometimes to take lunch. For these purposes Pontet Canet has a gigantic loft over the *cuvier*. It can seat no fewer than 600 persons. From the red-painted wooden balcony, there

is a fine view of part of the vineyard, at 185 acres one of the biggest in the Médoc. Two-thirds lie immediately around the château, the remainder a little way off.

The grapes enter via the loft where they undergo *égrappage* — the removal of the stalks and are lightly bruised (this latter process is called *foulage*). The grapes are then pumped into the fermentation vats.

A cathedral for newborn wine

Most of the vats are of dark oak, with a few of concrete. This, ex-*régisseur* Ardiley tells us, was purely a question of tradition. The wooden vats in fact require much more attention than other types — they are more difficult to clean, and dry out, which makes extra maintenance necessary. Another disadvantage is that the fermentation temperature is difficult to regulate. With modern stainless-steel vats, all that you need do, so to speak, is press the button; with oak — and often with concrete — vats with their thick walls, the temperature is hard to influence from the outside. At Pontet Canet I saw a small, old-fashioned coal-burning stove standing between the vats for raising the temperature of the wine a little on cold

January mornings. This is done in order to allow malolactic fermentation to proceed unhindered. Immediately behind the *cuvier* is the first-year cellar. It is one of the tallest I know, at least in Bordeaux. There are many surface cellars of this kind in Jerez de la Frontera, where they are called *bodegas*. There, in southern Spain, a great deal of air and ventilation are needed to promote the development of certain bacteria; at Pontet Canet the space was created to rid the wine of the carbonic acid gas that is produced in the first year.

On a still, summer's day, the atmosphere in this large cellar with its tall white walls is almost religious, rather like a cathedral: a cathedral of wine where the latest Pontet Canet spends the first year of its life. It is cleaned up now and again by racking (*soutirage*), but after that it slumbers on.

An average of 300 tonneaux

If you walk through the first-year *chai* you reach the rooms where the casks are cleaned and the wine for the estate staff is stored. To see it, you would say that they are fond of a glass at Pontet Canet! However, taking wine is not regarded as 'drinking' in Bordeaux. A

Château Pontet Canet

man can drink seven pints a day and still happily claim that he does not drink. By drinking they mean drinking spirits and, anyway, you are so used to wine that you hardly notice it.

The second-year cellar does actually lie below ground. Unlike the building above, space is very limited here. The *barriques* lie stacked one on top of the other in relatively narrow, parallel vaulted passages.

Above ground, you were briefly reminded of Spain, here below, of Burgundy. The wine itself, however, disclaims any association with other districts. Because when you are offered the one-year-old wine in a glass here in the dim light, it is a real Pauillac, a true Médoc, a genuine Bordeaux. The average yield is 300 *tonneaux*.

A rather more supple vinification

I tasted the 1973 in the cellar with former *régisseur* Ardiley. The wine was clear in colour, not too dark, with a bouquet with a somewhat sultry, fruity scent and a relatively developed taste. The latter surprised me because I consider Pontet Canet a traditional Pauillac (from 70% Cabernet Sauvignon, 10% Cabernet Franc and 20% Merlot) and consequently not very forthcoming in its youth. Ardiley rather confirmed my observation. Because the consumer may have neither the facilities nor the patience to let wine lie for years, they had decided at Pontet Canet to vinify the wine in such a way that it would become a shade more supple and easy. Ardiley (who has now moved to Château du Glana) thought this was a pity, but he understood that it was in line with the times.

The 1973 referred to was certainly already agreeably drinkable around 1978. This also applies to the relatively light, elegant 1972. The very good wines of 1975 and 1976 will become drinkable during the 1980s. Of the older vintages, I can recall the 1962, a real beauty. It hung to the glass, had a splendid heavy bouquet and a sturdy, round taste. Perhaps not a finely mannered marquis but at least a hearty country squire.

The 1966 is a wine to be left for a good long time yet. When I saw the rather velvety colour, with just a hint of brown, I was already expecting a decently developed wine. However, the taste proved the contrary. On the tongue, I detected plenty of strength, and the wine will continue to develop well into the 1980s.

As regards recent vintages, I cannot avoid the impression that Pontet-Canet changed course towards the end of the 1970s, because from the 1978 on all the vintages I tasted were really outstanding. The former quality seems not only to have returned, but even to have been surpassed. The supple style of the early 1970s had been abandoned for relatively dark wines, rich in tannin, fruit, flesh and nuance. Not only was I particularly impressed by the 1978, 1979 and 1981, but I also found the wine of the lighter 1980 to be delicious. Pontet-Canet is among the best wines of that difficult year. Everything shows that Château Pontet-Canet again fully deserves every attention.

Château
Haut-Bages Libéral

GRAND CRU CLASSÉ EN 1855

APPELLATION PAUILLAC CONTRÔLÉE

1972

SOCIÉTÉ CIVILE CHARREULES PROPRIÉTAIRE

MIS EN BOUTEILLES AU CHÂTEAU 73 cl

Château Haut-Bages Libéral

5e Grand Cru Classé

It says on the Château Haut-Bages Libéral label that the property belongs to the Société Civile Charreules, but in fact this simply means the Cruse family. It was they who in fact bought Château Haut-Bages Libéral in 1960 and turned it into a company of their own for administrative reasons. I mention this because the family actually once succeeded in raising a fifth *cru* — Pontet Canet — above its status, and so it is possible that in due course they will achieve a similar result with Haut-Bages. I purposely say 'in due course' because that kind of thing takes a great deal of time, not to mention money.

Within only 14 years of the takeover, in 1974, the *chai* and the *cuvier* had been entirely updated. Unlike the traditional approach to Pontet Canet, everything at Haut-Bages Libéral is super-modern. They have the very latest type of *égrappoir*, a dozen stainless-steel fermentation tanks, and a fine series of cellars. In addition, they are busy reconstituting the vineyard in order to simplify working. At first the percentage of Cabernet Sauvignon was as much as 89%, but this was gradually reduced to 70% (with 25% Merlot and 5% Petit Verdot).

Increasingly better results

Perhaps rather spoiled by Pontet Canet, Batailley, Grand-Puy-Lacoste, Mouton Baronne Philippe and other *cinquièmes* at Pauillac, I found the wines of Haut-Bages Libéral something of a disappointment to begin with. The 1967 and 1969, for example, seemed to me rather like high-jumpers who just failed to qualify by half an inch or so. They lacked charm, and seemed rather meagre. Fortunately, under the new management, the wines have improved greatly. I can particularly recall the excellent 1973, the similarly succesful 1974, the outstanding 1975 and the supple, fruity 1976. Each of them has style and a certain charm. I think that the gradually increased percentage of Merlot has something to do with this, the age of the vines also plays a part. I also had a positive impression of the 1978 and 1979 vintages, while 1980 was well balanced, with a hint of blackcurrant.

The Haut-Bages Libéral château lies about half a mile from Château Latour, and the vineyards of the two estates adjoin each other. Altogether, the Haut-Bages Libéral vineyard covers some 64 acres. The yield has recently fluctuated between 59 *tonneaux* in 1980 and 99 in 1979 and 1982.

Château Mouton Baronne Philippe

5th Grand Cru Classé

No-one entering the park of Mouton Baronne Philippe can fail to be struck by the surrealistic appearance of the château. It is only half a house, with only the half of a pediment beneath the roof. Work on the building started between 1820 and 1830 but was never completed. This is very typical of the times before the refined vinification techniques of today. The growers were entirely dependent on the weather and, in consequence, were rich and poor by turns. It was not only the weather but also the economic situation that determined the owners' weal or woe. This was very evident during the crisis years in the 1930s when even the greatest names were in serious

difficulties. The fifth *cru* Château Mouton-d'Armailhacq was no exception to this rule and Baron Philippe de Rothschild, who 11 years earlier had taken on the management of the adjoining Mouton-Rothschild, bought it in 1933. By so doing, the baron reunited two estates under one owner; Mouton-d'Armailhacq had in fact been split from the great Mouton vineyard during the French Revolution and ended in the hands of the Armailhacq family, and later of the Comte de Ferrand.

Château
Mouton Baron Philippe
Grand Cru Classé
Pauillac
APPELLATION CONTROLEE
Baron Philippe de Rothschild
PROPRIETAIRE A PAUILLAC
MIS EN BOUTEILLE AU CHATEAU

Château Mouton Baronne Philippe

No expansion at Mouton-Rothschild

Baron Philippe would have been legally entitled to merge the Mouton-d'Armailhacq vineyard completely with the Mouton-Rothschild and thereby appreciably increase the output of this much more famous and expensive *cru*. However, that did not happen for the simple reason that the baron wanted to do nothing that might reduce the quality of Mouton-Rothschild by as much as a whisker. So the vineyards remained divided. Baron Philippe certainly did everything to raise the wine from his new acquisition to a higher standard according to his own strict standards. The size of the vineyard was reduced from 185 acres to 124, replanting was undertaken where necessary, new *chais* were built and good equipment was installed. It was not until 1956 that the baron considered the wine of Mouton-d'Armailhacq good enough to be included in the family and the name changed to Mouton Baron Philippe. There were in fact two other reasons for this change. The vitally important English-speaking world could pronounce the name of d'Armailhacq only with the greatest difficulty and the baron feared an unfortunate confusion with the wine distillate Armagnac.
But did Baron Philippe buy this *cinquième grand cru classé* only because it was another Mouton? Evidently not. For the baron, the fact that Mouton-d'Armailhacq was separated from Mouton-Rothschild by walls, barriers, gates and trellis, which greatly hampered access to his château, had for long been a thorn in the flesh. The purchase of Mouton-d'Armailhacq enabled the construction of the park and the long drive that now gives entry to both Moutons. However, the baron's plans had to wait until d'Armailhacq's capricious owner died, in 1938, and then the work was postponed until after the war.

An individual style and a high standard

The first wine to be offered as Mouton Baronne Philippe was the 1956, not a particularly fortunate year because the frost had been especially heavy. Since 1975 the château has been called Mouton Baronne Philippe, out of respect for the late Pauline de Rothschild, Baron Philippe's American-born wife. The Mouton Baronne Philippe wine (yield 180 to 220 *tonneaux*) has a quite personal style which differs significantly from Mouton-Rothschild. Now and again, it even tends more towards the style of Lafite than of Mouton. One of the reasons is undoubtedly the relatively high percentage of Merlot (20%), which makes the Mouton Baronne Philippe much softer, more cheerful and drinkable sooner than Mouton-Rothschild. The wine is vinified in the estate's own *chais* and here, too, there are differences from the parent château. The fermentation vats are of concrete instead of wood, and mainly three-year-old casks from Mouton-Rothschild used for maturing the wine. It sometimes happens when the vintage is large that there is not enough room for all the wine to be stored in the *barrique* type of cask. In such years they proceed to store part of the noble juice for a year in very large 2,200 (2,640 US) gallon casks: another practice that differs from Mouton-Rothschild.
The wines of Mouton Baronne Philippe are impressively good. The 1966, for example, has a perfume so full of depth and nuance that you might almost forget to drink the wine. A similar *bouquet extraordinaire* and a fleshy, juicy taste are also characteristic of the recent good years of this estate (1975, 1976, 1978, 1979, 1981 and 1982). You can easily tell that the wine is related to Mouton-Rothschild, but it is not for nothing that the Mouton Baronne Philippe motto is '*Bon sang ne peut mentir*', which is just another way of saying 'good breeding will out'.

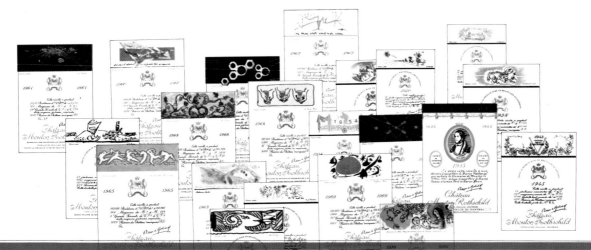

Left:
Since 1945 celebrated artists such as Jean Cocteau (1947), Salvador Dali (1958), Henry Moore (1964) and Marc Chagall (1970) have designed labels for Mouton. It is said that the illustrations often reflect the quality of the vintage: thus Chagall's colourful gouache was a perfect, striking symbol of the exuberance of the 1970. Baron Philippe's business friends are sent a New Year's card reproducing the latest of these miniature works of art.

Below:
The Mouton-Rothschild vineyard comprises 178 acres. There are no plans for expansion. The average annual production is about 250 tonneaux.

Château Mouton-Rothschild

1er Grand Cru Classé

Mouton-Rothschild is one of the most fascinating properties in the Médoc. Each year it attracts 30-40,000 tourists and more than any other château it has been the subject of countless articles in newspapers and magazines. This interest is in no small way due to the 118 years that Mouton spent struggling against the 1855 classification. To its owners' great dismay, Mouton was not admitted to the *premiers grands crus classés* but had to be satisfied with top place among the second *crus*. The reason for this was perhaps one of time. The Domaine de Mouton was bought in a relatively neglected state by Baron Nathaniel de Rothschild in 1853 (two years before the official classification, that is). And he had no opportunity within so short a period to make the estate and the vineyard respectable. Mouton was then no more than a farmhouse and only in 1880 did Nathaniel's son James make a move towards a real château. He built an elegant dwelling, now known as Petit-Mouton, adjoining the *chais*.

Baron James died at the age of 37 in 1881, but the Rothschilds continued to manage the property through his wife. The fortunes and misfortunes of Mouton were off-loaded onto her son Henri in 1920, but he was more interested in literature and the theatre and after two years transferred command to his then 21-year-old son, Baron Philippe. The reputation of Mouton-Rothschild had already transcended that of the other two estates but Baron Philippe was to be the first of the British Rothschilds to attempt seriously to raise Mouton to a *premier grand cru*.

For decades, as a protest against the 1855 classification, Mouton bore the motto: 'Premier ne puis, second ne daigne, Mouton suis' (First I cannot be; second I do not deign to be; I am Mouton'). After the château's promotion to premier cru the motto was changed: 'Premier je suis, second je fus, Mouton ne change' (I am first; I was second; Mouton does not change').

It is not generally known that the foundations of the private museum collection were laid by Philippe's father, Baron Henri, who managed to acquire many art objects when the collection of Baron Carl Mayer de Rothschild de Francfort came under the hammer.

This museum has two stars in the Guide Michelin, meaning 'worth a detour'.

Cyril Ray, who had already published a book about Lafite, wrote a 90-page book about Mouton in 1974. It was published by Christie's of London.

In the centre of Pauillac are the offices and cellars of La Baronnie, the marketing organization of Baron Philippe de Rothschild GFA. Its Mouton-Cadet brand is a best-seller around the world, accounting for 70% of La Baronnie's turnover. This wine carries the Bordeaux appellation and is of a very reliable quality. But it has nothing to do with the wine of Mouton-Rothschild, except for a resemblance in label and name.

Far right:
Bust of Bacchus by Giovanni della Robbia, 16th century; one of the art treasures of the private museum.

Below:
A 17th-century silver vase, from Augsburg.

Bottom right:
Wine bowl in silver and gold, Persian, 5th century.

Bottom left:
Map of Mouton-Rothschild. A cellars, B museum, C the large cellar, D Petit-Mouton, E visitors' car park, F private apartments, G Grand-Mouton complex. A new large chai has been extended from A, over the road; it can accommodate 700,000 bottles.

Above:
Two Persian beakers of the 9th and 8th century BC.

Château Mouton-Rothschild

A wine of high quality

One of the first things that the young owner did was to introduce mandatory château bottling — a fairly revolutionary step for those times. It gave him and his team an opportunity to give wine drinkers the world over an absolute guarantee of genuineness and quality. The eternal rival, Lafite-Rothschild (belonging to the French branch of the Rothschild family), followed the example within a year. Every attention was, of course, paid to the quality of the wine. Highly characteristic of Mouton is the very high percentage of the noble Cabernet Sauvignon grape: approximately 85%, with 10% Cabernet Franc and the remainder Merlot.

The baron also began to move his château into the limelight in other ways. From 1934, the exact number of bottles of the vintage was stated on all labels, and from 1945

(l'année de la victoire) the upper part of the label was designed each year by a different artist. The one exception to this was 1953, as the wine and label for that year were devoted to the first three Rothschild owners of Mouton in celebration of the centenary.

A unique museum

Baron Philippe's most spectacular deed was to open his private museum in 1962. With his American wife Pauline he assembled a unique collection of art objects in a former cellar, each of them in some way associated with wine. The collection includes precious glass in many forms, remarkable old flagons, wine stoups from 8th-century Persia, antique furniture upholstered with vinous designs, paintings by Picasso and the Dutch masters, tapestries and objets d'art from

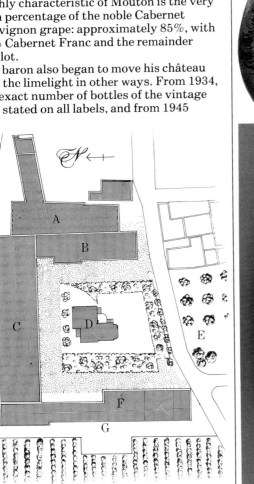

In addition to Mouton's own
wine its cellars contain about
100,000 bottles of wine from
other famous châteaux in the
Médoc, Graves, Sauternes,
Saint-Emilion and Pomerol. In
many instances Baron Philippe
has examples of vintages of
fellow owners that they
themselves no longer possess.
The collection starts with the
1859 vintage. The bottles are
recorked every 25 years.

The names of Mouton-
Rothschild, Lafite-Rothschild
and Cos d'Estournel all contain
the same idea: Mouton comes
from motte de terre ('mound'),
Lafite from la hite ('the hill')
and Cos from coteaux or côtes
('slopes').

In September 1978 I was able
to taste a number of recent
vintages. There was no doubt
at all about the class of the
1975. I was very curious about
the 1976. It proved to be a
substantial wine with more
charm than its predecessor; a
remarkable wine in the style of
1959. The 1973 has in the
meantime developed into a
simply excellent wine, one of
the best of that year. I prefer it
to the 1974, which was
nevertheless good. A number of
venerable Moutons were tasted
by a group of wine lovers in
1978. The 1945 was still not
fully developed, in contrast to
the 1947. The 1949 was ready
for drinking, and it is expected
to last for a good time yet.

When I asked the baron
whether designs for Mouton
labels had ever been rejected he
replied, 'At least a dozen. Often
even ones by very great
artists.' An accepted design is
usually valued at ten cases of
Mouton-Rothschild, five from
various mature vintages, and
five from the year in question.
One case is the payment for a
rejected design.

From 1924 to 1928 Philippe de
Rothschild directed a Paris
theatre, and also successfully
filmed Vicky Baum's Hell im
Frauensee.

Vivre la vigne is the title of
Baron Philippe's
autobiography, published in
1981 by Presses de la Cité.

Château Mouton-Rothschild

---

such far-off countries as Tibet, Russia and
Egypt. It is all extremely tastefully
exhibited in the right surroundings, with the
right lighting. All visitors to Mouton are
made heartily welcome, but without their
cameras.

Among the leaders at last

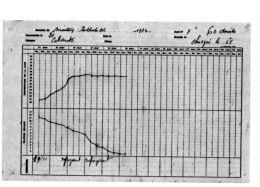

Baron Philippe's flair for publicity and his
persistent attempts to make a first *cru* of
Mouton were finally successful in 1973.
With the consent of the four other *premiers*,
Mouton-Rothschild was admitted to the
select group, but only after a number of
battles had been fought, particularly on
paper. Philippe Cottin, a director of Baron
Philippe de Rothschild CFH, knows all about
this — his file weighs 150 pounds, and it
only goes back to 1959!
How right it was to promote Mouton is clear
from the fact the wines have now been sold

Château Mouton-Rothschild

for 50 years or more at the same prices as other *premiers grand crus*. Since the Second World War, even more has often been paid for Mouton. In 1971, for example, the starting price for Lafite was 100,000 francs per *tonneau* of 198 gallons, and that for Mouton 120,000 francs. Although a big banquet was organized for all employees, the promotion of Mouton was not really a reason for wild rejoicing. To quote Philippe Cottin, a few days after the minister had signed the order, 'We really regard this only as confirmation of an established fact.'

A wine to reverence

In the Mouton cellars everything has been done to impress the visitor. First of all, you are conducted along the large oak fermentation vats by the *maître de chai*, Raoul Blondin (or his brother Pierre), and are then admitted to the enormous cellar where the wine from the previous harvest lies maturing in some thousand brand-new casks. The atmosphere is almost devotional, and even loudly clad day trippers speak in hushed tones, afraid perhaps to disturb the wine in its slumber. If you are lucky, you can taste a little of the hard purple juice that is destined to become one of the world's greatest wines.
The wine of Mouton-Rothschild has been lauded by many. The description given by the British Master of Wine Clive Coates in *Wine Magazine* is typical. 'The concentration of flavour, the sheer opulence, the massive amount of fruit, allied with the unmistakable seductive cedar-woody aroma of mature Mouton makes truly exhilarating drinking; bended-knee wine indeed.'

The great Mouton

The most impressive Mouton that I have ever tasted was the 1961, a year that comes in the same, singularly high category as the 1870 and 1945. Raoul Blondin had brought the wine to exactly the right temperature and decanted it to perfection. I can still remember what he said when handing me the first glass: 'Et Voilà le grand Mouton'. There was not an ounce of exaggeration in those words because it truly was a great wine. First came the disconcertingly deep colour. Then the pent-up, deep and rich bouquet, followed by the round, woody, fruity taste, and finally the long, lingering aftertaste that was still present half an hour after the tasting. Even Raoul Blondin, who has tasted quite a fair amount of Mouton in his time, refused to spit out this wine.
People sometimes say that the *premiers grands crus* are too expensive, but wines like the Mouton Rothschild 1961 are simply priceless. Besides, the yield in 1961 was pitifully low, only 9 hectolitres per hectare. Another memorable Mouton was the 1952, chiefly because it was a highly characteristic year with all the good properties of this great wine. At Mouton the 1952 vintage was rated even higher than the 1953. The wine of that classic year quite clearly displayed the *goût de capsule* mentioned by so many wine writers. However, I feel that the taste is not so much of 'capsule' as of iron. There is in fact iron in the subsoil of Mouton's vineyard and in dry years like 1952 the roots seek their nutrients at great depth.

The best wine of an exceptional year

The Mouton 1970 is majestic, and acclaimed by the critics as the best wine of an already exceptional year. It is a rich wine in every respect, with tones of cedarwood and spices. Because selection is so strict at Mouton-Rothschild, excellent wines are often produced in the less good years. Particular examples are the 1962 and 1967. However, no one is infallible and even Mouton has poor vintages. Particularly notorious was the 1964, and the 1969 tasted relatively thin. I also found the 1973 somewhat lacking in class, even though this was so memorable a year for Mouton. Fortunately, however, wines of this kind are very much the exception.

Right:
This image appears on the label that the baron and baroness themselves designed for Clerc Milon. The model was a silver German wedding beaker dating from 1609. The bowl between the figure's hands can turn, and the lower part of the figure is hollow. The idea was that bride and groom could drink from the beaker at the same time, one from the top, the other from the bottom.

Below:
One of the modest château buildings.

Opposite page:
The Clerc Milon cork and label.

Château Clerc Milon

5e Grand Cru Classé

Over the years the château has had a number of names. In Bordeaux et ses vins of 1850 it is listed as Château Clerc, in the 1868-98 editions as Clerc-Milon, and from 1908 to 1969 as Clerc-Milon-Mouton. Baron Philippe has returned to the form Clerc-Milon: Clerc was the first owner, Milon the hamlet where the château is situated.

The wine matures for 22 to 24 months in oak casks. About 20% of the casks are replaced each year.

1970

Château Clerc Milon

Grand Cru Classé

on Philippe de Rothschild

PROPRIÉTAIRE A PAUILLAC

APPELLATION PAUILLAC CONTRÔLÉE

Château Clerc Milon

'Notre château bourguignon' — 'our little Burgundy mansion' — is what Baron Philippe de Rothschild's people call the château at Clerc Milon. They mean that everything about this *cinquième cru* is in miniature — except for its wine. This small property lies in the hamlet of Mousset; the vineyards have the doubtful honour of being the closest to the depressingly large oil refinery at Pauillac. There is no real Château Clerc Milon, more a collection of cottages and cellars.

A wine château in miniature

The *cuvier* is a tall room in which eleven metal fermentation vats stand side by side. They bear the highest numbers of all the *cuves* in Baron Philippe de Rothschild's château; Clerc Milon's eleventh vat ends the sequence with number 54.
The *chais* are pocket-sized, but as clean as a new pin. I saw a first-year cellar painted a bright white inside. The only other noticeable colour apart from the brown of the casks was the black of the beams and the sculpture of a man in the corner. It seems that it was bought many years ago by Baron Philippe in New York but on arrival at Pauillac it failed to please its purchaser. So it disappeared to one of the many cellars and was really only discovered by chance during a spring clean. Baron Philippe bought Clerc Milon in 1970 for a very reasonable price. The property was not in the pink of condition, but the baron would hardly be the baron had he left it at that. A great deal of money was put into it.

Rationalizing the vineyard

Work was not limited to the *chais* but extended to the vineyard as well. Here, a rationalization took place and in particular a start was made with regrouping the very scattered *vignoble* plots. At present, Clerc Milon has about 74 productive acres planted with 80% Cabernet Sauvignon and Cabernet Franc and 20% Merlot, with a dash of Petit Verdot. The yield in the first year, 1970, was 60 *tonneaux*, but in subsequent vintages this rose to an average of 130 *tonneaux*. Although the baron is always full of plans, he seems to have no desire to enlarge the vineyard substantially in the near future. Much will also depend on the small growers who own plots of land on which he has his eye. If their price is reasonable, then he may do business, but if their demands are exorbitant (because, after all, the name Rothschild is associated with money) then Clerc Milon will probably stay as small as it is — so says a spokesman for Baron Philipppe de Rothschild GFA. But expansion or not, the first thing will be to make a very good wine at Clerc Milon and give it the reputation it deserves. That is the number one project, and for this alone Clerc Milon is reckoning on 20 years.

From primitive power to sophisticated style

It has so happened that on many occasions I have drunk bottles of Clerc Milon from the period when the estate still belonged to its previous owners. I can remember the 1960, 1962 and the 1963. The 1960 was somewhat thin in the mouth, reasonably *tuilé*, with a nice fragrance and pleasant aftertaste. I preferred the 1962 whose distinctive bouquet momentarily reminded me of an old Latour. The wine had a rich, penetrating taste and was obviously more elegant than the Pontet Canet served on the same occasion. The 1963 was much sturdier than I had expected — and I am speaking now of a ten-year-old wine from a practically failed year. The wine was even on the robust side and showed no signs of a premature deterioration. Nearly all Clerc Milon wines contain a kind of primitive strength, which gives the wine a long life: only after many years have passed does a sophisticated *cru* result with an aroma that often reveals a hint of blackcurrants.

Youth its only fault

The first wine that Baron Philippe made here with his Mouton team was also the best, the 1970. For me it was a perfect Pauillac, complete, balanced, full of colour and fragrant. The only fault you could find with it was its youth. I later heard that this 1970 gained the highest score from among 15 wines at a Californian *grand cru* tasting (when all the *premiers* were present), which does not surprise me. The wine was becoming ready for drinking in about 1983. The 1971 has also developed well. Wines of at least the same class as the 1970 were made in 1975 and 1978; wines with plenty of fruit and a lingering taste. I also found the Clerc Milon 1976 surprisingly good, an unusually attractive wine. The 1979, too, deserves a mention. The Clerc Milon style shows a certain kinship with that of Mouton-Rothschild — the wine could be described as '*un petit Mouton*'.

Château Lafite-Rothschild

1er Grand Cru Classé

Visiting the Médoc without seeing Lafite-Rothschild is like 'doing' the Louvre without seeing the Mona Lisa, or the Rijksmuseum in Amsterdam without looking at Rembrandt's *Night Watch*. Lafite is the *crème de la crème*, the holy of holies. It is a wine, a château and name that appeals to the imagination of every Bordeaux *aficionado* the world over. Lafite represents the very best that wine can be. It is not so much a name as a concept. And certainly not only for the lucky few who have drunk this wine but also for the countless people who hope one day to drink it — a bottle, a glass, a sip, perhaps more, at least once in their lives. Lafite-Rothschild is a Mecca for wine drinkers and it could undoubtedly receive tens of thousands of people more each year than it does. It is just that it does not care to. Lafite and Mouton are very different. At the latter château everyone is welcome; Mouton is a symbol of hospitality, Lafite is very

Left:
It is odd that Bordeaux's greatest wine should have the smallest label: only 3¾ by 2¾ inches.

Below left:
Part of the long second-year cellar.

Below right:
Cellarmaster Robert Revelle who succeeded his father Georges in 1966. Revelle senior spent all his life at Lafite. In recognition of his services he received the medal of the Chevalier de la Légion d'Honneur from the hands of Baron Elie de Rothschild in 1959.

We know to the last centime what a Dutch syndicate paid for Lafite in 1796: 1,286,606 francs, 25 centimes. The purchase cannot have been very profitable: in 1803 Lafite was sold again, to Ignace-Joseph Vanlerberghe for 1,200,000 francs. His family kept the estate until it was bought in 1868 by Baron James de Rothschild for 4,440,000 francs (exclusive of 400,000 francs in taxes and other charges).

Since the 1974 vintage Lafite has had a second wine again: Moulin des Carruades, mostly made from vines less than ten years old.

Château Lafite-Rothschild

reserved. Visitors are tolerated, but no more. Spontaneous cordiality is lacking and at no other château is it more difficult to taste anything older than the wine in the cask. From their former Paris home (Rue Lafite) the French Rothschilds have built up a central administration that exercises an extremely strict regime. Even when I visited the château by appointment for this book the *régisseur* could not let me taste a bottle. It is to be hoped that the policy will be somewhat more flexible now that Eric de Rothschild has taken over the day-to-day management from his uncle Barone Elie. How I envied Cyril Ray who was given dozens of wines to taste for his excellent book *Lafite*.

A visit to Lafite

A visit to Lafite begins in the mighty *cuvier* where 27 casks of Bosnian oak are arranged in two rows beneath a wooden ceiling, covered with roof tiles. We then enter the first-year *chai*, a spacious room 70 feet long, with round white pillars at the centre. The air is pleasantly heavy with a mixture of new oak and wine. Like the other *premiers*, Lafite uses only new casks for every vintage. This means 1,000 to 1,200 each year, and all topped up three times a week and racked every three months. Twelve months later the wine is removed to the much smaller second-year cellar. Shaped like a tunnel, it was built beneath the inner courtyard between 1947 and 1953. Immediately before being moved to this underground *cave* the wine is fined with egg white. A record six to seven eggs is used per cask at Lafite. After doing its time in the second-year cellar, the wine sometimes goes to the third-year cellar for a further six months. This, too, is underground, and the oldest part of the château: this *cave* was built some 200 years ago. Bottling generally begins in February and may continue to June. Every bottle of Lafite is therefore nearly three years old before it reaches the point of sale. For example, the *mise en bouteilles* of the 1972 was begun in February 1975. From February it can still take several months before the wine has recovered from its bottle sickness and arrives at its destination.

A vineyard in three parts

The Lafite *vignoble* covers no less than 272 acres, of which 90% is in production; 148 acres lie round the château, particularly the majestic knoll that rises above buildings to the south. A second part is located a quarter of a mile further west and a third part, barely 12 acres in size is to be found, oddly enough, in Saint Estèphe. However, it is entitled to the Pauillac *appellation* because it has been in Lafite-Rothschild's ownership for centuries.
The vines live to a venerable age — the *régisseur* estimates an average of 30 years. Together with the Cabernet Franc, the

Château Lafite-Rothschild

Cabernet Sauvignon represents some 83% of the planting. The output is generally 250 to 280 *tonneaux*. Most of this is exported, chiefly to the United States.

The Rothschild regime

In the château stand two busts of Baron James de Rothschild, the man who bought Lafite in 1868 but never lived to see it. At the time of buying it he was already old and sick. But what moved him to add Lafite to the family possessions? Cyril Ray writes that it was not the old Baron James who wanted all this but his three sons. As members of the European élite, Alphonse, Gustave and Edmond liked the idea of pouring Lafite, already the world's most prestigious wine, as their own. The more so since Nathaniel de Rothschild of the British branch was already the owner of Mouton, then still the first of the second *crus*.
After the purchase, the French Rothschilds and their friends undoubtedly greatly enjoyed Lafite's wine, but the revenues rather less so. In fact, for 80 long years not a penny was earned from Lafite — and that is quite something for a banking family! Only in 1948 was a profit made for the first time, two weeks after Baron Elie (born 1917, and a fervent polo player) had taken on the management at the request of his nine fellow owners. He is still ultimately responsible for Lafite. Because of his many commitments in the world of international finance, however, he is not in a position to live at the château more than four or five times a year, and then generally for a few days only.

Stylish interior

The actual château itself has only four rooms of any importance downstairs, and not one of them is particularly large. From the hall you enter the *salon rouge*, which lies in the south-west corner of the château and has three windows. On the walls hang four of the five Rothschilds, the brothers who left the Frankfurt ghetto in Napoleon's time to seek and make their fortunes in five different

Château Lafite-Rothschild

countries. The chairs and sofas in the salon are upholstered in red damask and in the middle of the carpet stands the small table at which Bismarck dictated the terms of armistice that led to the Treaty of Frankfurt (1871) and the end of the Franco-Prussian War.

Adjoining the large salon is the *salon d'été* (the summer salon) with its large french windows opening out on the terrace. White garden chairs are put out here in the summer but the view of the Gironde, once so beautiful, is now marred by the notorious Pauillac oil refinery. The interior of the little salon is entirely attuned to warm days. The wooden panels painted with pretty flowers and the soft brown undertones suggest a benign and shaded coolness.

The library, on the other hand, makes a warm and snug impression. Here green damask and easy chairs are dominant. In the dining room the woodwork is painted in friendly white and green shades that contrast well with the pink and blue-green Bordeaux porcelain on which the food is served.

The wine itself

Writing about Lafite wine is like photographing the Empire State Building in New York. Not only have countless people done it before you, but no ordinary mortal will ever succeed in giving a complete picture. Let me quote a few distinguished writers. Edmond Penning-Rowsell in *The Wines of Bordeaux*: 'In successful years Lafite is the acme of fine claret, well-balanced, elegant and supple with a delicious aroma.' Alexis Lichine in his *Encyclopaedia of Wines & Spirits*, already mentioned, says: 'In great years, when Lafite is successful, it can be supreme. It has great finesse and a particular softness imparted by the Merlot grape. The wine tends to be firm yet supple, with an eventual lightness developed in age. Lesser vintages are still excellent wines, lighter than those of great years, but always showing breed, fragrance, and depth of flavour.' Frank Schoonmaker's views appear

in his *Encylopaedia of Wine*: 'The wine of Lafite varies, as all Bordeaux wines vary, from one year to another, although Lafite less than most, but of its best vintages it is hard to speak except in terms of the highest praise. Rarely over 12% alcohol, they have an astonishing authority, impeccable breeding, fruit and fragrance and depth of flavour, all the qualities with which a great claret should be endowed.' And the favourite quotation of the eminent Cyril Ray is one by P. Morton Shand, who wrote in his *Book of French Wines*: 'Its flavour and bouquet are considered so grand and sublime as to afford a symposium of all other wines.' What can one add to this? Nothing, really, except a glass of the wine itself.

The best years

What is striking about Lafite is that it is nearly always a lighter wine than other Pauillacs of the same year. The wine is often so fine that in character it is much nearer to Margaux than to Latour or Mouton. I have always found Lafite above all a wine of charm, feminine, elegant and refined. And despite the tremendous complexity in aroma and taste, all the components — the colour, the bouquet, the fruit, the body — fit perfectly with each other, as if carefully selected piece by piece by a *couturier*. Lafite is an almost perfect wine.

At least, a *good* Lafite — and that was not always the case in the early 1970s. Six years after harvesting, the 1971 was already surprisingly mature and far from impressive. The 1972 was relatively thin and incomplete. The 1973 was attractive and charming but without great depth, and the 1974 was rather light for its year. Lafite again showed its outstanding class with the 1975: perhaps a less powerful wine than others of that year, but still rich in aroma and taste, a wine of great distinction. The 1976 is perhaps still better, with much fruit and elegant meatiness and superb balance. The 1977 was a great disappointment but the 1978 was impressive, as was the delicious 1979. Thanks to strict selection, the 1980 proved

very acceptable, and the 1981 has much allure. Expectations of the 1982 are also set high. Lafite-Rothschild once again fully lives up to its status as a *premier grand cru*.

For a long time Duhart-Milon-Rothschild belonged to the celebrated Castéja family, whose possessions include Batailley and Lynch-Moussas, two other Pauillac grands crus classés.

At around 114 acres the vineyard is reasonably large, but the total estate covers 198 acres: mostly woodland. Only about 25 more acres could be converted into vineyard.

There are 25 people permanently employed at the estate, under the leadership of Jean Crété, manager of Lafite-Rothschild.

Duhart-Milon-Rothschild wines are usually bottled 2½ years after vintage in their third winter. About a third to a half of the casks are replaced each year. Used casks come mainly from Lafite.

The château's second wine is called Moulin de Duhart.

Below left:
Duhart-Milon-Rothschild does not have a château, just a few cellars. The photo shows the completely new chai, built under the direction of André Portet of Lafite-Rothschild; it was brought into use in 1974.

Below right:
The Duhart-Milon-Rothschild label shows a strong family likeness to Lafite's. The building in the engraving is purely symbolic.

Château Duhart-Milon-Rothschild

Baron Philippe de Rothschild reserves his family name only for the very best. That is why Château Clerc Milon will never have 'Rothschild' added to its name, no more than happened with Château Mouton Baronne Philippe. The French branch of the Rothschild family clearly has different ideas. The owners of Lafite have not hesitated to attach their prestigious surname to the *quatrième grand cru classé* they acquired in 1962, Château Duhart-Milon. But the Lafite barons did not do so, of course, before

making sure that Duhart-Milon was again producing wine entirely in keeping with its official status.

New cellars at Pauillac

To achieve this, a good deal had to be done because at the time of the sale the property was in a lamentable state. The former owners lived partly in Bordeaux, partly in Madagascar, and had clearly neither the time nor the desire to make really good wine.

Right:
New steel cuves.

Below right:
The wooden vats which were still used as late as 1974, but for only part of the harvest. Nowadays only steel vats are used.

Below centre:
The second-year cellar of Duhart-Milon-Rothschild, where the casks are stacked high. This chai was the only storage space when the estate was bought.

Bottom:
One of the many testings the wine undergoes as it matures, to keep a close watch on its development.

Château Duhart-Milon-Rothschild

The vineyard covered only 40 acres and the *chais* were hopelessly soiled.
Duhart-Milon-Rothschild is now managed by Jean Crété, the *régisseur* of Lafite. His predecessor, André Portet, completely cleaned up the neglected cellars. Nowadays, there is little to be seen of Duhart's past, neither in the cellars nor in the vineyard. The latter lies on the Carruades plateau and adjoins that of Lafite. It measures not quite 114 acres. The vines stand in neat rows because they are tended by the tried Lafite method. There have been some changes to the *chais* as well, great improvements that allow sufficient room for the wine. The brand-new first-year cellar is very large and tall, as it should be, and the *cuvier* contains a number of new steel fermentation vats. The *chais* are in fact a mile and a half from the vineyard, in the middle of Pauillac. When I asked my host whether this location might not cause space problems because of the possible increase of production, he answered that he still had 60 square yards of land in hand, enough for future requirements. Duhart-Milon has never had a château of its own. The only building with claims to this status was the owner's house on the quayside in Pauillac, but this was sold after the Second World War.

No family resemblance

The Duhart-Milon-Rothschild wine comes from a vineyard bordering on Lafite, is made by Lafite people, and matures in second-hand Lafite casks. You would therefore expect at least a family resemblance. But in fact Duhart is a completely different wine from Lafite; it has more colour, more body, and is harder, with less finesse. One morning I tasted Lafite-Rothschild and Duhart-Milon-Rothschild of the same year and the differences were quite incredibly big.
This can be ascribed in no small measure to the soil, because although the two vineyards adjoin, the subsoil is quite different. But then there should be a difference between a first and fourth *cru*.

Merlot needed for balance

The proportions of the grape varieties differ somewhat from Lafite (63% Cabernet Sauvignon, 15% Cabernet Franc, 18% Merlot and 4% Petit Verdot), but because the Duhart soil produces a much harder wine, it is particularly important that the Merlot should have its full effect. If not, the wine will be uncompromisingly hard. This was noticeable with the 1971 and the — subsequently wrongly bottled — 1972. In normal years, on the other hand, the quality of the wine can be quite surprising. At the end of 1977, the Duhart 1973 was tasted with nine other wines of the same vintage, including even *deuxièmes grands crus*. The Duhart-Milon-Rothschild achieved the highest score. True, the wine was found to be on the hard side, but its unmistakably aristocratic qualities were appreciated. Good wines were produced here in 1975, 1976, 1978, 1979, 1981 and 1982 (a strong Merlot year). This Pauillac estate produces some 150 *tonneaux* annually.

Château Cos Labory

5e Grand Cru Classé

With Cos Labory we enter the land of Saint-Estèphe, a commune famous for its powerful, vinous wines. Although it is one of the most important towns in the Médoc, two cars can barely pass on the road linking Pauillac and Saint-Estèphe. The road starts between the châteaux of Cos Labory and Cos d'Estournel and as soon as you have passed the boundary fences of the two, you seem to enter a different wine world, very far from the sophistication of our society.
Saint-Estèphe. is pure French *campagne*. In the ear-assailing quiet, there is nothing but green vine-covered hills, a château or two, and a few winding lanes. A restful landscape, where people have been busy for generations with just one thing — making good wine.

Restoration and rebuilding

Cos Labory once had the same owner as the almost adjoining Cos d'Estournel. His name was Martyn, and he lived in London. No doubt, a Labory gave his name to the estate long ago, but the present owner, François Audoy, knows nothing about him. In fact, it is hard to find out anything about the history of Cos Labory at all. Where other owners overload you with interesting documentation, all they can do at this château is shrug their shoulders in the nicest possible way.
The château was entirely restored during the 1970s. The greater part of the adjoining *chais* was also rebuilt. But not all the storage space is at the château — there is a bottling cellar and bottle store half a mile down the road. The people at Cos Labory must have had their work cut out when all the wine began to be bottled at the château. Labory wine spends about 18 months in the cask. Twenty new casks are bought each year, often complemented by second-hand casks from Lafite.

A quick-maturing wine

The average annual yield from Cos Labory is 65 *tonneaux*. To store this quantity 240

Château
Cos Labory
GRAND CRU CLASSE
CLASSEMENT DE 1855

1970
SAINT-ESTÈPHE MÉDOC
Appellation St-Estèphe Contrôlée
AUDOY, Propriétaire à Saint-Estèphe (Gironde)
MIS EN BOUTEILLES AU CHÂTEAU

casks are required, with the space to keep them; four casks with the customary capacity of about 50 (60 US) gallons together form one 200 gallon (240 US) *tonneau*. The wine comes from a vineyard of 37 acres, divided into three plots within a radius of less than a mile from the château. Noteworthy in this case is the high percentage of Merlot planted: 40% Cabernet Sauvignon, 20% Cabernet Franc, 35% Merlot and 5% Petit Verdot. Because the yield from Merlot is higher than from Cabernet, this means that in normal years half the juice is obtained from it. This in turn explains why Cos Labory is generally a relatively soft wine and can be drunk fairly soon. I had the impression that the château has been through a difficult period. The 1970, for example, which I was served from a magnum at the château, appeared oxidized. However, the patient seems to have recovered. A tasting I attended at the *chai* in September 1978 left a relatively favourable impression. The first wine to be poured was the 1977. It had a very deep, healthy colour and its fair share of tannin. I thought it lacked roundness and body, while the taste was on the dry side. But in view of its difficult year, it was by no means a disappointing wine. The 1976 had a lighter colour than the 1977 and more charm, although I would have preferred rather more fruit. François Audoy said that he would like to make a wine like this 1976 every year. This wine will develop quickly, but the 1975 much more slowly. It is a strong wine whose bouquet had not yet opened out. Apart from strength, it had a certain flexibility. I thought it lacked somewhat in refinement. I made similar notes later about the 1982, among others. Not a particularly exciting wine, Cos Labory is rather short on breeding and finesse, but it is far from unpleasant at table.

Château Cos d'Estournel

2e Grand Cru Classé

The story of Cos d'Estournel could start 'Once upon a time . . .' because it is the most fairytale château in all the Médoc. Well, there was once a Louis Gaspard d'Estournel who started planting the family property in the hamlet of Cos, just to the north of Pauillac, with noble varieties of grape. In the course of time he succeeded in producing a good wine. This was partly sold in the ordinary way, but also used for barter because d'Estournel's other occupation was that of horse dealer. In fact, he bought many Arab horses in the Middle East and used his own wine as payment in kind.

One fine day he was unable to buy sufficient horses so that he had to return to Bordeaux with some of the wine he had taken with him.

Back home, he opened one of the bottles and discovered that this much-travelled wine had developed remarkably well. So well, in fact, that d'Estournel had the bright idea of transporting all his wine to the Middle East and then back again, and only then putting it up for sale. But this had, of course, to be done in style. Everything to do with his wine had to acquire an oriental character. So d'Estournel had an exotic park laid out at the centre of Bordeaux where people could buy his wine and he also had a château in wholly oriental style built by the vineyard. And so it was done, albeit with much delay. The fantastic project proved so costly that it took 20 years before the château was finished. In the meantime, it had even been

sold once and then bought back. But the results are there to see. When now you drive northwards from Lafite-Rothschild, a white building suddenly rises up before you looking for all the world like a Chinese temple or a stage set for an oriental dance company. I doubt whether anyone would really be convinced that Cos d'Etournel is a wine château until they actually saw the long, reassuring rows of casks inside.

A wine palace

During the Second World War the Germans did a lot of damage during their stay at Cos d'Estournel (and among other things stole the golden pagoda bells), and there was good

Château Cos d'Estournel

reason for pulling down the architectural curiosity, to replace it with a more conventional wine château. However, that was not done. On the contrary, Cos d'Estournel has been fully restored. The talented co-owner and *gérant* Bruno Prats told me why. 'To me, Cos d'Estournel is not just an ordinary château but a wine palace. An extraordinary home for an extraordinary wine. That is why we have done everything to recapture the old lustre.'

The vineyard where this wine is born stretches over some 133 acres of fairly hilly country, and is planted with 56% Cabernet Sauvignon and 31% Merlot, plus 13% Cabernet Franc. Vinification takes place under the personal supervision of the *ingénieur agronome* Prats by traditional methods applied in a very modern way. This enables him to direct the fermentation process on extremely natural lines in such a way that very acceptable results are achieved even in moderate years. Cos d'Estournel 1968, for example, was an undeniably successful wine, and they can tell you that particularly in Denmark, since that is where much of that vintage was sold. In sunny years Cos d'Estournel always produces sinewy, concentrated wines that may develop over dozens of years. A majestic example is the subtle 1961, and the 1966 and 1970 are also broad, mouth-filling wines. Cos d'Estournel is often a wine that seems to mature quickly in the cask, but whose development in the bottle seems almost to stand still for the first few years. Only then does the wine begin gradually to unfold.

Of more recent vintages, the 1975 is somewhat on the light side. I prefer the fuller, more complete 1976. The 1977 is certainly successful, and the 1978 has a fine, juicy taste, overtones of ripe fruit and a good balance. I found the 1979 really excellent (much colour, aroma, taste). The 1981 also impressed me with its deep, dark colour, its roundness, its tannin and its structure, and in the exceptional year of 1982 Cos made a glorious wine. The estate has been advised since 1975 by the well-known Professor Pascal Ribereau-Gayon.

'That's the kind of wine I should like to make each year' is what Bruno Prats said of the 1971 vintage. It produced a wine with excellent balance, a deep colour, an attractive perfume and a complete, but not exaggeratedly full or powerful taste, with

Far right:
A proud Bruno Prats standing in front of the two fantastically sculpted doors which form the main entrance to the château. These hand-made doors were once part of the Sultan of Zanzibar's palace and were bought by Bruno at an auction in Nîmes — he was bidding over the telephone. Once again they make a fitting entrance to a palace, this time a wine-palace.

Right:
The façade of Cos d'Estournel. The main entrance, graced by the great wooden doors, is under the central tower.

Below:
A bird's eye perspective of this exceptional château. Cos Labory is just to the left.

Château Cos d'Estournel

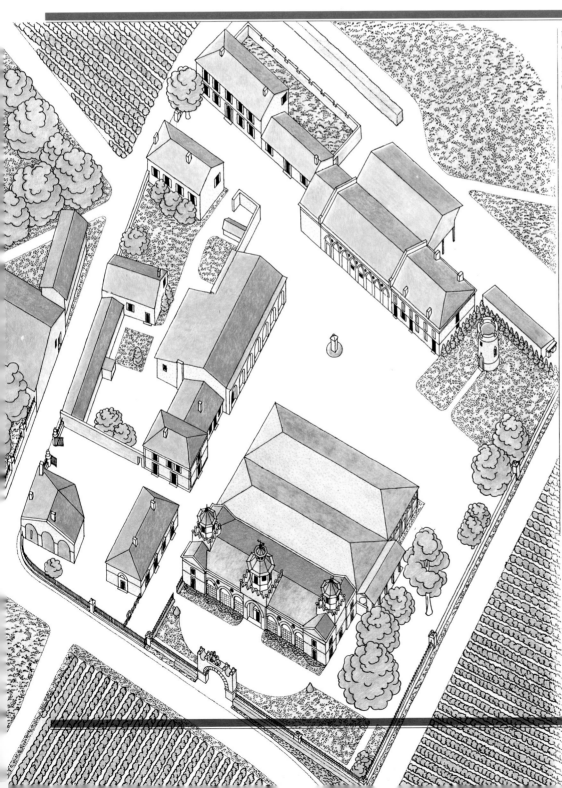

traces of ripe fruit; a really great wine. But do not drink it before 1984. And even then there is no need for hurry, because the wine is bound to stay at the same high level of quality for at least 10 years more.

Over the years, some 60% of Cos d'Estournel has been sold to America and 20% to Britain. The remainder went to a large number of other countries, including Belgium, Switzerland and Japan. The average yield is about 200 *tonneaux*.

Permanent staff

It is a noticeable fact that the staff at Cos (which is always pronounced with the 's') have always had deep roots in the estate. Altogether there are 40 permanent employees, headed by a *maître de chai*, and a *chef de culture*. Many were born at Cos d'Estournel and their families have known quite a few generations of owners. It is interesting to note that Cos has special accommodation for pensioned staff, who pay no rent and who can therefore, if they wish, spend their last days on the land where they have worked all their lives. There are some who have never even been to Bordeaux. These deep roots are partly due to the fact that the Cos vineyard is traditionally divided into *sadons* of 800 vines, and each *vigneron* is responsible for a number of these pieces of ground, always the same ones. For years now Cos d'Estournel has had a system of flexible working times. The vineyard workers fix their own hours, provided of course that the vines are well tended. The wine proves irrefutably that they are.

Below right:
Manager Paul Bussier with glasses in his hands for a dégustation of Lafon-Rochet's recent vintages.

Below:
Few people realize that the château is a completely new building. The cuvier and chais are situated behind the château on the right. On the left is the entrance to the private cellar of owner Guy Tesseron.

Château Lafon-Rochet is completely surrounded by its vineyards, which cover 100 productive acres. Lafon-Rochet has a second wine produced from young vines and sold under the name Château Vieille Chapelle (there is an old chapel in the park).

It is a very old estate which, in the 17th century, belonged to Monsieur Lafon, counsellor to the parlement of Bordeaux. The château remained in the family until 1880, then changing hands several times until bought by Guy Tesseron in 1960.

Château Lafon-Rochet

4e Grand Cru Classé

As far as I know, Lafon-Rochet is the only Médoc château to be built from scratch on its present site since the beginning of this century. You would hardly think it from its classical lines. The owner, Guy Tesseron, let his architect go on searching until he had found a form that fitted this vineyard and the atmosphere of the Médoc. It is characteristic of the exemplary single-mindedness with which Tesseron has since 1960 devoted himself to improving Lafon-Rochet and its wine. When a good owner spends large sums of money on his château, you can be sure that the vineyard and *chais* will already have received the same kind of attention, if not more. The assumption seems to be very right in this case because the wine was attended to first, and only then the people.

Not only was the vineyard area expanded by

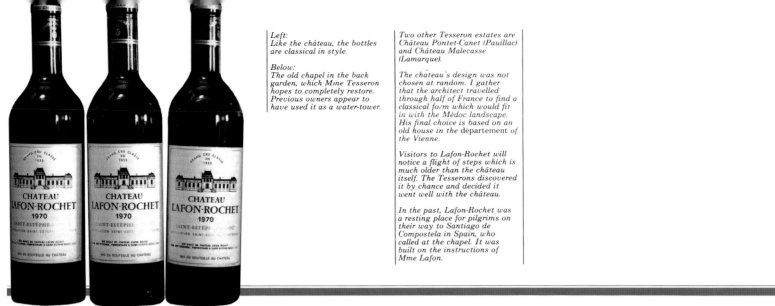

Château Lafon-Rochet

about 62 valuable acres, but it also underwent a radical face-lift. When the estate was bought, the percentage of Merlot grapes was found to be unusually high and although the plants were still in the prime of life, Guy Tesseron decided to replace them with the much superior Cabernet. In the *chais* an entirely new fermentation area was built with spotless oak vats, a new first-year cellar, a renovated second-year cellar and an underground storeroom for bottles. Everything was carried out to perfection and with an eye for detail; for example, the bottles in the cellar do not rest on concrete but on a gravel floor, so they can still breathe a little. Beneath the château itself a further, second cellar has been built, entirely for private use. Neither effort nor expense was saved here either. The wines are in recesses along a narrow, white vaulted passage that comes out by the one element in this well-groomed environment that is not quite perfect — a statue without a head.

Wine and brandy interests

Guy Tesseron is a dedicated, energetic man who divides his time between his three estates and his other profession, that of brandy wholesaler. So the Tesserons have a busy life and are continually on the go. Their ideal is one day to go and live peacefully at Lafon-Rochet, but there is little prospect of their doing so at the moment.
Madame Nicole Tesseron descends from the ancient wine-growing family of Cruse (her father was Emmanuel Cruse, and her mother owns Château d'Issan) and is naturally closely involved in everything concerning Lafon-Rochet. Although the interior of the château had not yet been completed at the time of my visit, she told me with great enthusiasm of the other plans for the garden and its little chapel. Guy Tesseron now receives a good deal of assistance from his son Alfred.

The Cabernet begins to show

Because a vine takes at least four years before it produces mature grapes that can be used for a *grand vin*, the effect of the Cabernet planting at Lafond-Rochet began to be felt only from 1966 (the 1964 was still just too early, and 1965 was a failed harvest). The 1966 vintage produced a deep-toned wine, rich in tannin, whose taste and aroma had only just begun to lose something of its hardness when I tasted it. Other wines with much colour, strength and tannin were made in 1970 and 1971 and other years. The present vineyard proportions are 70% Cabernet Sauvignon, 8% Cabernet Franc, 20% Merlot and 2% Malbec.

Although neither the 1974 nor the 1975, nor even the 1976 were noticeably good, or bad, for their years, I have tasted a series of remarkably good wines starting with the 1978. The 1978 itself was a blackish, broad wine with a taste you could almost chew, very intense and with a great deal of tannin; wine to put down and forget about for decades. The 1979 was rather more austere, with an overemphatic Cabernet presence. Although it had some fruit as well as wood, the wine lacked flesh and charm. Only after years of rest will this 1979 become attractive. The 1980 was a pleasant surprise, being more svelte than usual, but still sturdy in taste and colour. The 1981 was a concentrated, powerful wine, dark in colour and rich in tannin. I was struck by the great purity of all these wines. Between 120 and 190 *tonneaux* of this distinctive Saint-Estèphe are produced each year. Before it is bottled, the wine generally matures in oak casks for 22 months, a third of which are new.

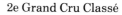

Château Montrose

2e Grand Cru Classé

The slapdash approach is quite unknown at Montrose. Here, everything is the ultimate in organization and neatness. You notice this as soon as you arrive. Where other châteaux leave motorists to drive around at random, at Montrose they have gleaming signs to show the way to the reception area. The lanes between the buildings are clean and some are even named. I saw an Avenue du Mulhouse and a Rue d'Alsace. The *cuvier*, the *chais*, the château, the park and, of course, the vineyard are immaculately maintained.

Montrose has always had dedicated owners; from the earliest days, in 1778, much love has been lavished on the estate. It has expanded substantially in the course of time.

In 1825 Montrose had only 12 to 15 acres to its name, but by 1832 it had nearly 80 and just over 180 by 1880. The present area is 166 acres.

The era of Mathieu Dollfus

The one man who more than any other set his stamp on the estate is Mathieu Dollfus. The present cellars, for example, date from his time and still bear his initials. For their period — late 19th century — they were very modern and that is perhaps why they still do excellent duty today. Dollfus also erected a wind pump, to have sufficient drinking water available in the summer. The well was more than 650 feet deep and was worked until

139

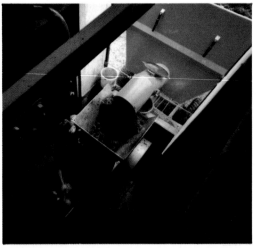

Château Montrose

1960. The vanes were blown off a few years later, but the metal frame still stands and serves as flagpole and lookout tower. Dollfus was also a progressive man from the social aspect. He distributed 10% of his profit among his staff, paid all his workers' medical fees and introduced an exemplary financial scheme for pregnant wives. Dollfus died without issue and his possessions were sold to Jean Hostein, then also the owner of Cos d'Estournel. He passed the property on to his son-in-law Louis Charmolüe in 1896, and it is his descendant, Jean-Louis Charmolüe, who at present runs Montrose in such exemplary fashion.

Perfection to the smallest detail

It is often the small things that show an owner to be greatly concerned with the welfare of a château, his people and his wine — his mastery of his calling shows in the detail. At Montrose there are examples in abundance: the tiled floor in the *cuvier* and the first-year cellar which Jean-Louis Charmolüe specially had laid to facilitate cleaning; or the polished wooden fermentation vats; or the five to six egg whites with which the wine is fined (elsewhere, they often use only three or four); or the mini-bus that takes all the small children to school each day; or the clean accommodation for the pickers and the modern kitchen installed for them; or the continuous improvements to all buildings, from the bottle cellar to the château.

The pink hill

The Montrose vineyard lies on a slope not far from the Gironde. It is this hill that apparently gives the château its name. Where the vines now stand in serried ranks there was nothing but bramble and wild heath in the 18th century, and when the heath was in flower on these 200 or so acres the land acquired a pink hue all over — hence the name *Mont Rose*. On the estate's 166 productive acres, the Cabernet Sauvignon takes pride of place at 65%. It is followed by Merlot (25%) and Cabernet Franc (10%). The average yield is 250 *tonneaux*. The wine matures for 23 to 25 months in wood. About one fifth of the barrels are renewed each year.

Fleshy and vinous

Château Montrose has bottled all its own wine only since 1969. Consequently two versions circulate of most earlier vintages, the *mise du château* and that bottled by the importer. There could be great differences between the two, and certainly not all of them in favour of the château bottling. But practice made perfect, and in recent years the *mises* have displayed the château wine in all its glory — honest, fleshy and vinous. A wine that I can unreservedly recommend is the 1970. Its tannic, generous, lingering taste is preceded by an intense aroma and an almost black colour: a wine with much personality and great solidity. It is perhaps the sturdiest of the Saint-Estèphes of its year and will not be ready before 1985. I also found the 1974 impressive in more than one respect, a deeply dark wine with a lot of class for its year. The 1975 was an astringent wine, concentrated, aromatic and fairly hard. The 1976 offered more fruit and meatiness and will be ready for drinking much sooner. The 1977 was very hard (the Merlot was conspicious by its absence). Since 1978 the Montrose wine has seemed more accessible, more supple and less astringent than formerly, but also less intense in colour. This was evident in all vintages from 1978 to 1982. Chance, or a deliberate change of course? Time will show.

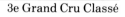

Château Calon-Ségur

3e Grand Cru Classé

With Calon-Ségur we are briefly taken back to the days of antiquity. In Gallo-Roman times, Calon was the villa from which the parish of Saint-Estèphe was later to develop. The name is derived from an old word meaning wood, the small boats that once used to carry timber to the soldiers being called *calones.* How closely Calon is linked with the history of Saint-Estèphe is also clear from the fact that until the 18th century the parish was called Saint-Estèphe-de-Calon, or sometimes Saint-Estèphe-Caloneis. There can be no doubt that in this northernmost commune of Haut-Médoc, wine growing started at Calon; documents have been found that refer to taxes on the vines in the 13th century.

Calon-Ségur acquired its present name when a century or two ago it became the property of the Marquis Alexandre de Ségur. President of the Bordeaux *parlement*, he was also the owner of Lafite, Latour, Mouton, de Pez and other estates. But despite the luxury of the already famous first *crus,* the Marquis preferred Calon. He apparently said, 'I make wine at Lafite and Latour, but my heart is at Calon.' This sentiment is symbolically represented on the Calon-Ségur label by a heart.

Better than its classification

But just as the Marquis lost his heart to Calon, so equally did Philippe Capbern-Gasqueton. He is today's forthright, dedicated *administrateur* with only one aim in life — to make the best wine possible. It has taken quite a few years, but he has succeeded. There was a period when Calon-Ségur produced great, classic wines. One example is the wine of 1973. In that year, according to Capbern-Gasqueton, he considered 30% of the Médoc harvest as successful and 70% as less so: something that would make the buyers very cautious. And this lack of enthusiasm would only be strengthened by the general economic decline and by the large stocks of 1971 and 1972, still available. His own Calon 1973 proved to be so good, however, that he had already sold the entire vintage before the *mise en bouteilles.* It was certainly a very promising wine. It showed a remarkable amount of fruit in its nose and taste, was very well rounded, and was extraordinarily balanced. In my opinion, this Calon-Ségur was one of the best Médocs of its year, no mean achievement for a *troisième grand cru classé.* That Château Calon-Ségur often produces wines that deserve better than their present status is also confirmed in *Bordeaux et Ses Vins* of 1982, which says '*actuellement supérieur à son classement*' (at present better than its classification).

Château Calon-Ségur

Vineyard in one piece

Long ago, the Calon vineyard was Saint-Estèphe's largest. But that was centuries ago. Almost one third — 2,700 acres — of this commune of 9,280 acres is planted with vines. Calon-Ségur accounts for 148 of these (119 productive), in one continuous piece of land, most of it walled.

The soil is very gravelly and generally fairly heavy, as can be tasted in quite a few of the vintages up to 1975. The grape varieties are listed as 60% Cabernet Sauvignon, 20% Cabernet Franc and 20% Merlot. The wine matures a full two years in casks; a third of these are new. Calon-Ségur is not filtered, and is clarified only with fresh egg white. As at Château du Tertre, the other *grand cru* managed by Philippe Capbern-Gasqueton, production at Calon-Ségur is on the low side. Partly because there are many old vines that are well past their best, and partly because the rather less successful wines are

ruthlessly separated out of the rest. Altogether, the 119 acres yield an average 140 *tonneaux* of the château's *grand vin*. It is sold chiefly to the United States and Britain, although Belgium and the Netherlands also regularly import Calon-Ségur. Saint-Estèphe has in fact always had close ties with Holland because the Dutch were called in to drain the marshes.

Recent impressions

There is something odd about Château Calon-Ségur because it often makes better wines in ordinarily good years than in the excellent years. I personally preferred the 1967 to the 1966. The 1967 was a wine with plenty of fruit, an intense bouquet and a respectable strength. The 1966, on the other hand, was on the light side for that extraordinary year. Similarly, I would sooner spend my money on the 1973 than on the 1971 — although the latter wine was very

correct in taste. The 1972, like the 1974, was very successful for its year. The 1975 (only 40 *tonneaux*) was a good, somewhat austere wine with subtle gradations of aroma and taste. My notes are less positive about the later vintages. I found the 1976 smooth and easy going, the 1977 very light, the 1978 less firm and full than expected, and the 1979 rather wanting in breeding and depth. The Calon-Ségur of today seems less exciting than that of the past — although this could be a question of personal taste.

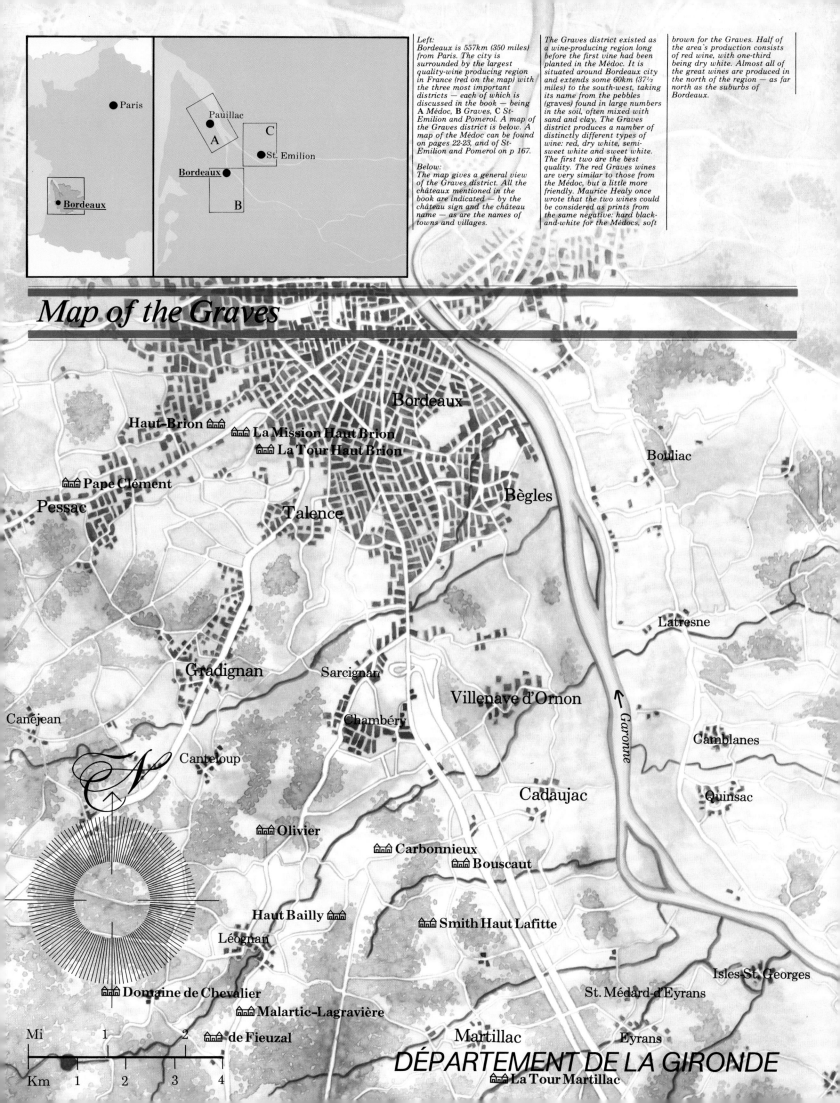

Map of the Graves

Left:
Bordeaux is 557km (350 miles) from Paris. The city is surrounded by the largest quality-wine producing region in France (red on the map) with the three most important districts — each of which is discussed in the book — being **A** Médoc, **B** Graves, **C** St-Emilion and Pomerol. A map of the Graves district is below. A map of the Médoc can be found on pages 22-23, and of St-Emilion and Pomerol on p 167.

Below:
The map gives a general view of the Graves district. All the châteaux mentioned in the book are indicated — by the château sign and the château name — as are the names of towns and villages.

The Graves district existed as a wine-producing region long before the first vine had been planted in the Médoc. It is situated around Bordeaux city and extends some 60km (37½ miles) to the south-west, taking its name from the pebbles (graves) found in large numbers in the soil, often mixed with sand and clay. The Graves district produces a number of distinctly different types of wine: red, dry white, semi-sweet white and sweet white. The first two are the best quality. The red Graves wines are very similar to those from the Médoc, but a little more friendly. Maurice Healy once wrote that the two wines could be considered as prints from the same negative: hard black-and-white for the Médocs, soft

brown for the Graves. Half of the area's production consists of red wine, with one-third being dry white. Almost all of the great wines are produced in the north of the region — as far north as the suburbs of Bordeaux.

Paris

Pauillac

A

St. Emilion

C

Bordeaux

B

Bordeaux

Haut-Brion

La Mission Haut Brion

La Tour Haut Brion

Bouliac

Pape Clément

Pessac

Talence

Bègles

Latresne

Gradignan

Sarcignan

Villenave d'Ornon

Canéjean

Chambéry

Camblanes

Canteloup

Garonne

Cadaujac

Quinsac

Olivier

Carbonnieux

Bouscaut

Haut Bailly

Smith Haut Lafitte

Léognan

Isles-St. Georges

Domaine de Chevalier

St. Médard-d'Eyrans

Malartic-Lagravière

Mi   1   2   de Fieuzal

Martillac   Eyrans

DÉPARTEMENT DE LA GIRONDE

Km   1   2   3   4

La Tour Martillac

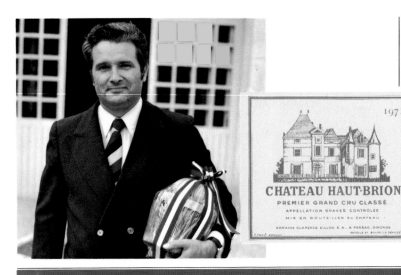

Château Haut-Brion

1er Grand Cru Classé

When Samuel Pepys drank Haut-Brion in the Royal Oak Tavern on 10 April 1663 he noted, 'And here drank a sort of French wine called Ho Bryan; that hath a good and most particular taste that I ever met with', this was in all probability the first time that the wine of an individual *cru* was mentioned by name. Not until the early 18th century do we begin to find other names. Haut-Brion can therefore justify its claim to be the first Bordeaux *cru* to become well-known.
The estate developed out of the Maison Noble d'Aubrion which in the 16th, 17th and 18th centuries was the property of the Pontac family. It was the Pontacs who planted the vineyard and exported the wine to England. They had an eye for the right kind of publicity. For example, in 1666 François Auguste de Pontac opened an exclusive tavern in London, called Pontac's Head, which soon became the meeting place for the aristocracy — and where, of course, a great deal of Haut-Brion was served.

Acquisition by Clarence Dillon

Haut-Brion passed out of the family at the end of the 18th century and the property was to change hands many times after, until it was acquired by the American financier Clarence Dillon. That was in 1935 and the story of the sale is an interesting, and possibly true one. It is said that to start with Dillon was interested not in Château Haut-Brion but in Cheval Blanc, because during these crisis years this famous Saint-Emilion estate was up for sale, like many other *grands crus*. But Clarence Dillon wanted to see the château before the deal was struck. And so, together with Dubaquié (director of the Station Oenologique) and Seymour Weller (chairman of Domaine Clarence Dillon SA) he got into his car. As chance would have it, however, the weather was cold and on the way the company had to stop to buy blankets — which hardly appealed to Clarence Dillon, not known for his patience. Then the fog descended and they became hopelessly lost. This apparently was the last straw — Dillon had had more than enough of

the remote and elusive Cheval Blanc and decided to abandon the purchase. Of course, the American continued to be interested in buying a wine estate and after further consultations he chose Haut-Brion.
With hindsight, the perspicacious, clever financier seems to have acted very wisely because Haut-Brion, lying close to Bordeaux, is now worth far more than Cheval Blanc. Clarence Dillon transferred Haut-Brion to his son Douglas in 1962. After the latter's death, his daughter Madame la Duchesse de Mouchy became chairwoman of the *société anonyme* that manages Haut-Brion. Day-to-day management is in the hands of Jean-Bernard Delmas, one of the most expert wine makers I know.

A question of soil

I asked Delmas how it happened that the Haut-Brion wine was not just the only non-Médoc wine to be included in the 1855 classification, but also had much in common with a Médoc? His answer was, 'It is not just a question of quality and seniority, but also of soil.' In prehistoric times, rivers carried stones and gravel to the Bordeaux estuary. Here a complex layer was deposited originating partly in the central Pyrenees, partly in the Massif Central and partly in the valleys of the Lot and the Aveyron. However, in the Haut-Brion area these deposits, ideal for wine growing, were later covered with a thick layer of wind-borne sand from the Landes. Only at the spot where Haut-Brion now stands did the sand fail to settle. Two small streams on either side of what is now the estate washed the sand away in the course of time. The famous gravelly ground therefore remained available as a subsoil for the roots of the vines, explaining the Haut-Brion phenomenon. The geologist Henri Enjalbert has also pointed out that the Haut-Brion subsoil is very like that of Latour.

Separating out unripe grapes

The Haut-Brion *vignoble* is planted with 55% Cabernet Sauvignon, 20% Cabernet Franc and 25% Merlot. Altogether, 124 acres are available, of which 109 are under cultivation. There is also a patch of ground where white Sauvignon and Sémillon grapes are grown for the dry, very fruity Haut-Brion Blanc. The vineyard lies on two softly rolling hills, one just behind the château, the other on the far side of the railway line where La Mission Haut Brion also has land.
One of the countless details that go to make up a great wine is the state of ripeness of the grapes. Ideally, the fruit must be really ripe, even, so Jean-Bernard Delmas thinks, a fraction over-ripe. So it is particularly important that under-ripe grapes should be separated out from the rest before fermentation. At Haut-Brion, attempts were made to have the pickers do the selecting, but this proved impracticable, so Delmas thought up a different method. As the grapes arrive, they are unloaded before *égrappage* on two or three stainless-steel tables attended by eight workers. This group picks out the unripe grapes and, particularly, any leaves that may have been included by mistake. A particularly strict pre-selection had to be made in 1962 and 1972, and in some other years

Pioneers of stainless steel

Haut-Brion was one of the pioneers in the use of stainless-steel fermentation tanks. The first of these was brought into use in 1961, at Delmas's initiative. Haut-Brion's wooden *cuverie* had to be replaced and he looked for a type in which he could adjust the temperature to his own requirements during the first fermentation. Temperature is an important factor for the wine's colour and tannin, among other things. Moreover, the new casks would have to last for a good time, but not differ too greatly in shape from the wooden ones, because he did not want to spend further money on drastic rebuilding. The problem was simply that the *cuves*

Château Haut-Brion

Delmas was looking for did not yet exist. With Professor Peynaud and others, he began to experiment. Stainless steel seemed a possible solution, but that was very expensive and its effect on wine was unknown. They had to be sure. Jean-Bernard Delmas can recall many trials, e.g. with wine to which enormous doses of sulphur were added, more than could ever occur in reality. This was intended to show whether it could affect the metal. In the same way, the neutrality was assessed, the right thickness of wall decided, and so on. The shape of the first steel *cuve* was designed by Delmas himself. Because of the height of his existing *cuvier*, and for various other reasons, he went for a relatively broad shape, with as large a diameter as possible. As wine ferments, a cake of skins starts to float on top. It is important for the wine to stay in contact with this, because the skins give the juice its colour. So, a broad tank allows greater contact than a narrow one.

At Latour, however, this line of reasoning was not followed. Priority was given to cooling, which is of course easier and faster if the *cuves* are tall and narrow. Whose decision was the right one is difficult to say, but it seems as if Haut-Brion took the path of least risk. Painstaking selection is made from among the various wines after fermentation. Each wine is firstly fully

Château Haut-Brion

Château Haut-Brion

analysed and then Jean-Bernard Delmas tastes it several times on different days because the occasion, the weather and the taster's own state of mind can influence the outcome. A wine that is considered too light will be offered non-vintage as Château Bahans-Haut-Brion. This is exclusive to the firm of Johnston. The average yield of 120 *tonneaux* at Haut-Brion is sold to some 20 *négociants* who ship the wine mainly to the United States (around 40%), Britain, Belgium and Japan.

Less reserved than a Médoc

In the second half of the 19th century the English writer Cyrus Redding said of the wine of Haut-Brion, 'The flavour resembles burning sealing wax: the bouquet savours of the violet and raspberry'. And the somewhat bemused Edmund Penning-Roswell comments on this appraisal in *The Wines of Bordeaux*, 'These parallels are nearly always lost on me, but I pass this one on, in the hope that it will strike a chord with others.' Either hyper-acute senses or a lively imagination are required if we are to recognize Redding's properties in the wine. Rather more understandable and to the point is P. Morton Shand's dictum, nearly a century later, in his *Book of French Wines*: 'Indeed, many connoisseurs used to consider it out and away as the greatest of the four and the finest wine on earth, with its stately harmony and massive volume of round, regal flavour.' Haut-Brion is certainly a full wine, with a round, noble taste. It is, moreover, a wine with a personality all of its own, quite different from the Médocs. Compared with the Médocs of the 1855 classification, you can already taste in Haut-Brion the friendliness of the Graves. Haut-Brion is generally a less reserved wine than the Médocs — although it is the red Graves that correspond most to the Médocs in terms of character. A good Haut-Brion always offers a fine, velvety quality in addition to its strength and depth, which gives it a disarming charm later in life. Here are some more specific tasting impressions.

I found the bouquet of the 1964 very fine; it was rich, creamy and strong — with a taste to match; perhaps on the light side for Haut-Brion, but still very fine. The 1966 was a pronounced success and the same could be said of the 1967. In 1968, Jean-Bernard Delmas succeeded in making perhaps the best red Bordeaux of that year, no mean achievement in view of the competition. Much the same was achieved in 1977. The best wines of the 1970s are undoubtedly the 1975 and 1978. I regard the 1975, in particular, as one of Haut-Brion's greatest vintages, with a velvety richness, highly sophisticated tannin, and an aftertaste lasting for minutes. The 1978 is rather more accessible and is characterized by seductive nuances of fruit. The 1974 was more successful at this château than the 1973, although the latter wine offers much charm. Charm is also there in abundance in the 1979, and the 1980 offers prime quality. Red Haut-Brion normally matures for 27 months, always in casks. This *premier grand cru* is lightly filtered after fining with fresh egg white.

CHÂTEAU
LA MISSION HAUT BRION
APPELLATION GRAVES CONTRÔLÉE
Grand Cru classé
1964

SOCIÉTÉ CIVILE DES DOMAINES WOLTNER
PROPRIÉTAIRE

BORDEAUX
FRANCE
MIS EN BOUTEILLES AU CHÂTEAU

Left:
The cross of St Vincent de Paul, founder of the religious order which owned La Mission Haut Brion, can be seen all around the castle — including on the gates.

Below:
La Mission Haut Brion has a small ornamental garden. Entry to the old chapel, which has been turned into a small museum, is gained through the main building.

There is a story that Napoleon one day developed a craving for some La Mission wine and despatched a messenger post-haste to the château to fetch some. The then owner, however, believed that his wine did not travel well and that it should be tasted only at the château itself. Accordingly, Napoleon's messenger was told, 'If your master wants to drink La Mission, he must come to the cellar.' It seems an understandable reaction, as Napoleon was known for his uncivilized drinking habits: it is said that he used to water down his Chambertin!

The wine is usually left to mature in wood for 22 months, with one-quarter of the casks being renewed at each harvest.

The wine of La Mission is not filtered, but it is fined with egg white.

Francis and Françoise Dewavrin-Woltner travel widely in Europe and to America. They have opened a wine-import business in California and are also co-owners of the Conn Creek Winery in the Napa Valley. They also own a vineyard on Howell Mountain.

The Woltner estates are owned by four people, one of whom lives in Basel, Switzerland.

Château La Mission Haut Brion

Cru Classé des Graves

Henri Lagardère is undoubtedly one of the very few *régisseurs* with prayer stools in his office — but then La Mission Haut-Brion is an estate with a strongly religious history. In earlier times, it formed part of the great Haut-Brion domain, but in 1682 passed via a bequest to a religious order founded by St Vincent de Paul and known as the Preachers of the Mission (*Précheurs de la Mission*). The monks enlarged and improved the vineyard. In addition, they built a small chapel, consecrated on 26 August 1698 and still standing today. It is arranged as a small museum to which all successive owners have made a contribution. The congregation had

to leave La Mission Haut-Brion at the time of the French Revolution and as a result the estate passed into private hands. However, memories of the hard-working monks persist, in the chapel, in the cellars and on the bottles; the cross of the order is still encountered everywhere.

A confined estate

As might be expected, La Mission Haut-Brion lies close to Haut-Brion, and the latter's vineyard cuts into that of its neighbour. Altogether, La Mission has 54 acres in production, planted with 65%

Cabernet Sauvignon, 5% Cabernet Franc and 30% Merlot. The *vignoble* is divided into four parts by a road and the main Bordeaux—Spain railway line. The largest piece, nearly half, lies round the château. Expansion as in the Médoc appears quite impossible because, like Haut-Brion, La Mission lies in the suburbs of ever-expanding Bordeaux. 'We have in fact to be very careful', says Henri Lagardère, 'that none of the vineyard is lost to urban sprawl.' Part of the *vignoble* is still just within Pessac, but most of the land and the château itself are in the commune of Talence

As a rule, the wines of La Mission Haut Brion are about 20% cheaper than those of Haut Brion.

Cardinal Richelieu appears to have been extremely fond of La Mission Haut Brion wines — so much so that he drank more of it than was good for him. When the Cardinal's doctor told him he should drink less, Richelieu answered, 'Why should God forbid drinking when he has made the wine so good?'

Right:
The menu for a typical, well-balanced dinner at the château.

Far right:
The interior of the old chapel with its magnificent stained-glass windows. All the owners have contributed to the collection of church objects and furniture which visitors admire. The château has another two collections: one of Holy Water basins, and one of Bacchus statues, assembled by Henri Woltner. This unique Bacchus collection was borrowed for display at the 1958 World Exhibition in Brussels.

Below:
The château seen from the back. The cuvier is in the right wing of the building.

Château La Mission Haut Brion

Henri Woltner's involvement

After the First World War, La Mission was bought by Frédéric Woltner. He was followed by his two sons Fernand (the elder) and Henri and by their sister Madame le Gac. Henri, in particular, devoted his whole life to La Mission. He was one of the owners most closely involved in the life of Bordeaux, and very particular about the reputation of his wine; for example, twice each year he toured several large châteaux to discover how his wine compared with the others. Woltner was also a gifted taster, one of the five best in Bordeaux according to Lagardère. He also had a great knack for looking into a wine's future, to make forecasts. Lagardère remembers how Henri Woltner was one of the first to rate the 1966 vintage higher than the 1967 — a prophecy that few would accept, though proved true in the course of time.

For Henri Woltner, quality stood paramount and he was prepared to make sacrifices for it. In 1968, for example, he suggested to his *régisseur* that all the bad grapes should be cut away. Lagardère pointed out that he would have a third less wine', to which Woltner retorted, 'I want quality'. And so the rotten fruit was cut out and the La Mission Haut-Brion 1968 was one of the most successful of Bordeaux wines that year.

A quarter century of experimentation

Henri Woltner worked and studied at the Station Oenologique and was regarded as an expert on vinification matters. It is therefore hardly surprising that the *cuvier* at La Mission is unique in that part of the world. At no other château are such fermentation tanks to be found. They are of metal, angular and low, spray-painted white on the outside. But the wine does not come into contact with

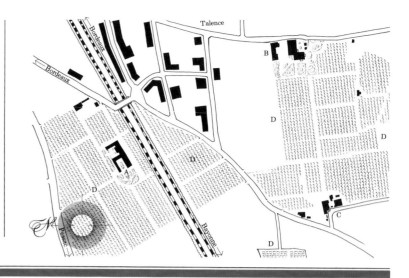

Château La Mission Haut Brion

the metal because inside the tanks have a vitreous lining. At first sight, the *cuvier* seems very new. In actual fact the first tank dates back to 1926. For 25 years, Henri Woltner experimented with his steel *cuves* until he was absolutely convinced that the results were not only equal to fermentation in wood but even better. The irony is that Woltner discovered these fermentation vessels in a brewery! This is clearly an example of how careful they are at La Mission with everything that can have some influence on the ultimate quality of the wine. Another vinification device that proves this is the cooling apparatus bought in 1971. This keeps the temperature at no more than 30°C (86°F) during the first fermentation — 28°C (82°F) is regarded as ideal at La Mission — by passing the juice through stainless-steel tubing. The juice comes into contact only with the stainless steel and is not subjected to any sudden movement.

Henri Woltner died on 9 October 1974, unfortunately just before this great *viticulteur* would have made wine for the 50th time at La Mission Haut-Brion. Henri's brother Fernand died shortly after.

Humble Cellars

Fernand's daughter Françoise Dewavrin now is the *gérante* of the estate. She and her husband Francis live in Paris but she has frequent contact with Henri Lagardère, who has worked at La Mission since 1954. He is assisted by his son Michel, a qualified oenologist. Because the yield from the estate is not particularly large — 70 to 100 *tonneaux* in good years — the *chais* does not have the imposing aspect of some Médoc châteaux. Perhaps that is why they are so appealing. The first-year cellar is a low, whitewashed building, and you go down steps to the second- and third-year cellars.

Outstanding class

There is no more ideal place for tasting the more mature vintages of La Mission Haut-Brion than the château's own table.

Hospitality is very generous and I recall the lunch I had there which consisted of *soles du bassin* (small sole from the Arcachon estuary), *boeuf grillé, fromages, fruits, desserts, café* and *alcools*. I drank La Mission 1949, a wine with a deep colour and soft, luxurious bouquet and a full, ripe taste. The overall impression was that of an elegant, velvety nectar without the slightest trace of tiredness. Other, older vintages of repute from La Mission Haut-Brion are the 1953, 1955, 1959, 1961, 1964 and 1970.

The memorable 1975

Henri Woltner's indifferent health was one of the chief causes for the drop in quality of the wine between 1971 and 1975. However, from 1975 La Mission Haut-Brion again shone in full glory. As at Haut-Brion, a fabulously good wine was produced that year, very rich, very deep, very long, a wine with a great deal of strength yet also a wealth of nuances. It is not expected to become drinkable until around 2000. I also greatly enjoyed 1976, a much more supple wine, generous in aroma and taste, and of excellent quality. Great wines were also produced in 1978, 1979, 1981 and 1982, and the 1980 must be regarded as one of the best of that vintage. The La Mission Haut-Brion style is different from that of Haut-Brion: firmer, broader, with more tannin and *terroir*, and initially more reserved — but masterly in recent years nonetheless.

Left and below:
The cross on the label of La Tour Haut Brion is turned through 45° so as to underline the difference between it and La Mission.

Bottom:
The château, which is now an old people's home.

The name La Tour Haut Brion is a compound of two of the greatest names in Bordeaux: Latour and Haut-Brion. However, its wine bears no resemblance to either, having its own distinctive personality. Prices are generally 25% lower than those of La Mission Haut Brion.

Recommended vintages are: 1966, 1975, 1976, 1978, 1979, 1981 and 1982.

The vineyard borders that of Laville Haut Brion, which was bought by the Woltners in 1978.

CHÂTEAU
LA TOUR HAUT BRION
APPELLATION GRAVES CONTRÔLÉE
Grand Cru classé
1963
SOCIÉTÉ CIVILE DES DOMAINES WOLTNER
PROPRIÉTAIRE
BORDEAUX
FRANCE
MIS EN BOUTEILLE AU CHÂTEAU

Château La Tour Haut Brion

Cru Classé des Graves

Like La Mission Haut Brion, La Tour Haut Brion is the property of the Société Civile des Domaines Woltner. At the beginning of the present century it belonged to a certain Cousteau, the same person from whom Frédéric Woltner bought La Mission. He continued to live a short while at La Tour Haut Brion after the transaction, until the Woltner family took over in 1924.
The two châteaux lie cheek by jowl — only the railway really separates them — and because La Mission had both a good team and good equipment, the Woltners decided to have the La Tour Haut Brion wine vinified at La Mission.
The rather unimaginative, angular château was let and now serves as an old people's home. A pleasant park surrounds the château, practically hiding it from view when the leaves are out.

La Mission's second wine

The *vignoble* borders the building on two sides and is very small, only 11 acres in fact. It is something of a minor miracle that no tower blocks or other blessings of civilization have yet been erected on this land — although I thought the white buildings of the University of Bordeaux were already alarmingly close. There may well have been a period when the grapes at La Tour Haut Brion were vinified separately, but they are now mixed with those of La Mission Haut-Brion. The latter's 54 acres in fact include the 11 at La Tour Haut Brion. Château La Tour Haut Brion is nothing more nor less than Château La Mission Haut Brion's second wine — a fact that was publicly disclosed only in 1980.

A good standard

That La Tour Haut Brion nevertheless deserves the status of a *cru classé* is proved by its wine. This is generally somewhat less full, more austere and harder than La Mission, and less complete and complex, but still of very high quality. Selection is strict. In 1980, for example, wine for La Tour Haut Brion was also rejected. What was left produced an elegant wine, lighter than usual. Generally speaking, La Mission's good vintages are also good vintages for the second wine.

Château Pape Clément

Cru Classé des Graves

Archbishop Bertrand de Goth may have been a most worthy churchman but he still loved the good life. And so, in 1300, he started his own vineyard. Tradition has it that a grand feast was once held at the château attended by Philipe le Bel, a fair number of attractive women, and a great quantity of wine. That was perhaps the normal way of life among the clergy in those days. In any event, the archbishop was elected pope in 1305. Four years later, he moved the Holy See from Rome to Avignon (where he long enjoyed the wine) and passed his vineyard on to Arnaud de Canteloup, hi successor at Bordeaux. Because the new pope had adopted the name Clement V the vineyard was soon called Pape Clément.

Complete reconstruction

Pape Clément was in dire straits in the 1930s. The owners went bankrupt and a firm of bankers specializing in land speculation became the new owners. They completely neglected the vineyard and to make matters worse, the vines that were still sound were destroyed in the spring of 1937 by an unusually heavy hailstorm.

The estate was saved in 1939, when it was acquired by Paul Montagne, devoted wine grower and talented poet. He put all his energies into replanting the vineyard and repairing the buildings. It took a good ten years before production began to return to normal but what was made in the way of wine in all those years was quite creditable. His heirs now possess an outstanding vineyard of 67 acres, whose yield varies from 86 to 182 *tonneaux.*

The soil is very ferruginous and has a lot of clay. Couple this with a high percentage of Merlot — 40%, supplemented with 60% Cabernet Sauvignon — and you will understand why Pape Clément produces consistently muscular, meaty, generous wine. Pape Clément's athletic strength is further accentuated by a generally strong wood-and-vanilla aroma; this red Graves normally spends two years maturing in casks of which 30-40% are new. Classic successes of this estate were the 1961 and 1962, together with the 1970, 1971, 1975 and 1978. But even in less sunny years, Pape Clément makes splendid wines, as was clear from such fine vintages as the 1973 and 1974 (one of the best wines of that year).

Château Olivier

Cru Classé des Graves

The white wine from Château Olivier — a medieval castle standing amid 395 acres of woodland and arable — has long been better known than the red, and no wonder. The output of red wine used to be small and was sold almost entirely to the United States. Nowadays, however, there are far more acres of black than white grapes — about 45 as against 40. It took a great deal of money and time to achieve this. Most of the vines were planted in the early 1970s. On my first visit to Olivier, in January 1975, I saw row upon row of one and two-year-old vines much damaged by rabbits from the adjoining wood. Only two varieties of grape had been planted, Cabernet Sauvignon (80%) and Merlot (20%). After being rather light at the start, the red Olivier has gained somewhat in depth. Nonetheless, it is still an elegant wine, even if rather lacking in depth and length. The most complete of recent years included the

1975, 1978, 1979, 1981 and 1982. The red wine — which like the white belongs among the *crus classés* — usually spends up to 18 months in wooden casks. A quarter of the casks are renewed each year. The wine is filtered twice.

The white wine

Olivier Blanc is based on three varieties of grape — 70% Sémillon, 25% Sauvignon and 5% Muscadelle. The wine is rather lacking in body and therefore not particularly exciting. Even so, it is a pleasant table drink, with the softly fresh, gravelly, taste of the Sémillon. Record quantities of white were harvested in 1976 and 1982, 110 *tonneaux*. The nadir was in 1977, with only 49 *tonneaux*. The output of red fluctuates between 50 and 115 *tonneaux*. Both wines are now bottled at the château.

Changing the watch

Early this century the wine merchants Louis Eschenauer took a lease of the estate, and, of course, sold the wines exclusively. This situation changed slightly in 1982, when the owners, members of the Bethmann family, decided they would again run the vineyard themselves. Jean-Jacques Bethmann acts as administrator and manager. What effect this will have on the wines is not yet clear at time of writing. I do not expect too much, at least in the immediate future. Messrs Eschenauer have in fact retained exclusive selling rights and will therefore continue to sell Olivier in the same markets, to the same customers.

Left:
The noble produce of this well-known château.

Below left:
The elegant inner courtyard, where receptions are sometimes organized in summer.

Bottom:
The old engraving of Carbonnieux which adorns the label. It was once an imposing castle surrounded by a wall with 12 towers. The château takes its name from a certain Carbonnieux family, which has been traced as far back as 1234 when a Ramon Carbonnieux was baptized in the church at Léognan.

Château Carbonnieux

Cru Classé des Graves

When in 1741 the Benedictines of the Abbey of Sainte Croix de Bordeaux became the new owners of the Château Carbonnieux they set to work in a most practical fashion. They sold the white wine not only to Christians in their own country but also to the Moslems at the Turkish Court. The only problem was that Moslems are forbidden to consume alcoholic drinks and could not therefore openly purchase wine. However, Benedictines found a solution: when the casks arrived at Constantinople, written on them in large letters was *'Eau Minérale de Carbonnieux en Guienne'*.

154

Château Carbonnieux

This ruse, so they tell you at the Château, satisfied everyone, monks, thirty customers, God, Allah and Bacchus! Could modern oil sheikhs not also be induced to buy mineral water from Carbonnieux?

From Burgundy via Algeria to Bordeaux

The French Revolution forced the monks to hand Carbonnieux over to the State. Since then, the estate has been in secular hands. The family of the present owners have been making wine for a century or more. The Perrins came from Burgundy but were obliged to leave the country in 1840 for political reasons. They moved to Algeria —

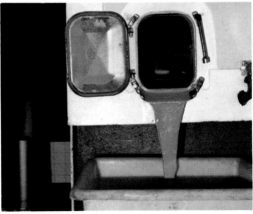

then still a French colony — and again started up in the wine-growing business. In 1962 they had to move once more, but meanwhile, in 1956, Marc Perrin had had the good sense to buy Château Carbonnieux. When he bought it, the château, the vineyard and the cellars were in a very sorry state. The building had stood abandoned since 1910, the *chai* and the *cuvier* had been badly maintained, and of the 74 acres of vineyard no less than 90% had to be completely replanted.

White wine maturing in steel

Visitors to Carbonnieux today are unaware of this former sad state of affairs. Marc Perrin and his son Antony have thoroughly restored the estate to its earlier glory. To the right of the gravelled inner court — one of the finest in the district — is the *cuvier*. I remember how this was buzzing with activity during the sunny autumn of 1970 — a tractor discharged its load, juice was transferred to the cool underground fermentation tanks, a white grape press was working overtime, and the air was heavy with the fruity sweetness of the fresh must. We were served a cool, crisp white 1969 from the tilted *barriques* and seldom has a wine tasted so good. Carbonnieux Blanc is never left to ripen in oak casks but, for a year or more, in steel tanks. The reason for this is that the wood might have three undesirable effects. First, the wine takes on a darker colour; second, it is more likely to maderize; and third, it loses something of its *fraîcheur*. Of the present 173 acres of vineyard, half are planted with white grapes. The varieties grown are Sauvignon (65%), Sémillon (30%) and Muscadelle (5%). The average output of white wine is 150 *tonneaux*. Carbonnieux Blanc is beyond doubt a good wine, but to my mind it lacks that excitement which turns a good wine into a great one. The colour is very pale, the nose is often somewhat wanting, and the taste is clear with a dash of fresh acids. All recent white Carbonnieux have tended to resemble one another.

At Carbonnieux the area devoted to the production of red wine has gradually risen to the present 86 acres. There are no plans to expand further. Planting comprises 55% Cabernet Sauvignon, 30% Merlot, 10% Cabernet Franc and 5% Malbec. Unlike the white, the red wine matures in the wood, generally for two full years. A quarter of the *barriques* are renewed each year. Both the white and red Carbonnieux are filtered. While many red Graves taste on the soft side and can be drunk early, Carbonnieux usually needs rather more patience. An example is the 1969 which began to loosen up only during 1975 but had still not fully developed three years later. The perfume of a ripe, red Carbonnieux is soft without being very deep or complex; and the taste often has a piquant undertone. A wine which I can recommend wholeheartedly is the 1973, nicely full for its year and very pleasant. The 1975 was also successful, though I found it a little on the light side for its year, lacking body and fruit, but with some nuances. The 1978 was rather lean for that great year, but the 1979 offered an attractive taste, with elegance, fruit and good balance. There are better, finer red and white *crus classés* at Graves but if they are unobtainable, the wines from Carbonnieux will provide a good substitute.

Château Haut Bailly

Cru Classé des Graves

I shall certainly remember my first visit to Haut Bailly. It was a sunny winter morning and I was received by Daniel Sanders, a charming man with silvery-grey hair. He allowed me to taste his 1966, an elegant, delicious wine, in his sparsely furnished, unheated château. I have since then purchased Haut Bailly regularly for my own cellar. Daniel Sanders is now dead but his son Jean acts as *gérant* for the various heirs. Daniel bought Haut Bailly in 1955 for a relatively small sum. 'Anyone in Bordeaux,' he once said, 'could have bought it then, but no one wanted to. The property had in fact gone down in the world. However, as a wine merchant, I had bought a good deal of the 1945, a fantastically good wine. So I knew what Haut Bailly was capable of and it was thanks to that one wine that I took it on.'

Specializing in red wine

Unlike the other *crus classés* at Léognan, Haut Bailly specializes in red wine only. The vineyard covers 62 acres and is planted with 60% Cabernet Sauvignon, 30% Merlot and 10% Cabernet Franc. Soil and grapes together produce a wine characterized by a soft, stylish elegance. The softness can be tasted early, even when the wine is still in cask. This texture does not mean that Haut Bailly will not keep; on the contrary, Haut Bailly wines show their character when young but maintain it for many years. According to M. Sanders, the secret of the wine lies not only in the soil and careful vinification but also in the age of the vines — one-quarter are more than 40 years old.

Half the casks renewed

The annual yield of 90 to 160 *tonneaux* of red wine is kept for some 20 months in open casks, about half of which are new. It is not filtered. Haut Bailly's great wines were, in addition to the 1966 already mentioned, the 1970, 1978, 1979, 1981 and 1982. The 1975 was a shade lighter than at other estates because of hail damage. In the early 1970s the château produced a series of relatively light wines, perhaps due to the new plantings. Even so, I enjoyed the 1973, for example, for a good long time.

Château de Fieuzal

Cru Classé des Graves

When travelling round a wine district you notice that the wine is sometimes better housed than the people who look after it. The workers often have to make do with humble, uncomfortable houses, while the wine lies resting in a spacious well-kept cellar. I have not seen the cottages where the staff live at Fieuzal but their accommodation certainly cannot be as palatial as that of the wine. In fact, the only resident at Château de Fieuzal is *Monsieur le Vin*. On entering the château, it seems as if they are awaiting the arrival of some VIP because everything is bright, clean and shining. In the first-year cellar, for example, not only the walls and ceilings are painted white, but even the floor; and the gleaming, varnished wooden *cuves* are not cleaned with water but with brandy! Everything at Fieuzal breathes perfection, and that is why the wine has gained such a strong reputation since the Second World War.

Theatre manager turned wine grower

The man behind this success was Erik Bocké, a tall, lean man whose boisterous laugh I shall never forget. He was born in Sweden but left for America in 1918, to serve as a volunteer in the army which was then fighting the Germans in France. Two years later he married, in France, the daughter of Abel Ricard, owner of Château de Fieuzal. In 1940, he and his wife left the country to live in Morocco for the duration of the Second World War. When he returned in 1945 his father-in-law had died, the vineyard was neglected and the cellar ransacked. As former manager of the Alhambra Theatre in Bordeaux, he knew nothing about wine-making but set to work getting everything repaired. His efforts were crowned with success and on 1 January 1974, Bocké at the age of 80 or so and after the death of his wife, sold Fieuzal for a sum of 10 million francs to

Georges Nègrevergne. Nègrevergne, in turn, appointed the highly capable Gérard Gribelin as his *administrateur*. The vineyard has been gradually expanded to 57 acres and the addition of a further 24 is planned. Mainly red wine is produced. Since 1974, it has gained in elegance, with fruit and wood in the bouquet and taste. It is a nicely vinified wine, not noticeably sophisticated, but with an unmistakable distinction. The 1975, 1978 and 1979 had much class and the first impressions of the 1981 and 1982 are highly positive. In its youth, the white wine often tastes and smells of juicy peaches.

Bottom left:
The chais, where the wines of Malartic-Lagravière mature and are bottled. This large chai is some distance from the château itself, in the centre of Léognan, in the same building as de Fieuzal's warehouse, situated on the left, outside the picture.

A few years ago, Brigitte, the charming daughter of the Marlys, was taking an important group of visitors around the estate and facing many questions to which she hardly knew the answers. She remembers one of the guests asking what was the most prevalent grape variety in the vineyard. With a straight face she replied, 'Mildew'. It was gratefully noted down.

Bottom centre:
Here, many times enlarged, is a reproduction of a bottle of Malartic-Lagravière which is part of the château's advertising material.

The name of the estate is engraved in beautiful lettering on the façade of the chai in Léognan.

Opposite page right:
The château, situated at the foot of its vineyard.

Opposite page bottom:
An old drawing of the château, the vineyard and the cuvier, all of which have hardly changed. This drawing is reproduced on the label.

The red wine usually matures in wooden casks for 20 months; the white for seven. Both are filtered.

Below:
Some of the labels used by the château. M. Marly had one printed in mirror-writing, because he is also a mirror manufacturer, but the trade insisted that he withdraw it.

Château Malartic-Lagravière

Cru Classé des Graves

CHAIS DE VIEILLISSEMENT

When I visited Malartic-Lagravière, the owner Jacques Marly pointed out a weathercock which did not turn with the direction of the wind but stood at right-angles to it. 'That', said my host, 'is our family. We are always the odd ones out and refuse to run with the crowd.'

This unorthodox attitude was quickly evident when the subject of quality versus quantity was raised. Unlike nearly all his colleagues, M. Marly holds that the two go hand-in-hand — at least in his vineyard. It therefore often distresses him that in certain years much good wine of Malartic-Lagravière has to be declassified, simply because he has produced more per acre that year than is legally permitted. Another matter close to his heart is the character of his wine. Malartic-Lagravière cannot be said to be an immediately appealing wine and more than once Jacques Marly has been asked to make his wine a little more subtle by some other method of vinification. But he certainly has no intention of doing so: 'In the long run all wines will seem the same! It would be ridiculous to expect me not to make Malartic the way I want to!'

New vats

However, time has not stood still on the estate. The *cuvier* contains 19 shining stainless-steel fermentation tanks (total capacity 264 gallons). For this small, independent château, it must have meant an enormous outlay but Jacques Marly considers the expenditure very much worthwhile. The modern *cuves* will last for a long time and enable him, better than any other type, to control the temperature during fermentation. At Malartic-Lagravière one-third of the wine goes into new casks, both the 70 to 90 *tonneaux* of red and the 6 to 8 of white.

Only Sauvignon for white wine

The vineyard lies immediately behind the château, on a long, broad slope. The surface area is 36 acres. The black grape varieties are

Château Malartic-Lagravière

relatively traditional (50% Cabernet Sauvignon, 25% Cabernet Franc, 25% Merlot), but for the white, only the Sauvignon has been planted; there is no Sémillon. According to M. Marly, the Sauvignon on its own produces a fruitier and more aromatic wine than a mixture of the two. To prove it, he had me taste it and I must admit that the result was very successful, fresh, light and fragrant.

A marvellous range of wines

I had the particular pleasure of tasting several vintages of the red wine at a lunch in the château. It happened to be a Saturday, a day when the château is 'at home' to the nine children and their families. They talk and play billiards, and in the afternoon the tables are put up for bridge. However, the main event is the meal, a sumptuous feast at which spectacular wines are often served. The apéritif in this case was a dry champagne, with a white wine for the first course, followed successively, with the lamb and the cheeses, by a red 1973 (preparing the way for the wines still to come), the 1964, and 1953 and a magnum of 1929. Not a bad selection for just an ordinary Saturday! Although it needed considerable discipline and a firm hand to make legible notes during this family celebration, I succeeded in doing so. I also tasted several of the same (and other) wines elsewhere, so that my impressions are not based merely on this visit.

The 1929 was a perfect wine — for about a quarter of an hour. Then it suddenly ended and oxidation set in at lightning speed. But in that precious brief period I immensely enjoyed the magnificent colour, the powerful bouquet and the sublime flavour. The 1953 was not yet at its best. The wine was on the austere side and will continue to develop for years yet. I found the 1964 especially good. Looked at with hindsight, it was probably the most typical of Malartic-Lagravière's wines. Supple in taste, but with a hard, fairly tough core. Other good reds were made here in 1966, 1967 (still somewhat reserved in 1983), 1970, 1971, 1975, 1976 (more subtle than elsewhere), 1977, 1978 and 1979. The Marly family was very optimistic about 1981 and 1982.

Domaine de Chevalier

There is little concern for outward appearances at Domaine de Chevalier. The house is low, small and modest, the word 'château' is not used and the property as a whole has a distinctly rural character. What is more, the estate lies away from the other great names, is situated in a clearing deep in the woods behind Léognan, not far from a sand quarry. All this might lead you to suppose that they make a pleasant wine here, rather than a great one. The facts are otherwise. Domaine de Chevalier produces excellent red and white wines which are among the best in the district. I personally consider the white Domaine de Chevalier as one of the world's greatest, if not *the* greatest, white wines. I have tasted the wine together with Le Montrachet but the white Graves stole my heart.

Extraordinarily low yield

The estate is 42 acres in size, of which less than 7 acres are planted with white grapes (70% Sauvignon and 30% Sémillon). Anyone else would be tempted to profit as much as possible from such a small area but not owner Claude Ricard. By very severe pruning of all the vines, the yield at Domaine de Chevalier is perhaps the lowest of all the estates producing table wines in Bordeaux. In 1970, for example, Claude Ricard was the only grower in the Gironde *département* with a crop below the statutory maximum per hectare. His highest yield to date was in 1973, 27.5 hectolitres to the hectare. In good years, the Domaine de Chevalier produces 40 *tonneaux* of red and 8 *tonneaux* of white.

Acme of perfection

Both wines are made with obsessive attention to detail, even more care being devoted to the white than to the red. The white vineyard is, in fact, so small that Claude Ricard can reach the acme of perfection with it. The white grapes are generally picked in three separate stages.

First of all, any rotten grapes are removed. Then only the fruit which is sound and ripe is picked, and this process is repeated a few days later. The grapes should not be over-ripe because the wine then loses something of its firmness. The grapes are then pressed and only the first pressing is used for the *grand vin*. Claude Ricard has carried out extensive trials to see whether anything could still be used from subsequent pressings, but even a 2.5% addition could be detected in the taste, so delicate and subtle is the white Domaine de Chevalier. After pressing comes the fermentation. This takes place in casks, which makes it easier to keep the temperature down. New *barriques* are not used for the white because the young wood again influences the taste. Claude Ricard told me that in 1955 he had too few old casks so that part of the wine had to go into new ones, 'but you could taste the wood

Bottom left:
The modest cellar of the estate.

Bottom right:
Manager R. Tahon has been
working at the Domaine de
Chevalier for some 10 years
and — together with Claude
Ricard — took a course in
oenology given by Professor
Peynaud. Although they are
both totally different in
temperament, they always
agree when faced with
important decisions.

Far left:
Different bottle sizes of the
Domaine de Chevalier's great
wines, making up a small 'still
life.'

Left:
The label of Domaine de
Chevalier which, rather
unusually, shows a
photographic reproduction of
the estate instead of an old
drawing.

Domaine de Chevalier

in it for years afterwards'. There are of
course many other detailed procedures in the
wine-making operation but there is
insufficient space to discuss them all here.

Every other cask is new

The red wine comes from 65% Cabernet
Sauvignon, 5% Cabernet Franc and 30%
Merlot. After light crushing and de-stalking,
the wine is left to ferment in 20 steel tanks
each holding 2,200 gallons. The wooden
fermentation casks of yesteryear
disappeared during the 1970s.
Claude Ricard has different views about the
temperature during the first fermentation.
While many châteaux do their best not to
exceed 28°C, M. Ricard considers it
necessary to reach 30°C.
The red wine lies in cask for two years. After
lengthy experimentation M. Ricard has

concluded that half of the casks should be
renewed in every normal year; they lie
alternately in the small *chai*. Only in the very
outstanding years does the entire crop go
into new *barriques*.

Refined and aristocratic

For me, the white Domaine de Chevalier is
the quintessence of refinement. It is one of
the world's greatest dry white wines,
virtually unequalled in its sophisticated
wealth of nuances — while just the aftertaste
of this wine is an experience in itself. The
exceptional class of Domaine de Chevalier
Blanc can be experienced in wines such as
the phenomenal 1979, and the rather fuller
1978 or 1981 (when the estate produced only
16 casks of white). This white Graves can
mature at length. I remember the 1964
which I was given to taste in 1982 and which

was still completely vital, with an abundance
of subtlety in both fragrance and taste.
The red Domaine de Chevalier must be left to
mature. This wine as a rule requires some 10
years to develop; for great years such as
1964, 1966, 1970, 1975 and 1978 even 20
years' waiting may be required. Give it
patience, and the result will be an
aristocratic, stylish red wine, refined, elegant
and redolent of ripe fruit. Even in the less
great years, the quality of the red Domaine
de Chevalier is exemplary.

Mis en Bouteille au Château

1973

Château Bouscaut

GRAND CRU CLASSÉ

APPELLATION GRAVES CONTROLÉE

Domaine Wohlstetter - Sloan

S.A. du Château Bouscaut

PROPRIÉTAIRE
à CADAUJAC près BORDEAUX

WHITE BORDEAUX WINE   PRODUCT OF FRANCE

Left:
A detail of the chai. Château Bouscaut is in the commune of Cadaujac, which apparently means, 'I stop here'. For the wines of Le Bouscaut, perhaps?

Bottom:
The beautiful château in all its glory. It was built as a maison bourgeoise in 1710, with the sturdy round tower being added in 1847. There is a lake in front of the château, and a swimming pool at the back.

Opposite page left:
One of the magnificent tapestries in the dining room.

Opposite page right:
The table has been set and everything is ready for a superb meal in the Bouscaut's dining room.

Opposite page bottom centre:
The ouillage, the topping-up of the casks, is a process which is repeated about three times a year.

Bottom right:
A garden view.

Château Bouscaut

Cru Classé des Graves

To my mind, Château Bouscaut is one of the most fascinating estates in the Graves. What they have achieved in a short space of time verges on the unbelievable. Bouscaut was purchased in 1969 for a sum of one million dollars by a group of 10 people assembled by the American Charles Wohlstetter. What they obtained for their money was really little more than the certainty that Bouscaut would be able to make good wine. Apart from that, the estate was badly run down. The cellars had been poorly maintained, the vineyard was almost bare, the château lacked every vestige of comfort and the staff accommodation was primitive. But all that soon changed. The Americans took on Jean-Bernard Delmas from Haut-Brion as their manager and gave him and his charming wife Anne-Marie a free hand to renovate Bouscaut from top to bottom. Jean-Bernard was to see to the cellars and everything to do with the wine, Anne-Marie to the château. Together they made it into something tremendous.

First-class hotel comfort

First of all provision was made for the workers. In a space of four years 10 houses were built for the families of the permanent staff. Then came the château's turn, and here Mme Delmas worked wonders. Downstairs, the château contained a large reception room, an excellently equipped kitchen, a dining room and a library with a large grate for an open fire in winter. Upstairs, there is a television room with books and all kinds of games. Also on the floor is a kitchenette with a refrigerator always filled for thirsty or hungry guests. There are also bedrooms and bathrooms provided with every convenience. Bouscaut thus offers the comfort of a first-class hotel — with ten times as much atmosphere. Last but not least, there is an outstanding cook, who tempts the guests with all manner of imaginative dishes. Life is certainly pleasant at Bouscaut, at least for anyone not on a slimming diet.

$400,000 for vineyard and cellars

The cellars also required a great deal of attention, as is clear from the amount spent — $100,000. That was just a start, because at a later stage Jean-Bernard Delmas replaced the wooden fermentation casks with ordinary and stainless-steel tanks of the type used at Haut-Brion. The de-stalking machine is likewise identical to the one at Haut-Brion. A great deal has also been done to the vineyard. The 103 acres had to be almost entirely replanted, costing a further $300,000. This gigantic outlay did not

Château Bouscaut

perhaps produce the anticipated income for some of the Americans since, in January 1980, the majority of shares was transferred to Lucien Lurton of Brane-Cantenac and Durfort-Vivens fame. It is rumoured that the transaction involved some 15 million French francs.

Crisp and dry white

As at the other Graves châteaux, Bouscaut makes both red and white wine. The yield is 80 to 170 *tonneaux* of red wine and 16 to 40 *tonneaux* of white. These quantities will rise further in the future as the vineyard is to be extended. The black grape plantings will increase from 79 to 96 acres, and the white from 24 to 38 acres. White Bouscaut tends to be an aromatic, pleasant, softly fresh wine with a crisp, clean taste. I have enjoyed it both with oysters from Arcachon and with

ham from Bayonne. The grape varieties for this wine are 52% Sémillon and 48% Sauvignon.

Red that keeps well

Red Bouscaut is obtained from 55% Merlot, 35% Cabernet Sauvignon and 10% Cabernet Franc. The high Merlot content leads one to expect the wine to have a soft, round, fleshy taste and, in particular, to be ready soon for drinking. This is not the case. Red Bouscaut, in particular, is a rather reserved wine, even austere in its youth, with much tannin, and thus suitable for keeping. The 1969 for example — the first wine from the Delmas period — had more strength than most of that year and should really have been drunk only after 1980. The 1970 is a wine which can stay around much longer — dark and rich in tannin. Bouscaut also made good wines in

1971, 1973, 1974, 1975 (only 56 *tonneaux* of red wine owing to hail damage), 1976, 1978 and 1979. The latter two years should not really be opened before 1990. It is still too early to obtain a clear impression of the type of red wine that Lucien Lurton has been making since 1980, but it is evident that Bouscaut is becoming more supple, with a little more charm and fruitiness. Since the 1980 vintage the estate has been advised by Professor Peynaud. Red Bouscaut matures for 18 months in oak casks, nearly a third of which are new. Both the red and white wine are very lightly filtered before bottling. The estate also has a second brand, Château le Valoux, chiefly for the wines from the young vines. This was also used in the past for the less successful vintages, so that a fairly large part of the red 1972 was sold under that label.

GRAND VIN DE GRAVES SEC

1972

EXTRA DRY — TRES SEC

CHATEAV
SMITH HAVT LAFITTE
MARTILLAC
APPELLATION GRAVES CONTRÔLÉE

LOUIS ESCHENAUER S·A·PROPRIÉTAIRE
A MARTILLAC (GIRONDE) FRANCE
Mise en bouteilles par
LOUIS ESCHENAUER S. A. · BORDEAUX
PRODUCE OF FRANCE

Château Smith Haut Lafitte

Cru Classé des Graves

It could be said that Smith Haut Lafitte is enjoying its second youth. A great deal has been improved on this estate since the end of the 1960s — as was done earlier, in the latter half of the 19th century. Under the energetic management of M. Duffour-Duberger, former mayor of Bordeaux, the three original parts of the Smith Haut Lafitte estate were reunited. The resulting vineyard was regarded in those days as a textbook example. For example in 1876 Château Smith Haut Lafitte was awarded the prize for the best maintained vineyard in the entire Gironde *département*.

The estate changed hands many times after M. Duffour-Duberger died. The archives contain, among others, the names of a German firm and the French Treasurer-General of Indo-China. The only constant factor for many years was the Louis Eschenauer house which has had exclusive selling rights for the wine since 1902. The company purchased the vineyard in 1957, (but not the château) and Smith Haut Lafitte's star has since then risen in the heavens for a second time.

Enthusiastic re-building

Much was achieved in a relatively short time in the capable hands of Eschenauer's technical director, René Baffert. The vineyard was enlarged from a miserable 15 to 25 acres to 126 acres (still 37 acres less than the area cultivated in 1860). In addition, an imposing, entirely new cellar complex was built, completed in stages. There was rather too much initial enthusiasm, for the concrete fermentation vats intalled in 1962 lasted barely 15 years. They have now been replaced by steel vats which experiments have shown to produce better results.

Outside the *cuverie*, Eschenauer built a gigantic *chai* on the site of some earlier living quarters. It is 230 feet long and 82 feet wide, and provides storage space for at least 2,000 casks. Other buildings included a second-year cellar, a bottling hall a bottle store, a cleaning area for 6,000 casks annually, and much else. 'You could call it enthusiastic reconstruction,' says M. Baffert, and I agree with him wholeheartedly. Work is not in fact limited to what is needed for wine-making. Thought is also being given to the outward appearance of the estate. A park has been laid down, an old tower has been reconstructed, a spacious reception hall has been added, and an old chapel has been restored.

Love it or leave it

The new château — because that is what it really is — lies amid the vines at the top of a gentle slope. Of the 126 acres, 111 are planted with black grape varieties and 6 with white, Sauvignon only. White Smith Haut Lafitte is a decidedly fresh wine, often with a rather green taste. Some 30 to 38 *tonneaux* are normally harvested but that is not nearly enough to meet demand; which is why Eschenauer has launched the Les Acades de Smith label. This, too, is a white Graves, but obtained from other producers. The quality is markedly lower, but the taste is softer, more friendly, with less breeding.

Elegant and pleasant

While White Smith Haut Lafitte has no special classification, the red wine from this

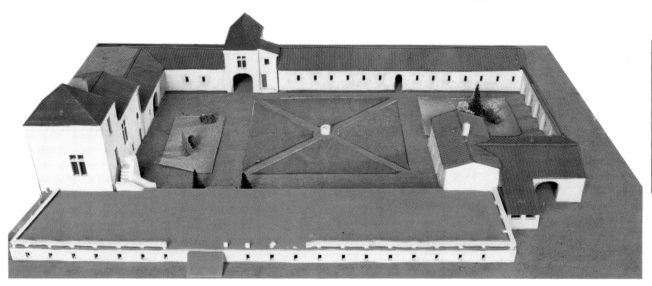

Château Smith Haut Lafitte

estate is amongst the *crus classés*. It is made from 73% Cabernet Sauvignon, 16% Merlot and 11% Cabernet Franc. The yield is between 170 and 275 *tonneaux*. Normal maturing takes some 18 months; half the casks are new. The wine is clarified with fresh egg white and it is filtered before bottling. The first wines after the renovation — end 1960s to early 1970s — were influenced by the young plantings; they lacked depth and the colour was generally on the light side. The wines began to fill out from 1975 although they still remained elegant. I regard them as too supple and insufficiently complex for the status of *cru classés*: they smell and taste balanced and pleasant but they do not provide a real experience. There is also a second label for the red wine, Les Hauts de Smith Haut Lafitte.

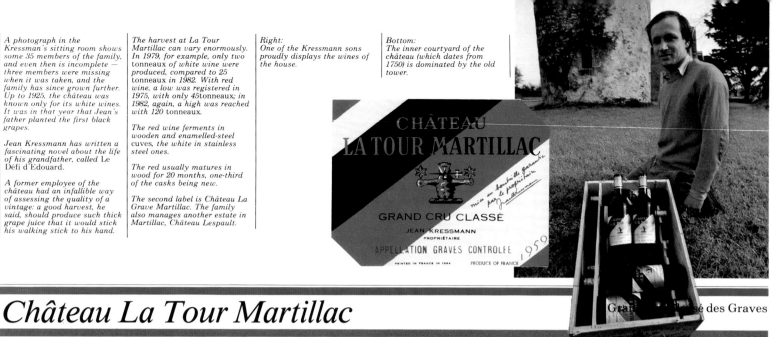

Château La Tour Martillac

Château La Tour Martillac lies in an idyllic spot in the Graves region. The shady back garden offers a vista of the gently undulating vineyard which extends in the distance to the edge of a wood. On warm summer days it is blissfully silent and the everyday world seems far, far away, particularly, when you are peacefully enjoying a good wine and a fine entrecôte, grilled over glowing vine twigs, in the shade of the trees. It is not surprising that Montesquieu would have liked to exchange his gothic Château La Brède for the rustic simplicity of La Tour Martillac — but that he was unable to do because of his important position in the *parlement* of Bordeaux. It was understandable, therefore, that Jean Kressmann decided in 1965 to retire from the commercial firm of that name and live the life of a wine grower at this château.

Much effort and the white wine

Jean Kressman's first years at La Tour Martillac were not easy ones. He was not then a young men and recalls how, in 1968 and 1969, he was still driving the tractor himself in his 60-acre vineyard. The situation has now improved but they still work hard there. The 10 acres of white grapes, in particular, demand much time and trouble. Kressman himself says: 'My white vines are very old. So they take twice as much work and give half the yield. The quality of the white wine is good but I only get half as much for it as for my red. It is rather foolish of me to continue making my wine this way, and I fear that my sons will do it differently.' Thanks to Jean Kressman's perseverance, La Tour Martillac Blanc is a very pure, pleasant, light wine, which the Duke of Edinburgh drank with much pleasure with smoked salmon when he was admitted to the *Commanderie du Bontemps de Médoc et des Graves.*

Cool, sophisticated red wine

In the past, only 12% Merlot was used for red La Tour Martillac. The percentage is now 25%, supplemented with 60% Cabernet-Sauvignon, 6% Cabernet Franc, 5% Malbec and 4% Petit Verdot. Generally speaking, this red Graves is not an exuberant wine with a great deal of verve. Its fragrance is not outgoing but rather withdrawn. The taste has a cool, sophisticated personality without any noteworthy refinement or depth, but still decently composed and with more than a hint of class. The estate's red was apparently better in 1971 than in 1970, and I also found the 1979 to have more body than the 1978. The best red wine that the estate has produced in many years was the 1975.

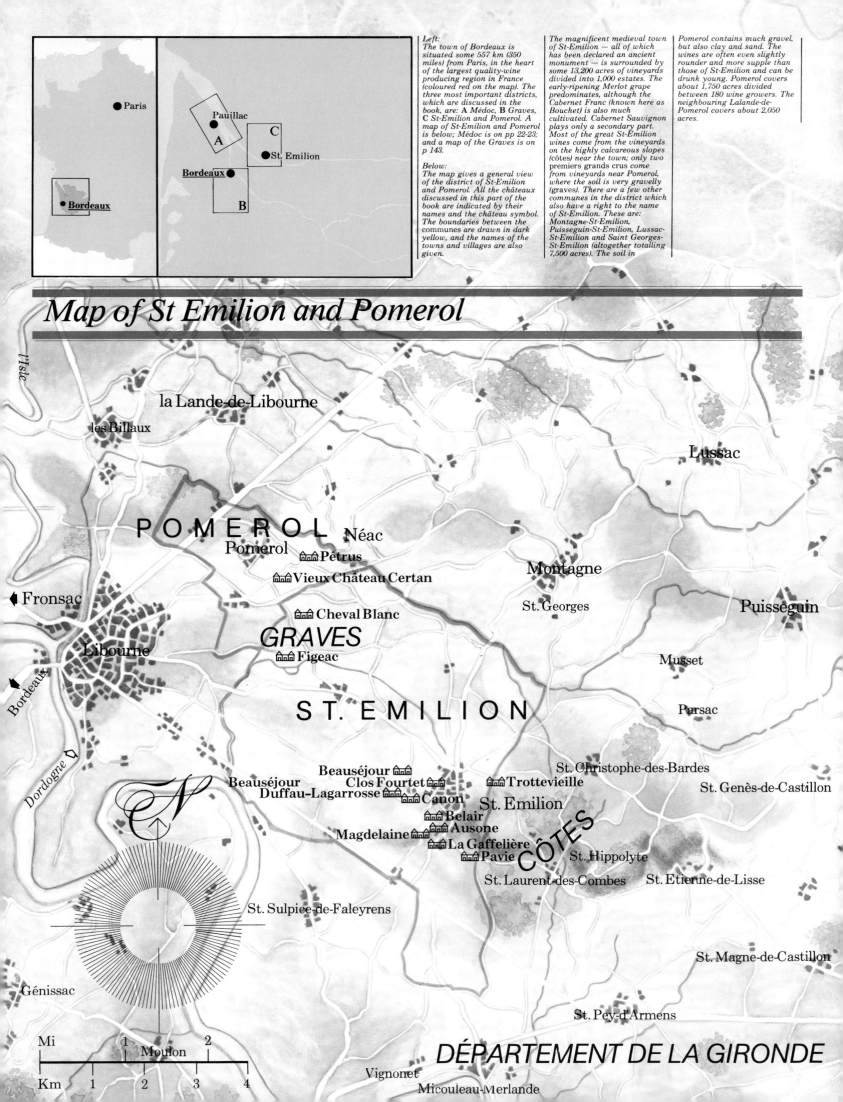

Map of St Emilion and Pomerol

l'Isle

la Lande-de-Libourne

les Billaux

Lussac

POMEROL

Néac

Pomerol

Pétrus

Vieux Château Certan

Montagne

St. Georges

Fronsac

Puisseguin

Cheval Blanc

GRAVES

Libourne

Figeac

Musset

ST. EMILION

Parsac

Bordeaux

Dordogne

St. Christophe-des-Bardes

Beauséjour

St. Genès-de-Castillon

Beauséjour
Duffau-Lagarrosse

Clos Fourtet

Trottevieille

Canon

St. Emilion

Belair

Magdelaine

Ausone

La Gaffelière

CÔTES

Pavie

St. Hippolyte

St. Laurent-des-Combes

St. Etienne-de-Lisse

St. Sulpice-de-Faleyrens

St. Magne-de-Castillon

Génissac

Mi   1   2
Moulon

St. Pey-d'Armens

DÉPARTEMENT DE LA GIRONDE

Km 1   2   3   4

Vignonet

Micouleau-Merlande

Château Cheval Blanc

Premier Grand Cru Classé

It is a remarkable coincidence that one of the best wines of St-Emilion is made on the extreme edge of the area. Cheval Blanc in fact adjoins Pomerol; the vineyard is separated by a country lane from that of Château La Conseillante A.C. Pomerol. The landscape is quite different from that round the little town of St-Emilion, some three miles down the road. Surrounding St-Emilion are fairly steep, rocky slopes, but round Cheval Blanc the terrain is softly undulating. But even sharper than the contrasts above ground are those underground. The *côtes* of St-Emilion contains a great deal of chalk and the soil around Cheval Blanc has a great deal of gravel. These two types of soil are separated by the *sables* — a strip of sand two miles wide. However, gravel is not the only soil component at Cheval Blanc. The vineyard extends over patches containing clay and iron. It is this unique diversity which gives Cheval Blanc its great class — combined, of course, with the grape varieties and human care.

No Cabernet Sauvignon

The vineyard covers 89 acres, of which 79 are fully productive. It was once much less; a map of 1834 shows it with less than half the present area. Through purchases of adjoining land during the previous century (mainly meadow and wood with a good subsoil) the vineyard has been brought up to its present extent.

The unorthodox planting of the vines is very characteristic of Cheval Blanc — Cabernet Sauvignon is entirely missing. The varieties planted are two-thirds Cabernet Franc, approximately one-third Merlot and 2½ acres of Malbec. This mixture was deliberate. Although changes could have been made in 1956 when a heavy frost destroyed most of the vines, this was not done. As few vines as possible were removed in the hope that they would in time grow again, and where replanting was unavoidable the previous varieties were restored.

Château Cheval Blanc

The yield in the disaster year of 1956 was only one cask, which was duly photographed.

Consistent quality policy

I believe that much of Cheval Blanc's reputation is due to the fact that the same family has conducted a consistent policy for quality for many generations. This is the Fourcaud-Laussac family, or more correctly, their successors. There are no owners any more with that name, just nephews, nieces and relations by marriage. Since 1970 the co-proprietor has been Jacques Hebrard, manager of Cheval Blanc. A giant of a man, he makes a somewhat laconic impression at first but I soon discovered that it was he who carried out many of the urgent improvements, such as building a new, cool, *chai* with a reception room above. He is very attached to his vineyard and is the first of all the owners in his family who lives at the château all year round. He is a great wine expert and has obtained practical experience of agriculture in central Africa.

The origin of the name

The château where Jacques Hebrard lives with his lovely wife perhaps lacks the *grandeur* of the *premier crus* in the Médoc but it is still a very comfortable home. They say that a post-house where horses could be exchanged once stood on the spot occupied by the present white-painted building. Evidently Henri IV stopped there one day on his way from Paris to Pau, his birthplace, in order to freshen up his white horses. After that the inn was called the Cheval Blanc. The truth of the story would be hard to confirm and is therefore best taken with a pinch of salt, the more so since there are those in St-Emilion who say that Cheval Blanc could not have existed at all during the time of Henri IV and that he would therefore probably have stopped at one of the other châteaux.

Château bottling since the 1974 vintage

From the house you can walk through to the cellars. The *cuvier* dates from 1964 and contains a number of concrete fermentation vats each of which can hold exactly the quantity of grapes picked in one day. According to M. Hebrard, this greatly helps to control the wine-making process. The cool, white first-year cellar is spacious and indirectly lit. The casks that lie there are renewed for each crop. The average time for maturing in cask is 20 months. The first vintage to be bottled in this new set of cellars was the 1974, the *mise en bouteilles* for all previous years having been at Libourne. The cellars in this wine village originate from the time when most of the St Emilion wines were brought there and were bottled or shipped further along the Dordogne river by the Libourne vintners.

Sharply fluctuating output

Cheval Blanc has a gentleman's agreement for its wine sales with five firms — Calvet, Delor, Cruse, J. P. Moueix and Horeau-Beylot. The chief customers are Britain, Belgium, Scandinavia, Holland and also the United States, France and Japan. The

Château Cheval Blanc

amount of wine produced each year fluctuates sharply, the yield lying between 23 *tonneaux* in 1977 and 185 *tonneaux* in 1982. The figures for several recent years are 90 *tonneaux* in 1978, 147 in 1979, 115 in 1980, and 100 in 1981. No Cheval Blanc was sold in 1965 and only 4,000 to 5,000 bottles in 1968.

A World of luxury

Whenever I drink Cheval Blanc — not nearly as often as I would like — I get a fleeting sense of great wealth. There is tremendous luxury in this wine. A good Cheval Blanc possesses a broad bouquet, often with a hint of spices, soft fruits, oak and other nuances. The taste is generous, velvety and round, with a sturdy backbone of tannin and plenty of style. I have excellent memories of the 1964 which I first drank in the château's intimate, blue dining room and which is still full of vitality. The 1966, 1970 and 1971 were also great wines, while the 1975 may be regarded as the greatest of all Cheval Blancs since the Second World War. The mouth-filling, very powerful 1978 is also a splendid wine, closely followed by the 1976 and 1979. It is a characteristic of Cheval Blanc that the château often produces good wines in difficult years. The 1972, for example, was one of the best of that vintage, while the quality of the 1980 is also high.

CHATEAU - FIGEAC
PREMIER GRAND CRÙ CLASSÉ
ST ÉMILION
Appellation St-Emilion 1er Grand Crù Classé Contrôlée
1964
MIS EN BOUTEILLES AU CHÂTEAU
A. MANONCOURT PROPRE A StÉMILION‹FRANCE›

Château Figeac

Figeac has always been overshadowed by its great neighbour Cheval Blanc, but undeservedly so. Figeac wines are in fact among the true aristocrats of St-Emilion and simply deserve proportionate fame. There are three reasons why Figeac is not so well known. The first is the existence of several châteaux which include 'Figeac' in their name (La Tour-Figeac, Petit-Figeac, Yon-Figeac, Grand Barrail Lamarzelle Figeac, and quite a few more). True enough, these make good wine but not to the same standard as Figeac. The second reason is that the owner's grandfather, Thierry Manoncourt regarded the château as a kind of holiday home because his job as a civic official in Paris prevented him from spending much time at St-Emilion. So the building was kept locked up and contact with the wine brokers — who in those days were still indispensable for trade — became sparse and infrequent. The third reason was the frost of 1956 which hit Figeac hard — much of the vineyard had to be replanted so

that output remained low for many years. Only in 1970 were the harvests back at earlier levels, namely 200 *tonneaux*, the same amount as in 1928.

Wide-ranging interests

Since Thierry Manoncourt took over the management of Figeac from his grandfather the estate's fame has increased by leaps and bounds. Not only did he improve the layout of the vineyard and build new cellars but he took every opportunity to get the trade and other interested people to taste his wine. Furthermore, M. Manoncourt is concerned with the affairs of St-Emilion generally. For over 10 years he has been *Premier Jurat* of the Jurade de St-Emilion, the oldest and perhaps the most authentic of Bordeaux's wine societies. Thierry Manoncourt is a taciturn, erudite man with wide-ranging interests — architecture, geology and history excite him just as much as wine-making.

Back to the 15th century

A visitor to Figeac is therefore more than likely to receive a long lecture on any of these subjects. Concerning the history of Figeac, for example, Thierry Manoncourt relates that once upon a time there were five *maisons nobles* around St-Emilion, of which Figeac was the largest. The names of these

Figeac has a second label, Château de Grangeneuve, named after a small château not far away.

With its 95 acres, Figeac is the largest wine estate of St-Emilion.

In 1832, the then owner of Château Figeac is said to have given part of the estate to an old employee — and it is this land which forms the basis of Cheval Blanc. In fact, when wine was first produced there it was sold as 'Vin de Figeac.' According to Thierry Manoncourt, the name Cheval Blanc was introduced — in 1854 — because the Figeac stables had been located there in the past.

Thierry Manoncourt relates how, in December 1966, he presented five bottles of the 1953 vintage to the Académie du Vin de Bordeaux. All five were Figeac wines, matured and treated in exactly the same way but each had been made from only a single grape variety. There was one bottle grown only from Cabernet Sauvignon, one from Merlot, etc. Most of the tasters preferred one wine above all others — a blend of all the grape varieties. The results of the tasting led M. Manoncourt to remove the Malbec vines from his estate, as they proved very disappointing. The Cabernet, on the other hand, produces excellent results even though it is not the best variety in St-Emilion.

The first conference of the associated makers of produits d'origine — natural products of legally controlled origin — took place in Bordeaux. As well as wine growers, the conference was attended by cheese makers, sellers of farm-bred chickens of Bresse, etc. Château Figeac was one of the three Bordeaux wines served at the gala dinner, along with Mouton-Rothschild and the Château d'Yquem (Sauternes).

Thierry Manoncourt's grandfather had little time for Figeac: one of his main concerns was the construction of the Paris Métro.

Right:
Owner Thierry Manoncourt. His family has owned Figeac for nearly a century. It has always produced good wine but its reputation — indeed, fame — has risen sharply during the past few years.

Below:
The château seen from the park.

The name Figeac is derived from the name of a Gallo-Roman called Figeacus, who had a villa in the area in the 3rd or 4th century. Figeac was probably one of the first estates in St-Emilion to de-stalk grapes. Maturation in wood lasts from 15 to 20 months.

Château Figeac

Château Figeac

seigneuries can still often be found linked to those of the châteaux. Corbin was also a *seigneurie*, and the name lives on in the Corbin and Grand Corbin d'Espagne estates. The Château de Figeac dates originally from the second half of the 15th century and one of the old walls containing a window certainly goes back to feudal times. More early architecture can be seen in an old turret and the two pillars at the main entrance. These date back to 1590 or thereabouts, at the end of the Renaissance period.

Impressive cellars

A modern feature is the set of cellars built up against the ancient *chai*. The transition between the two parts is great — to cross from the old, dark *chai* into the spacious, airy *cuvier* with its ten shining stainless-steel tanks is suddenly to bridge a century; behind you lies the 19th, before you the 20th. When the metal tanks were installed, the ten old wooden vats were not abandoned. In fact, the latter are still used for fermenting the wine, while the new tanks are used to hold any over production, which facilitates working. They are also used for cooling the must.

A project to extend the storage cellars came to fruition in 1972 and here, too, work has proceeded apace. Large first- and second-year *chais* were erected, together with a really impressive underground *cave*. Here the bottling takes place and there is space to store tens of thousands of bottles, in bins or in cases. It all goes to show that Thierry Manoncourt has proceeded with the utmost care, if not a touch of perfectionism. Neither expense nor trouble has been spared and Château Figeac can be proud of having the finest new cellars in the district.

As was the case with many estates, the expansion was a dire necessity. Early in the present century 90% or more of each crop was normally sold to the Bordeaux trade in casks after the first year. The châteaux therefore had little need for storage. Now, however, the châteaux are expected to mature and bottle their wines themselves.

Consequently three harvests instead of one must be accomodated in the cellar; two years in *barriques* and one year in bottles.

Gravelly plateau

The wine for the 125 to 180 *tonneaux* comes from the 94-acre vineyard. At its highest point, this lies 115 feet above the Dordogne and provides a magnificent view over the surrounding countryside. Cheval Blanc is nearby and the whole of the *graves de St-Emilion* area is in full view. In fact, the *graves* consists merely of a plateau with six ridges bearing two first-class vineyards, Figeac and Cheval Blanc. Thierry Manoncourt tells how the thick layer of gravel was chiefly carried down from the Massif Central by the Isle, a river which divides Fronsac from St-Emilion and Pomerol. My host added that apart from Ausone all the *premiers crus* at Bordeaux are born on very gravelly ground — Lafitte, Latour, Margaux, Mouton, Haut-Brion, d'Yquem, Cheval Blanc, and so on.

Of course, with soil like that, there is plenty of temptation to use every square yard for growing vines — understandable in St-Emilion since apart from the grape virtually nothing grows here nowadays. However, at Figeac they take the view that nature should not be forced; whatever is done must be done with respect for what already exists. That is why Thierry and his charming wife Marie-France refuse to sacrifice part of the extensive park or other agricultural land to wine-growing. 'We may perhaps be less sophisticated than other estates', says M. Manoncourt, 'but we happen to love nature'.

Full of velvety strength

Unlike Cheval Blanc, Figeac includes Cabernet Sauvignon — 35% of it. Cabernet Franc also accounts for 35%, Merlot for 30%. For this reason alone, Figeac is different from Cheval Blanc. Generally speaking, I find the many vintages which I have drunk rather more velvety than the same wines from their neighbours. They possess a soft,

elegant, Rubens-like roundness and an undeniable distinction. Here are some notes on several successful years.

The 1953 wine had a fine, ripe bouquet still with some restraint. The taste was soft and generous but less powerful than the 1955. The latter wine was very complete, extraordinarily sturdy and with an especially full bouquet — a beauty. The 1959 unfurled beautifully in the mouth. I found rather more sweetness than in the other wines (which was later confirmed by Thierry Manoncourt from his analysis). The 1961 was noteworthy for its rich, spreading perfume and voluptuous taste. I also placed positive comments against the 1970, 1971, 1972 (at least for that year), 1973, 1974 (among the better of that harvest), 1975 (much fruit and nuance; rather more reserved than normal for a Figeac), 1976 (generous and supple but with strength for maturing), 1977 (good wine from a deprecated year), 1978 (dark and deep, balanced, with a broad taste and subtle aftertaste), 1979 (charming, stylsh, sophisticated, for early drinking) 1980 (mouth-filling and sophisticated), 1981 (much colour and class) and 1982 (exceptionally good). This St-Emilion seems to have gained yet further in pure quality over the past ten years.

Left and below:
Since the firm of Jean-Pierre Mouiex took over the estate, the château is no longer inhabited. Magdelaine has its own well.

When Jean-Pierre Mouiex bought the estate in 1952, the vineyard covered about 22 acres. It has since been increased by 5 acres after some forest land was cleared.

The American west coast is by far the most important market for Magdelaine, taking more than half of the yearly production. Britain and Belgium are also faithful customers.

The 1961 Magdelaine was exceptionally successful, but is also very rare. It was much stronger than usual and still has a great future. Besides a deep colour and intense bouquet, it has a strong taste with a hint of liquorice and roasted grapes.

SAINT-ÉMILION 1ᵉʳ GRAND CRU CLASSÉ

CHÂTEAU MAGDELAINE
1971

Mis en Bouteille au Château

ETˢ JEAN PIERRE MOUEIX
PROPRIÉTAIRES A ST ÉMILION   PRODUCE OF FRANCE

APPELLATION SAINT-ÉMILION
1ᵉʳ GRAND CRU CLASSÉ CONTRÔLÉE

Château Magdelaine

Premier Grand Cru Classé

Some stalks retained

Throughout Bordeaux it is customary for the grapes to be de-stalked before they are fermented. However, at Magdelaine this is done to only 85% of the fruit; the rest goes into the concrete *cuves* with stalks, pips and all. Jean-Claude Berrouet, a qualified oenologist who is responsible for all the wines at the Moueix Château, told me why. He introduced the system to make the Magdelaine wines rather more sturdy; were he not to do so, they would tend to remain too light. At the end of the fermentation process — which sometimes takes 20 days, the wines are transferred to casks. Usually half of these *barriques* are new; they are prepared by Moueix in their own cooperage. After 20 months maturing, the casks are transported to Libourne where the wine is bottled.

Noble and complete

I count the wine from Magdelaine amongst my favourite St-Emilions. Not only because its quality seldom disappoints, but also because it is a very complete wine, a St-Emilion with much style, elegance and unmistakeable *noblesse*. A wine, furthermore, which thanks to the vinification and maturing in wood possesses a firm structure and, often, the light scent of vanilla imparted by new open casks. Some of the best Magdelaine vintages are the 1961, 1962 (remarkably good for that year), 1966, 1970, 1971, 1975, 1978, 1979 (perhaps even better than its predecessor), 1981 and 1982. I also had much pleasure from Magdelaine vintages of lesser standing, including the 1967, 1976, 1977 and 1980.

The 25-acre vineyard at Magdelaine lies roughly in a kind of half-moon along the top of a plateau, and partly on the downward slope. No less than 80% of the planting is Merlot, the remainder Cabernet Franc. The vineyard lies against a chalky slope and on a limestone plateau, with a top layer of clay (on which the Merlot flourishes). At Château Magdelaine harvesting starts only when the grapes have reached an optimum degree of ripeness. This has been possible since

Magdelaine was purchased in 1952 by the well-known firm of Jean-Pierre Moueix of Libourne. This *négociant-viticulteur* maintains a large group of its own pickers who can go out to work at a moment's notice so that all grapes are harvested within three days. Magdelaine is therefore often one of the last châteaux at St-Emilion to start the *vendange*.

Château Trottevieille

Premier Grand Cru Classé

By all appearances, Château Trottevieille is the most modest of St-Emilion *premiers grands crus*. The château is a low, relatively unsightly little building with a small garden behind it and the vineyard all around. There was once an inn here with an elderly but still highly active barmaid who brought the tired postillions, coachmen and passengers their meals at lightning speed. It is to her that the château is said to owe its name, because literally translated Trottevieille means 'the old lady who rushes about.'

Part-time manager

The *chai* with the small vathouse attached to it lies immediately alongside the uninhabited château. Although it contains concrete fermentation vats the entire 'château' is an example of rustic simplicity. Château Trottevieille has had M. Jean Brun as its manager since 1939 but the estate is so small that it cannot afford to hire him on a full-time basis. This is not uncommon in St-Emilion, and Jean Brun consequently has some seven châteaux under his wing. In addition to Trottevieille, they include, among others, Les Grandes Murailles and Croque-Michotte.

Sturdy character

The whole of the vineyard — 25 acres — was replanted after Marcel Borie took over the estate from Jean Guibaud in 1950. Preference was then given to Cabernet Franc, which for many years made up three-quarters of the planting. Nowadays, however, Merlot is the most important grape, at 60%. What is left is divided equally amongst Cabernet Franc and Cabernet Sauvignon. The yield fluctuates between 30 and over 50 *tonneaux*. The wine is left to mature for some 18 months in wooden casks of which one-third are new. Trottevieille is a sturdy St-Emilion which used to have a somewhat reserved taste — perhaps because of the then higher Cabernet content — but which today is rather fuller and rounder. The 1979 is a good example of this. This St-Emilion offers few nuances and little refinement but it fills the mouth in a most agreeable way. Among the successful vintages are 1970, 1971 (although a class below that of 1970), 1975 and 1978. The present owners are the Casteja family who not only also own Batailley and Lynch-Moussas in the Médoc but also run the Borie-Manous wine house, which markets the Trottevieille wines.

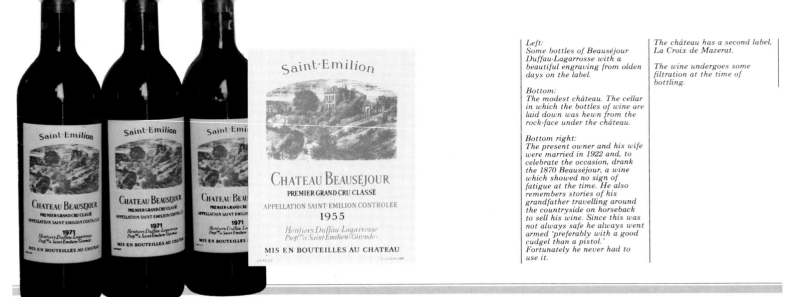

Château Beauséjour Duffau-Lagarrosse

Premier Grand Cru Classé

In 1869 M. Ducarpe divided his Beauséjour estate between his two children. Both received a more or less equal share and both were permitted to continue calling their vineyard Beauséjour. That is why there are still two Châteaux Beauséjour in St-Emilion. They lie immediately next to each other and are both *premier grand cru*. The direct descendants of Ducarpe's son still live at Beauséjour Duffau-Lagarrosse while the other Beauséjour changed hands long ago.

Family cooperation

As a château, Beauséjour Duffau-Lagarrosse has no pretensions whatever. It is a relatively extensive, simple building but nothing more; and that also goes for the people who live there. The Duffau-Lagarrosse heirs are friendly, very ordinary people who love their land, and do not regard their residence as a château but as a home for the family; and a family which is closely involved with the vineyard. Children and grandchildren all help as much as possible with working the land, harvesting and other tasks; and wherever possible, the children's friends also lend a hand. So there is no shortage of enthusiastic labour.

Made with concessions

The vineyard is small, some 17 acres. It lies beside the château on a fairly steep slope. The vines are 50% Merlot, 25% Cabernet Franc and 25% Cabernet Sauvignon. The grapes are allowed to ferment in one of the stainless steel or concrete *cuves* as soon as they have been picked, de-stalked and crushed. After fermentation, the wine used to mature in casks for 2½ to 3 years but this has now been reduced to 12 to 20 months.

One-third of the casks are new. The long maturing in the wood explains why the wines used to taste strongly of tannin and took years to develop. The 1961, for example, has still not fully relaxed, and the 1964 is only just becoming ready for drinking. The estate went through a difficult period towards the end of the 1960s and early 1970s. The wines were on the meagre side and not up to the level of a *premier grand cru classé*. Substantial improvements were introduced under the expert management of Jean-Michel Fernandez, particularly since 1978. The wines are beginning to show some fruit and charm in addition to the still ever-present tannin. The 1979 was a clear example of this. Beauséjour Duffau-Lagarrosse produces 30 to 43 *tonneaux* each year.

Château Beau-Séjour Bécot

Premier Grand Cru Classé

The first time I met Michel Bécot he ws bursting with eagerness to show me his new cellars. I would have done the same in his place because what this man has achieved within a short time is phenomenal. M. Bécot purchased the vineyard in 1969 in a very neglected state. The wine which was made there was so miserable that this Beau-Séjour (not to be confused with Beauséjour Duffau-Lagarrosse and other Beauséjours elsewhere) was on the short list for removal from the ranks of the *premiers grands crus*. In this unhappy situation, Michel Bécot set to work with tremendous energy to make rapid improvements. He spent all his time — and probably all his money as well — on reinstating or improving the cellars, the vineyard and the château. Beau-Séjour now houses a battery of ten of the latest model of stainless steel fermentation vats in a modern *cuvier*. Next door is a modern reception hall where 300 persons can eat, and with a beautiful *cave* cut from the rock beneath.

Land added

When Michel Bécot took over the estate the vineyard was barely 18 acres in size. The surface area is now 45 acres. Soil was added to the vineyard from adjoining estates — La Carte and Les Trois Moulins — which M. Bécot also inherited. Output at Beau-Séjour Bécot (as the name is now written) is about 70 *tonneaux* obtained from the following varieties: two-thirds Merlot, and one-third Cabernet Franc plus Cabernet Sauvignon. The wine matures for 18 months in 90% new casks.

Woody, meaty taste

Assisted by his children, Michel Bécot produces a woody, meaty St-Emilion, aromatic and often complex in taste. In some years, it has the fragrance of ripe fruit. The first great wine to be made by M. Bécot was the 1970, sparklingly deep in colour, concentrated in taste, and unfolding in the course of the 1980s. I also found the 1971, 1973, 1975, 1976, 1978 and 1979 to be good wines in relation to their year. The Beau-Séjour Bécot wines are distributed by Messrs de Luze. A second label is the Château la Carte.

CHÂTEAU
LA GAFFELIÈRE
1ᵉʳ Grand Cru Classé
SAINT-EMILION
+ 1971 +

Comte de Malet Roquefort
PROPRIÉTAIRE A St EMILION (GIRONDE)
APPELLATION SAINT-ÉMILION 1ᵉʳGRAND CRU CLASSÉ CONTROLÉE

Left:
Château Gaffelière dates from the 11th century, although the wings were rebuilt during the 17th and 18th centuries. During the 19th century, the château was extensively renovated to restore some of its original Gothic character.

Bottom:
A panoramic view of La Gaffelière. Remains of a Gallo-Roman villa were discovered on the estate in 1969, prompting the claim — along with Château Ausone — that it was already a settled area in Roman times. Perhaps the poet Ausonius himself lived there?

What is probably the largest cedar in the Gironde stands in the park of La Gaffelière — and it is guarded by some of the most aggressive swans in the department.

It goes without saying that Roquefort is rarely missing from Count de Malet Roquefort's cheeseboard.

Château La Gaffelière

Premier Grand Cru Classé

There are certainly more felicitous names for a château than La Gaffelière. Originally, the word meant 'leper colony' while *faire une gaffe* means 'to put your foot in it'.
One advantage of so odd a name is that it sticks in the mind. The owner, the Comte de Malet Roquefort, in fact tells how once a foreign letter reached him addressed to 'Château La Caféteière, France'. A post office official had written on the envelope 'France or Brazil?', and fortunately a search was first made at home. Actually, the road which cuts through the centre of La Gaffelière is also an asset. The château is separated from its cellars by a busy asphalt track and as a result all visitors to St-Emilion know where La Gaffelière is situated. The road was formerly a private one presented by Malet's grandfather (then mayor) to St-Emilion to connect the township to the railway station.

Two kinds of Soil

The La Gaffelière vineyard covers 62 acres planted with 65% Merlot, 25% Cabernet Franc and 10% Cabernet Sauvignon. About 25 acres lie on the slope near Ausone where the soil gives the wine its soundness. The remaining 37 acres lie at the foot of the hill, providing the wine with its suppleness. The total yield averages 110 to 120 *tonneaux,* but it always includes a proportion of substandard wine, which is sold under the second label Château de Roquefort. The owner exercises a strict selection. More than a third of the wine was not good enough in 1973, nearly a third in 1974. On average, some 60 to 80 *tonneaux* remain for La Gaffelière. The wine is sold chiefly to Belgium, Britain, Switzerland and the USA through five wine firms in Bordeaux and Libourne.

A visit to La Gaffelière is certainly worthwhile. The château has been tastefully fitted out with comfortable furniture, tapestries and old masters. On one wall I saw a canvas from 1486 showing Louis Malet, Admiral of France. Next to the tall château stands the modern *cuvier* which has been in use since the 1974 harvest. Here, a dozen stainless steel *cuves* stand glittering above a carefully waxed, crystal-clear tiled floor. For the *chais* you have to cross the road. Here the wine lies maturing for 22 months in oak casks, half of which are renewed each year. Château La Gaffelière is clarified with egg white, the wine not normally being filtered. Count Léo de Malet Roquefort is also the owner of Château Tertre Daugay in St-Emilion.

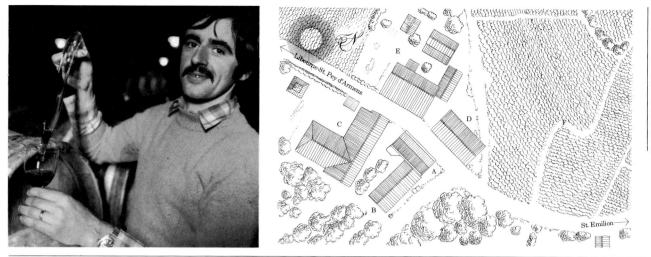

Château La Gaffelière

Private cellar

On a quest for some older wines during my first visit, my host and I visited his private cellar. This lies inside the château, next to the central heating boiler, but the temperature in the *cave* is not too warm thanks to a clever ventilation system which creates a kind of screen of cold air. As a result, the wine cellar is 10 degrees cooler than the temperature outside. Count de Malet Roquefort asked me to choose for myself and after some hesitation between the many good bottles which lay there I went for the 1961 and the 1947. After all, you should not be too shy in such situations because you may miss the chance of tasting wines that you may never encounter again.

Outstanding bottles

Both bottles were outstanding. After the oysters with champagne — they certainly know how to live at La Gaffelière — the 1961 was the first to be served. It was originally a wine with so much strength that the count had had to clarify it twice, once with four egg whites and then with three. As you might expect, the wine had a deep colour and full, supple taste. The bouquet was very fine, an abundance of rich gradations. The wine was at its most vital and even somewhat reticent, but without a hint of tiredness. After the perfect 1961 the 1947 was served. This wine, too, was a revelation, with tremendous class and surprising youthfulness.

My host told me that his father had made this wine and he himself the 1961. In his time, his father had advocated a short vinification to make the wine drinkable rather sooner. The son, on the other hand, is increasingly inclined towards long vinification which gives the wine great keeping qualities and also distinguishes it clearly from the many châteaux at St-Emilion where wines are now commonly produced for early drinking. The 1966 is not the only vintage to bear witness to the class that La Gaffelière can attain, but also the 1967, 1970, 1971, 1974, 1975, 1978 and 1979. The wines were supple yet sturdy, with an attractive perfume and much taste — though I found them somewhat lacking in depth and refinement compared with some other *premiers grands crus* in St-Emilion.

Clos Fourtet

Premier Grand Cru Classé

Every visitor to St-Emilion knows Clos Fourtet because the château lies immediately opposite the main car park near the church and a stone's throw from the famous Hotellerie de Plaisance. In earlier times, a minor fortification stood on this spot; the word *fourtet* means 'small fort'. Structurally, the château is not all that imposing. It is a pleasant country house covered with a green coat of ivy. The most interesting part of Clos Fourtet lies underground. This is the region of the *côtes*, the chalky cliffs around St-Emilion into which countless caves, passages and cellars have been cut. Beneath Clos Fourtet there are no less than three levels of galleries carved out of the rock. A small section of these is used for maturing the second year

wines, the major part for growing mushrooms. I was once told that in Bordeaux almost as many people are engaged in cultivating mushrooms as grapes.

Improved vinification

Clos Fourtet is the property of the Lurton family, four brothers in all. At one time André Lurton was the sole owner, but the general management of the estate is now in the hands of a *direction collégiale* which has obtained the advice of Professor Emile Peynaud. This led to improved vinification while changes were also made in the plantings. The percentage of Merlot was raised from 55% to 70%, the remainder being

split half and half between Cabernet Franc and Cabernet Sauvignon. There was a period when Clos Fourtet was a fairly tight, hard wine. However it has gradually become more supple in style, though not soft or velvety. The more successful vintages include, in any event, 1970, 1971, 1975, 1978 and 1979. The last two years in particular have great appeal. They show that Clos Fourtet has acquired a more open personality, with a fine fragrance and fruit in the taste. Clos Fourtet is once again living up to its status as *premier grand cru classé*.

Château Canon

Premier Grand Cru Classé

An estate which still uses horses for working the vineyard could hardly be expected to make its wine in any other but the traditional way — and this is true of Canon. There can be no question here of fermentation vats other than wooden ones since other systems are regarded as being too like a factory, and the rest of the process is also conducted along old, well-tried lines. The young administrator, Eric Fournier, stresses that keeping to the old ways is certainly not a question of economy. New wooden *cuves* today cost almost as much as stainless steel; and manual working is always slower and therefore more costly than mechanized labour.

Minimal replanting

The vineyard is spread round the château rather like an open fan. All the plots adjoin but are separated here and there by cart tracks or walls. In the distant past, much of the area was walled, the *enclos* being located immediately opposite the château. The total surface area is 44 acres, planted with 55% Merlot, 40% Cabernet Franc and the remainder with Cabernet Sauvignon and Malbec. The vines are often of a respectable age; quite a few have passed their 40th or 50th year, the average age being between 25 and 30. They take a thrifty approach at Canon and so replanting is undertaken only when absolutely necessary. This generally comes down to a patch of ground about one-third of a *journal* in size — a *journal* being the area of land that one man can work in one day, about four-fifths of an acre.

Generous and fragrant

The yield at Canon is an average of 55 to 75 *tonneaux*, all bottled by hand directly from the cask. Much of this is sold in France but some is also exported to Belgium, Britain, the United States and Japan and other countries. I regard Canon as one of the best wines of St-Emilion — generous, with a fine fragrance. The finest Canon that I ever drank was the 1961: extraordinarily aromatic and full of concentrated muscle. The best years were 1962, 1964, 1970, 1975, 1978 and 1979. It is fair to mention that Château Canon produced several weak wines between 1970 and 1975, not really up to the reputation of this estate. Fortunately, however, this seems to have been a momentary lapse. The wine normally matures for 20 months in cask; 30% to 40% of the *barriques* are renewed each year.

The magazine Paris Match is a sore point at Ausone. In the edition of July 21, 1973, it ran a long feature on Mouton-Rothschild illustrated with a full-page aerial photograph of a château that was supposed to be Mouton. It was, in fact, Ausone. Une grand scandale!

The general opinion at Ausone is that the wine should not be drunk before it is 10 years old.

Below right:
A display of Ausone bottles at the entrance to the cuvier.

Bottom:
The classic view of Ausone as seen by countless visitors approaching the small medieval town. Ausone is on the top of the hill on which the vineyard is planted. From the bottom of the hill, all that can be seen of the château is the outline of its roof.

Château Ausone

Premier Grand Cru Classé

The Roman poet Ausonius is said to have given his name to Ausone, but no one knows for certain whether his villa stood on the same spot as the château. Ausonius praised the wines of St-Emilion and it is easy to imagine the estate as a source of lyric inspiration. It is splendidly situated, high on the edge of a plateau from which the rows of vines run steeply down. From the little park with its palm trees there is a magnificent summer panorama over the hills of St-Emilion, decked in their thick coat of green vines. Far below motor cars sweep by, but the natural beauty is timeless.

The château itself is a rambling structure, and a rectangular tower with a steep pointed roof is its most characteristic element. It is obvious that the house has been extended by various owners in the course of the centuries so that it is now hard to discern its original shape. Mme J. Dubois-Challon and the heirs of Mme Cécile Vauthier (the joint owners) now live at Ausone. Mme Dubois-Challon is the widow of Jean Dubois-Challon, who died in 1974. He was born at Ausone in 1896, three years after his father-in-law to be, had inherited the property from an aunt of his wife. His widow is now carrying on his good work, closely assisted by her manager Pascal Delbeck, an extremely capable administrator. I also knew the former manager M. Chaudet, a wine maker of the old school who worked at Ausone from the 1950s to the end of the 1970s.

Ausone is fitted up like a real castle. In the large sitting room family portraits look down

CHATEAU AUSONE

SAINT-EMILION

APPELLATION SAINT-EMILION CONTRÔLÉE

1966

Vᵛᵉ C. VAUTHIER & J. DUBOIS-CHALLON
PROPRIÉTAIRES A SAINT-ÉMILION (GIRONDE)

MIS EN BOUTEILLES AU CHATEAU

Château Ausone

on you from three sides as you sit enjoying a glass of wine by the roaring open-hearth fire. The ceilings are high — there is a cabinet in the dining room whose top shelf cannot be reached without a ladder. Immediately behind the château lies the small vathouse with several wooden fermentation vats, presided over by St-Emilion's own patron saint, St-Valery.

Enormous stone gallery

The cellar is as grand as the vathouse is modest. A high cliff towers up behind the château, and into it is cut an enormous gallery. In this underground vault, with its squat, angular pillars, lies the wine. The air is damp, cool and at a constant temperature; even on the hottest summer day it is never more than 2° warmer than on the coldest day of winter. The passages date back to about 1580. As is often the case in St-Emilion, they were originally a quarry. Here, the wine

matures for 16 to 20 months in casks which are fully renewed every year. The purchase of new casks for each vintage is a long-established tradition at Ausone.

The cellar serves to store not only wine in casks but also bottled wine from both Château Ausone and from the adjoining Château Belair (partly jointly owned). In the twilight I detected several bottles from the earlier part of the 19th century, the oldest dated 1831.

High average yield

Cocks and Féret in their *Bordeaux et ses Vins* of 1969 write that the average output at Ausone is 25 *tonneaux*. The reason given for this low yield are the *vieilles vignes françaises* which have been retained thanks to, amongst other things, sparing use of insecticides. The writers mention century-old vines, which means that the plants survived the phylloxera. In any event,

Ausone has vines dating back to the 1903 to 1923 period. The average output has risen since 1969 to about 27 *tonneaux*. For a vineyard of 17 acres this comes to 35 hectolitres per hectare. (Figures based on the average from 1958 to 1978), a low but still acceptable yield. Another noteworthy fact is that Ausone has had a consistently normal crop since 1956 — the year of the great frost. Only two grape varieties can now be found in the small vineyard — 50% Merlot (it used to be 55%) and 50% Cabernet Franc. The few rows of Cabernet Sauvignon have disappeared. Incidentally, traces have been found at Ausone of wine-growing during Roman times. The owners in those days hacked long grooves into the rocky soil in which they planted their vines. How efficiently the Romans mastered certain techniques of wine-growing is clear from the fact that the rows at St-Emilion are still planted the same distance apart as in those days.

Château Ausone

A temporary lapse

Château Ausone, like most of the properties located on the *côtes*, is at the top of the St-Emilion classification, together with Cheval Blanc (of *graves* fame). These are the only two wines in Group A; the remainder of the *premier crus* are in group B. For some considerable time, nevertheless, Ausone did not really deserve its equal rating with Cheval Blanc. The highly respected English writer Edmund Penning-Rowsell states in one of the first editions of his *The Wines of Bordeaux*, '. . . since the war I have never met an outstanding Ausone'. Similar comments can be found in other books and articles. The auction prices at Christie's also show that Ausone's reputation was at a low ebb for a long time. With a few exceptions, such as the Ausone 1966, Cheval Blanc gained the higher ratings. Ausone produced few top-quality wines between roughly 1949 and 1976. Even years such as 1961, 1970 and 1975 were on the light side and lacked backbone. The best wine of that period was probably the 1964.

Back in the lead

The situation changed with the arrival of Pascal Delbeck in 1975. He pushed through a number of improvements, with the result that the 1976 became a very great wine. I consider this one of the best wines made that year on the right bank of the Dordogne. The wine has great style, breeding and allure, both in aroma and in taste, with exciting nuances and an excellent measure of tannin. Similarly outstanding wines were made in 1978 and 1979; I also found the 1977 and 1980 very fair for their years. With 1981 and 1982 as two other great years, it would seem that Château Ausone has moved right back into the lead.

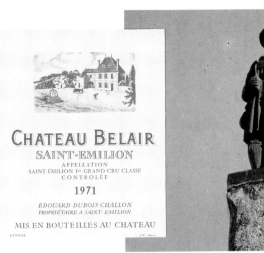

Château Belair

Premier Grand Cru Classé

While Ausone belongs only partly to Mme Dubois-Challon, she is sole owner of Belair. The estates lie close together, no more than a few hundred yards apart. Like Ausone, Belair offers its visitors a fine panorama, though in this case more to the south than to the east.

The estate was for a long time in English hands, originally being owned by Robert de Knolles, then Governor of Guyenne. After Charles VII had driven out the occupying forces Robert de Knolles' descendants continued to live in the area and Belair remained in the family. However, the estate changed hands during the French Revolution and was purchased in 1916 by M. Dubois-Challon, the present owner's father-in-law. The only surviving relic of the English period is the old fortification next to the château.

A cave of wine

The vineyard covers 32 acres, 15 acres more than Ausone, but even this is not impressively large. The grapes, 60% Merlot, 40% Cabernet Franc, produce an average yield of 35 *tonneaux* a year. The wine matures in a cellar behind the château. As at Ausone, this was carved out naturally, long ago, from the chalky rock of the plateau above. The space is as large as that at Ausone but has the advantage of being more easily heated. Banquets were once held in the Belair cave for visitors to Ausone.

Lighter than Ausone

The Belair wine generally remains in the cool, dark cellar for about 18 months. One-third of the casks are renewed each year, and they also use vats from Ausone. Like Ausone, Château Belair went through a long period of mediocrity. I can remember the 1966, for example, which proved to be a powerful wine virtually everywhere, but was still light and thin at Belair. The 1967 was no more impressive. However, here too, matters took a marked turn for the better from the 1976 harvest. The wine that year was very successful, and again in 1978 and 1979. The Belair style is somewhat lighter and less complex than that of Ausone; the wine is also sooner ready for drinking. It is a crisp, fairly slender St-Emilion noted for its elegance rather than depth or muscle.

Right:
A corner of the cellar.

Below:
An old engraving of the château and its estate. Apart from the disappearance of the high rock wall rising behind the building, very little has changed. On the lower right is the cuvier of Pavie; at the left are the working areas, living quarters and office; and against the slope is the actual château.

Bottom:
A view from the vineyard down to the château.

Château Pavie

Premier Grand Cru Classé

Château Pavie

Château Pavie is undoubtedly one of St-Emilion's brightest stars. Both the vineyard and the building lie on a steep slope, with the *cuvier* at its foot, the château about halfway up, and the *chai* right at the top. The difference in height between the *cuvier* and *chai* is the best part of 60 feet, and considering that the annual output is a yearly average of some 600 casks (150 *tonneaux*), it is clear that moving all this wine to and fro involves an enormous amount of hard work.
The area where the wine spends at least 18 months in cask is an ancient cave dating back to the 11th century. The risk is evident, since the rain, in particular, has strongly eroded the chalk in the course of the centuries. The present owners have already experienced this twice when part of the cellars collapsed. The first time it happened was some 20 years ago, the second time, December 1974. It is to be hoped that this cycle will not continue because not only are workers' lives put at risk but some of the wine is lost on every occasion. The subsidence in 1974 took a toll of 43 casks full of wine.

Concrete vats from the 1920s

The vathouse at Pavie is the oldest of its kind in St-Emilion. The concrete vats go back to the early 1920s, when oak was still the norm. It must have been a revolutionary step to start working with this new material. The first models were lined with glass on the inside but this was abandoned because there was long-term danger of contamination. In addition to these vats, Pavie has several lined inside with plastic. The man responsible for wine making is *maître de chai* Pierre Rabeau, who has been with the estate since 1967. His counterpart in the vineyard is Gilles Clauzel, for many years now *chef de culture*. Some 20 persons are employed full-time at Pavie, an indication that the estate is an important one.

Many old vines

The Pavie vineyard is well situated from south-west to south-east. The surface area is 92 acres, of which 89 acres are productive. As at the other quality-conscious estates, every effort is made to keep the percentage of old vines as high as possible by replanting very carefully in small patches at a time. That is why Pavie still possesses gnarled stocks 80 to 100 years old. The yield from the vineyard tends to fluctuate. In 1974, 52 hectolitres were harvested per hectare, but in 1972 only 27. The composition of the vineyard is as follows — 55% Merlot, 25% Cabernet Franc and 20% Cabernet Sauvignon — traditional proportions for St-Emilion.

Supple, pliant wine

Director Jean-Paul Valette and his staff try to avoid making an intransigent, brick-hard wine which has to be left for years in the hope that it will soften in due course. On the contrary, at Château Pavie the aim is to make pleasant wines which are both powerful and supple. My personal impression is one of wines which lack that fullness of body and wealth of tannin. Pavie is already quite accessible in its youth. Although this St-Emilion does not offer great depth of taste, deep concentration or high refinement, it is an extremely attractive wine, of unusually reliable quality. Pavie quite rightly has many admirers. I have not drunk many old vintages of Pavie but still remember the 1962 with pleasure — not too broad but still delicious. The 1964 left an even better impression, a highly expressive wine with an almost sweet scent and brilliant finish. For its year, the 1966 was something of a disappointment but still had a pleasant, velvety, round perfume. Another good wine was the 1970, with deep colour, ripe fruit and other overtones in a splendid aroma, and a

reasonably sturdy taste. The 1971 seemed to be up to the same level. The celebrated years of 1975 and 1978 produced rather less powerful, less intense wines at Pavie than might have been expected, with some early signs of subtlety. I found the 1976 somewhat disappointing, but the fruity 1979, was a delicious surprise, the quality much better than its predecessor.

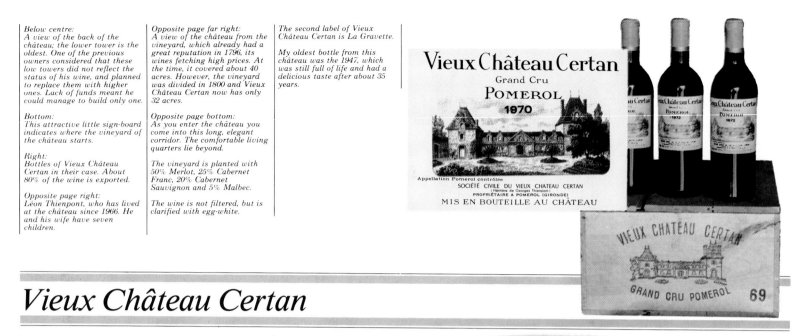

Vieux Château Certan

Vieux Château Certan lies near a crossroads which symbolizes the high quality of this area. Drive a few hundred yards towards the north-east and you come to Château Pétrus, the greatest of the Pomerols; and a little way south-west is Château Cheval Blanc, greatest of the St-Emilions. The vineyard's reputation is very high. Many regard it as Pomerol's second château after Pétrus. Whether that is correct is difficult to say because surrounding estates such as L'Evangile and La Conseillante also produce excellent wines. Be that as it may, Vieux Château Certan ranks among the great châteaux of Bordeaux.

The estate was purchased in 1924 by Georges Thienpont, a Belgian wine

merchant. Three years earlier he had taken over Troplong-Mondot in St-Emilion. He visited both châteaux three to ten times a year, but always stayed at Troplong. In 1935 he found it necessary to dispose of one of the two; but which? Emotionally, he felt closer to Troplong-Mondot, but financially he saw a greater future in Vieux Château Certan; and so it was Troplong which was sold.

Vieux Château Certan has been partly owned since 1957 by Léon, the son of Georges Thienpont. He lives with his son at the château the whole year round and it is he who has further increased the wine's reputation to its present level.

Vieux Château Certan

No hail insurance

M. Thienpont is proud of the fact that his
vineyard has its own microclimate. This has
the advantage that Vieux Château Certan is
hardly ever troubled by spring frosts. Nor
has the vineyard been plagued by hail since
1935. Vieux Château Certan therefore has no
hailstorm insurance. The vineyard lies round
the château and comprises 33 acres, three
more than when Georges Thienpont bought
the estate in 1924. The average yield
fluctuates around 60 *tonneaux,* which
generally go to Britain, the United States,
Japan, Australia and, of course, Belgium.
Léon Thienpont still has close ties with his
mother country, where other members of the
company owning the château still live, and
sold his entire 1973 crop to that country, For
the Belgians (and the Dutch) doing business
with M. Thienpont is a simple matter
because he speaks not only French but fluent
Dutch.

Wood more attractive

The cellars at Vieux Château Certan were
extensively rebuilt early in 1972. A new first-
year *chai* was installed with reddish-brown
tiles on the floor and also a new *cuvier.* This
contains a couple of stainless steel tanks but
most of the vats are of wood. The reason?
'Almost entirely because it is more
attractive; there's something traditional
about a wooden vat. I often get visitors who
are completely enchanted by my oak vats
after seeing all that cement and steel
everywhere,' says M. Thienpont. The large
wooden fermentation vats were not in fact
made in Bordeaux but come from the
cooperage at Rémy-Martin, the Cognac
dealers. The steel vats are seldom, if ever,
used for fermentation. They are used only for
assemblage at Vieux Château Certan, when
wines from the different varieties of grape
have to be mixed together into a single wine.
Altogether, the wine matures 22 months in
cask and about one-third of the *barriques*
used are renewed each year. The exact
percentage of new casks is known only after
the wine has been made. As at many other
châteaux, a fixed number of casks is ordered
each year — in this case 100 — but the
proportion of new ones varies according to
the size of the crop.

Distinctive capsule

In a restaurant, bottles of Vieux Château
Certan wine can easily be distinguished from
a distance, for they have a red capsule with a
gold bottom edge, an invention of Georges
Thienpont. Fortunately, this frivolous lead
seal is not the only thing that makes the
wine notable, as it has some quite particular
qualities. After the 1961 and the 1964, the
1966 was a great success, with a splendid,
velvety, deep colour, a fine bouquet and a
balanced taste. 1970 was also an excellent
year, producing a wine with much colour,
aroma and tannin. I was also impressed by
the 1971, one of the better wines of that year.
The same could be said of the 1973. The 1974
was a good wine but somewhat lacking in
body. The taste of the 1975 was intense, deep
and nuanced, while the 1976 possessed much
charm and delicate balance. I found the 1977
an attractive luncheon wine. the 1978 had a
deep, dark colour, with fruit and wood in its
unexaggeratedly full taste. 1979 was also a
very good year.

Château Pétrus

Cru Exceptionnel

It could be argued that everything about Pétrus is small-scale, except for its wine. The château, in particular, where this great, world-famous wine is created is of very modest proportions. In fact, it is little more than a reception room, a hallway, one or two little rooms above, and the cellars. The only eye-catching feature about the château is its turquoise shutters (almost the same as those at Prieuré-Lichine in the Médoc) and the tall flagpole with its large, gold letter 'P' which can be seen glistening in the sunlight a long way off.

The *cuvier* consists of a number of small concrete vats which are not lined with glass or plastic. The wine therefore is in direct contact with the bare concrete, or at least with the purple layer of sediment deposited by many years of vinification. The cellars in which the wine lies maturing in cask for 18 to 28 months are, like the rest of Pétrus, tiny. It is even necessary now and then to stack the wines of various years on top of each other for lack of space.

Clay is the secret

The label on the bottle shows St Peter with a key in his hand; naturally the key to the gates of heaven and not to the château, because the latter only has one, and that is kept by Christian Moueix who supervises all the Moueix properties and handles Pétrus with special care. Only half the estate belongs to Messrs Jean-Pierre Moueix, the remainder belongs to the two heirs of Mme Loubat, a lady responsible for building the reputation of the wine. She died in 1961. A painting still hangs in the reception room showing her at the age of 45. If you ask Christian Moueix for the secret of his wine, why Pétrus is so much more impressive than its neighbours, he answers quite simply: 'It's all in the clay.' Nature has endowed only the Pétrus vineyard with a clay topsoil, whereas the other châteaux in Pomerol have for the most part to make do only with gravel.

Old vines, speedy harvest

There are other secrets to its success. Pétrus' 28-acre vineyard contains virtually none but very old vines, the average age being no less than 35 years. That is thanks to Mme Loubat, who refused to replant after the frost of 1956 but allowed the plants to recover by themselves. Another factor which contributes to Pétrus' grandeur is the great speed of harvesting. This is done by the same group of pickers from Moueix who work at Magdelaine. They arrive as soon as Christian thinks the time is right, and then set to work with ten tractors and over 100 workers, men and women. In principle, picking is done at Pétrus only during the afternoon, preferably on dry, sunny days.

Château Pétrus

This is to prevent water affecting the wine. Despite these limitations, they still complete within four days. Another process which contributes to Pétrus' phenomenal personality is the restricted *égrappage*. The stalks are left on 30% to 35% of the fruit in order to give the wine some additional structure. Then, finally, there is the fermentation which takes a long time. In 1973, for example, it took 25 days.

A superlative wine

Because of the old vines, the Pétrus wine generally has a high alcohol content. By entirely natural means, the 1970 achieved more than 14% in the vat; and 13% is the rule rather than the exception. But that is not the only remarkable feature of the wine, since Pétrus is in every respect overwhelming. It is less a case of you taking the wine than the wine taking you. The wine contains such strength that it is virtually impossible to eat anything with it. Dominating almost every course, Pétrus is food and drink combined: and by no means only in good or outstanding years. Even with such a relatively light vintage as the 1962, the wine surrendered hardly anything in character. I saw an intensely deep colour, smelled a magnificent bouquet of inconceivable luxury and experienced such an overpowering taste that it leaves the mouth only reluctantly. The 1966 was of course still richer, more creamy and more powerful. This wine can be kept for many a decade without declining. I would also place 1970 among the successful years, together with the fabulous 1971. Other excellent vintages were the 1975, 1976, 1978, 1979, 1981 and the tremendous 1982.
Of all the red wines throughout Bordeaux, Pétrus is undoubtedly the wine with the most colour and the most muscle. It is therefore advisable to decant it long in advance — up to the 1949 one hour beforehand, from the 1949 to the 1962, two hours, and from the 1962, three hours. Alas, the yield of this masterly wine is only 40 *tonneaux*, so that its price alone brings it within the reach only of the fortunate few.

List of Further Important Growths

This final chapter contains a few brief notes on châteaux which for one reason or another are not included in the official main classifications of red Bordeaux wines but which are still well worth a mention, if only because they make good wine. The following is, of course, a selection and even then a very restricted one.

As far as the Médoc châteaux are concerned, it should be noted that the most recent official terminology has been adopted. This differs substantially from that of *Bordeaux et ses Vins* (1969 edition), the châteaux catalogue of Cocks & Féret. The reasons for this is that in 1978 a brave attempt was made to bring some order into the group of *crus bourgeois* once and for all. Until 1977, two different terminologies from two different classifications — the first of 1932, the second of 1966 — were used indiscriminately, which hardly made for clarity in communication. A clean sweep has now been made and it seems likely that most of the château owners will adopt the more recent terminology.

Altogether, 127 Médoc châteaux have now been classified. They have been divided into three quality groups, as follows:
Crus Grands Bourgeois Exceptionnels (18)
Cru Grands Bourgeois (41)
Crus Bourgeois (68).
The listed châteaux produce about a third of all the wine in the Médoc.

A small number of châteaux owners have refused a listing under the *Crus bourgeois*. The reason is often that they still cherish the hope and expectation to be included amongst the *grands crus classés* in due course. For them, acceptance of *bourgeois* status would be a moral defeat. Examples are Châteaux Gloria and Maucaillou. So no classification is given in these cases. The same applies to châteaux which were excluded from the new classification for other reasons. Nor have I mentioned outdated titles, although they still sometimes appear on labels.
For more details information on the *crus bourgeois*, see *The Good Wines of Bordeaux*.

MEDOC

Châteaux d'Agassac. *Cru Grand Bourgeois Exceptionnel, Ludon (appellation Haut-Médoc)*
The château is a splendid little castle complete with moat. It has survived the passage of time more or less intact and is thus one of the few monuments to the 13th century. The Capbern-Gasqueton family are the owners and entirely replanted the vineyard in 1960. This now encompasses 74 acres. The Cabernets predominate at 60%, Merlot accounting for the remainder. The yield is seldom more than 80 *tonneaux* because the owners apply very strict quality standards. The Netherlands, Belgium, the United States and France are the chief markets for this reliable, sturdy wine.

Château Labégorce-Zédé, *Soussans (appellation Margaux)*
This attractive estate became the property in 1979 of the Fleming Luc Thienpont, who is related to the Thienponts, owners of the well-known Vieux Château Certan in Pomerol. The quality of this solid Margaux has clearly risen since 1979. The vineyard covers 58 acres and is planted with 50% Cabernet Sauvignon, 35% Merlot, 10% Cabernet Franc, and 5% Petit Verdot. The wine matures in the wood for a year.

Château Siran, *Labarde (appellation Margaux)*
Wild cyclamen blooms in the Siran park in summer. The rest, however, is under strict cultivation and the Siran wines are certainly up to the level of a fifth *grand cru*. Owner Alain Miailhé has 62 acres at his disposal, planted with the traditional varieties. The yield varies from 100 to 230 *tonneaux*.

Château d'Angludet, *Cantenac (appellation Margaux)*
The château is inhabited by Peter Sichel and his family. Peter is the son of the famous connoisseur Allen Sichel and was the first Englishman to become chairman of the *Syndicat des Négociants et Vin et Spiritueux de Bordeaux*. The d'Angludet vineyard has

been virtually renewed since 1961, with 45% Cabernet Sauvignon, 15% Cabernet Franc, 5% Petit Verdot and 35% Merlot (20% for many years). Altogether the vineyard covers some 74 acres. The yield fluctuates sharply. 1971 produced 19 *tonneaux*, 1973 as many as 137 *tonneaux*. This consistently outstanding wine ferments in concrete vats.

Château Martinens, *Cru Grand Bourgeois, Cantenac (appellation Margaux)*
Unlike the majority of vineyards in Cantenac/Margaux, Martinens is all of a piece. The surface area is 74 acres, the yield 35 to 75 *tonneaux*. Grape varieties: 55% Merlot, 30% Cabernet Sauvignon, 15% Petit Verdot. The 18th-century château is inhabited by the owner, Mme Simone Dulos.

Château La Tour de Mons, *Soussans (appellation Margaux)*
This estate derives its name from the Marquis of Mons de Dunes who once possessed a château with a remarkable tower. This tower still stands, the remainder of the building being destroyed by fire in 1895. The manager is Bertrand Clauzel, who lives on the premises. The yield is 22 to 135 *tonneaux* a year. Altogether the vineyard comprises 64 acres, planted with 45% Cabernet Sauvignon, 40% Merlot, 10% Cabernet Franc and 5% Petit Verdot. Wooden fermentation vats.

Château Citran, *Cru Grand Bourgeois Exceptionnel, Avensan (appellation Haut-Médoc)*
Citran was once an important *seigneurie* and that is still quite evident from the size of the property — about 1,235 acres! Of course, only part of the land is planted with vines (207 acres). The yield lies between 250 and 500 *tonneaux*. It was once even greater. Grape varieties are 60% Merlot and 35% Cabernet Sauvignon. The wine matures in casks for 18 months.

Château Brillette, *Cru Grand Bourgeois, Moulis*
The owner, Mme Berthault, makes her wine

List of Further Important Growths

in concrete vats and allows it to mature in casks of which one-third are renewed each year. In 1974 output was 100 *tonneaux,* exactly double 1972. The wine comes from a 74-acre vineyard (with 55% Cabernet Sauvignon, 40% Merlot and 5% Petit Verdot). The estate's manager is Bertrand Bouteiller (of Pichon-Longueville Baron and elsewhere).

Château Chasse-Spleen, *Cru Grand Bourgeois Exceptionnel, Moulis*
Chasse-Spleen is a château with a tremendous and well-earned reputation. It produces consistently excellent wines, even in lean years. The 1969 was extraordinarily successful and the 1973 and 1974 live up to their great class. 1978 and 1979 were also excellent. The owners are two companies and a bank. Mme Bernadette Villars manages Chasse-Spleen very expertly. The cellars contain the vintages from 150 to 300 *tonneaux.* In the 148-acre vineyard, Cabernet Sauvignon accounts for 50%, Merlot for 40% and Petit Verdot and Cabernet Franc for 5% each. Half the casks are always renewed for the two-year maturation.

Château Poujeaux, *Cru Grand Bourgeois Exceptionnel Moulis*
About 60% of the wines of Poujeaux are sold directly in France by the Theil family: and despite the fact that no dealers are involved the wine has already been long enjoyed in French Government circles, which is a sure sign of quality. The vineyard covers 123 acres. The grape varieties are 40% Cabernet Sauvignon, 36% Merlot, 12% Cabernet Franc and 12% Petit Verdot. About 80 to 300 *tonneaux.*

Château Maucaillou, *Moulis*
The vineyard of the 'bad stones' (and therefore good wine) belongs to the Dourthe family. They produce very fine, elegant wines which can compete with the best of the Médocs. The yield in 1973 was 185 *tonneaux* but this will continue to increase as they have recently purchased and planted additional land. The grape varieties are 45%

Cabernet Sauvignon, 15% Cabernet Franc, 35% Merlot and 5% Petit Verdot.

Château Fonréaud, *Cru Bourgeois, Listrac*
The United States, Canada, Belgium and Britain are the chief customers of Fonréaud. Drastic changes were made in the vineyard between 1950 and 1965. The 108 acres are now planted with 52% Cabernets, 46% Merlot and 2% Petit Verdot. The fairly supple, pleasant wine normally matures one year in oak casks.

Château de Lamarque, *Cru Grand Bourgeois, Lamarque (appellation Haut-Médoc)*
This is one of the finest buildings in the Médoc. The château dates partly from the 12th and partly from the 14th century and is beautifully maintained by the owner Gromand d'Evry. So a visit is well worthwhile. The wine is left to ferment in plastic-lined concrete vats and matured for nearly two years in casks of which one-fifth are new. Grape varieties: 50% Cabernet Sauvignon, 20% Cabernet Franc, 25% Merlot, 5% Petit Verdot. Yield 110 to 270 *tonneaux.*

Château Lanessan, *Cussac (appellation Haut-Médoc)*
The Lanessan château reminds one rather of a haunted house but there is certainly nothing spooky about the wine. It owes its good name to the efforts of manager Hubert Bouteiller, whose family has held Lanessan since 1793. Output is 50 to 140 *tonneaux.* The 99-acre vineyard is planted with 75% Cabernet Sauvignon, 20% Merlot and 5% Cabernet Franc plus Petit Verdot. The wine is traditional in character and of an excellent standard.

Château Gloria, *St-Julien*
The legendary Henri Martin lives at Gloria where, together with his son-in-law, he makes a good wine which is sold at *grand cru* prices. The simple but comfortable château was built in 1888. Vinification takes place in steel vats and the wine then lies maturing in large barrels and small casks for 16 months. The vineyard at present covers 86 acres and

is planted with 65% Cabernet Sauvignon, 25% Merlot, 5% Cabernet Franc and 5% Petit Verdot.

Château Caronne-Sainte-Gemme, *Cru Grand Bourgeois Exceptionnel, St-Laurent (appellation Haut-Médoc)*
The vineyard of Caronne-Sainte-Gemme lies to the far south of the commune of St-Laurent, immediately adjoining Lanessan. Owner Jean Nony produces an average 175 *tonneaux* of generous, colourful wine there each year. The vineyard (65% Cabernet Sauvignon) covers 106 acres.

Château Larose-Trintaudon, *Cru Grand Bourgeois, St-Laurent (appellation Haut-Médoc)*
This estate to all appearances has the highest output of the Médoc — the 1973 harvest was no less than 719 *tonneaux* and the 1974 harvest 574 *tonneaux.* The owner Henri Forner has extensive — and successful — recourse to mechanical picking apparatus. Some 60% of the grapes consist of Cabernet Sauvignon, 20% of Cabernet Franc and 20% of Merlot. The vineyard already comprises 390 acres and there are plans to add a further 37 acres. Despite this area, the wine is surprisingly good. Vinification in stainless steel and concrete vats.

Château Fonbadet, *Pauillac*
This fairly unknown château produces very good wines. They are based on a 37-acre vineyard planted with 60% Cabernet Sauvignon, 15% Cabernet Franc, 19% Merlot and 6% Malbec plus Petit Verdot. The owner, Pierre Peyronie, produces 50 to 85 *tonneaux* each year.

Château Peyrabon, *Cru Grand Bourgeois, St-Sauveur (appellation Haut-Médoc)*
This pretty little château, the property of Jacques Babeau, dates from the 15th century. It is surrounded by a 131-acre vineyard. The grape varieties are 50% Cabernet Sauvignon, 23% Cabernet Franc and 27% Merlot. The wine, which cannot be faulted, matures for 18 months in cask.

Left:
The attractive façade of Château Siran in Labarde, near Margaux. In summer wild cyclamens abound in the park, which is otherwise very carefully laid out.

List of Further Important Growths

Château de Marbuzet, *Cru Grand Bourgeois Exceptionnel, St-Estèphe*
The White House in Washington and Château de Marbuzet are both built to the same model and so have some family resemblance. Marbuzet serves as second label for Cos d'Estournel (a classified *cru* from St-Estèphe and also owned by the Prats family). There is therefore no relation between the yield and the 25-acre area of the vineyard. 60 *tonneaux* were produced in 1972, 96 *tonneaux* in 1973. The quality of the wine is consistently very good.

Château Meyney, *Cru Grand Bourgeois Exceptionnel, St-Estèphe*
In times past — the annals go back to 1662 — Meyney was a monastic community. It now belongs to the Cordier family. The grapes ferment in stainless steel vats and then remain two years in casks, of which one-third are new each time. The 123-acre vineyard is planted with the following grapes: 70% Cabernet Sauvignon, 24% Merlot, 4% Cabernet Franc and 2% Petit Verdot.

Château de Pez, *St-Estèphe*
Pez has existed as a château since 1350 but the vineyard was put down only in 1749. The *Gérant* M. Dousson lives at the château and is very closely involved with his wine. Cabernet Sauvignon dominates the 57-acre vineyard at 70%, followed by 15% Cabernet Franc and 15% Merlot. The output of 100 to 160 *tonneaux* goes chiefly to Britain, the United States and Northern Europe.

Château Les Ormes de Pez, *Cru Grand Bourgeois, St-Estèphe*
This vineyard is the property of the same Cazes family which owns Lynch-Bages. The wine matures for 14 to 18 months in second-hand casks from Lynch-Bages or Latour. The vineyard covers 74 acres and is planted with 60% Cabernets, 30% Merlot and 10% Petit Verdot. Output: 25 to 165 *tonneaux;* hyper-modern cellar; very good wine.

Château Beau-Site, *Cru Grand Bourgeois Exceptionnel, St-Estèphe*
The average age of the vines in this 74-acre vineyard at Beau-site is 20 years. Here, too, the Cabernets have the main role at 65%; the remainder is Merlot. Output is between 80 and 215 *tonneaux*. The wine is still vinified in wooden vats. Messrs Borie-Manoux are the owners.

Château Phélan-Ségur, *Cru Grand Bourgeois Exceptionnel, St-Estèphe*
This estate lies just to the south of St Estèphe and is one of the largest in this commune. The total area is some 470 acres, of which a quarter is planted with vines. M. Phélan created the property by merging the Clos de Garramey and Ségur early in the 19th century. The yield is 170 to 250 *tonneaux* obtained from 50% Cabernet Sauvignon, 30% Merlot, 10% Cabernet Franc and 10% Petit Verdot.

Château Bel-Orme-Tronquoy-de-Lalande, *Cru Grand Bourgeois, St-Seurin-de-Cadourne (Haut-Médoc)*
A beautiful little château regularly occupied by the Quié family (of Rauzan-Gassies and Croizet-Bages). Many improvements have been made in recent years. The vineyard includes 53 productive acres and output fluctuates between 80 and 100 *tonneaux*. Bel-Orme is a wine which must be given a great deal of time.

Château Coufran, *Cru Grand Bourgeois St-Seurin-de-Cadourne (Appellation Haut-Médoc)*
This is the northernmost estate in the Haut-Médoc where the landscape begins to flatten out. The vineyard covers 158 acres and is chiefly planted with Merlot — 85%. The wine is therefore very supple for a Médoc. Output varies from 115 to 395 *tonneaux*.

Château Loudenne, *Cru Grand Bourgeois, St-Yzans (appellation Médoc)*
Loudenne is the headquarters of the Gilbey House. The British owners have replanted substantial parts of the vineyard since 1965.

It now covers 81 acres of black grapes (53% Cabernet Sauvignon, 40% Merlot, 7% Cabernet Franc) and 25 acres of white (50% Sauvignon and 50% Sémillon). The red wine is supple, elegant and harmonious, the white crisp and fruity. The production figures are 40 to 130 *tonneaux* and 0 to 20 *tonneaux* respectively. Gilbey's director Francis Fouquet lives in the pink château, which is surrounded with large lawns and an extensive complex of cellars.

Château La Tour de By, *Cru Grand Bourgeois, Bégadan (Médoc)*
The owner, Mr Pagès, prepares between 275 and 490 *tonneaux* each year in his very old vathouse. The wine comes from a 170-acre vineyard with 65% Cabernet Sauvignon, 33% Merlot and 2% Cabernet Franc. The first vines were planted in 1710; the château dates from 1876. The chief customers are the United States, the Netherlands, Belgium and Switzerland.

Château La Tour Bonnet, *Cru Bourgeois, St-Christoly-de-Médoc (appellation Médoc)*
A charming property including a 99-acre vineyard in a single piece. Planted with 50% Merlot, 27% Cabernet Sauvignon and 23% Cabernet Franc. The owners are Pierre Lafon and his daughter. Output: between 170 and 220 *tonneaux* per year.

GRAVES

Château Les Carmes-Haut-Brion, *Pessac*
This small estate of barely 8¾ acres lies right next to Haut-Brion. The Chantecaille family (of the eponymous firm) are the owners. Up to 15 *tonneaux* of its fine, aromatic wine is produced each year.

Château Laville Haut Brion, *Cru Classe des Graves Blanc, Talence*
Like the red La Tour Haut Brion, this white Laville is vinified at La Mission Haut-Brion. Fermentation takes place in oaken casks. Because the vineyard is only 15 acres in size, the yield is no more than 10 to 20 *tonneaux*. A characteristic of the wine is that it

List of Further Important Growths

continues to develop well in the bottle, sometimes for up to 12 years. Grapes: 40% Sauvignon, 60% Sémillon.

Château Couhins-Lurton, *Cru Classé des Graves Blanc, Villenave-d'Ornon*
This small estate has been separated from Château Couhins which is owned by the French Ministry of Agriculture. It has since 1979 belonged to André Lurton who makes 3 to 4 *tonneaux* of high-quality dry white wine (100% Sauvignon) and will also be producing 6 to 7 *tonneaux* of red Graves. The vineyard may expand to a maximum of 13¾ acres.

Château Larrivet-Haut-Brion, *Léognan*
The vineyard on this estate borders that of Haut Bailly. Altogether 15¾ acres, planted with 58% Cabernet Sauvignon, 14% Merlot and 2% Cabernet Franc, produce some 60 *tonneaux* of good red wine. The owner, Mme Guillemaud, also harvests up to 4 *tonneaux* of dry white Graves based on 50% Sauvignon and 50% Sémillon. Concrete and stainless steel fermentation vats and tanks.

Château de France, *Léognan*
The owner of the Château de France makes a red wine from 50% Merlot and 50% Cabernet. After vinification in stainless steel vats the wine matures for 12 months in cask. The output varies from 77 *tonneaux* (1979).

Château la Louvière, *Léognan*
One of the most imposing châteaux of the Graves district, La Louvière was designed by Victor Louis who built the Grand Théâtre at Bordeaux. The owner, André Lurton, makes some very successful white and red wines. The 118-acre vineyard includes 74 planted with black grapes (80% Cabernet Sauvignon, 20% Merlot) and 44 with white (85% Sauvignon, 15% Sémillon). The estate is well equipped, with, amongst other things, stainless steel fermentation vats. The château is unoccupied.

ST-EMILION

Château La Dominique, *Grand Cru Classé, St-Emilion*
The La Dominique vineyard (62 acres) adjoins that of Cheval Blanc. They produce 70 to 100 *tonneaux* which are vinified by modern methods in stainless steel vats. The owner, Clément Fayat, each year replaces one-quarter of the casks, in which the wine matures for two years. Grape varieties: 76% Merlot, 8% Cabernet Franc, 8% Cabernet Sauvignon, 8% Malbec.

Château Croque-Michotte, *Grand Cru Classé, St-Emilion*
Manager Jean Brun makes the wine here for Messrs Geoffrion-Rigal; an excellent wine which enjoys a good reputation even in St-Emilion itself. About 60 to 70 *tonneaux* is the annual yield. Merlot accounts for 90% of the vineyard, Cabernet for the remainder. Area: 37 acres. The wine matures for 6 to 12 months in cask.

Château Grand-Corbin-Despagne, *Grand Cru Classé, St-Emilion*
The output at this 62-acre estate is between 70 and 100 *tonneaux*. After fermenting in vats of stainless steel and concrete, the wine matures for 16 months in oak casks. The chief grape variety is Merlot (60%), followed by Cabernet Sauvignon (25%).

Château Corbin, *Grand Cru Classé, St-Emilion*
The foundations of the 14th-century feudal castle can still be seen at Corbin. The present structure dates from the 18th century. The vineyard altogether covers 37 acres, one-quarter of which is planted with Cabernet Franc, one-quarter with Cabernet Sauvignon and the remainder with Merlot. Output 18 to 75 *tonneaux* per year.

Château Fonroque, *Grand Cru Classé, St-Emilion*
Fonroque is a château well known for its reliable wines, which moreover retain a pleasurable vitality in the bottle for many

years. The 50-acre vineyard produces an average of 70 *tonneaux* each year.

Château Soutard, *Grand Cru Classé, St-Emilion*
The owner, Comte des Ligneris, is a highly enthusiastic wine maker who leaves nothing to chance. He also applies strict quality standards and voluntarily declassified much of his wine in 1973 and 1974. Contrasting with the romantic old cellar, Soutard has a *cuverie* with stainless steel vats. The vineyard covers 54 acres (60% Merlot, 35% Cabernet Franc and 5% Cabernet Sauvignon). Output varies between 50 and 110 *tonneaux*.

Château Troplong-Mondot, *Grand Cru Classé, St-Emilion*
For St-Emilion, this estate has a quite remarkable output — 100 to 180 *tonneaux*. The vineyard covers 71 acres, planted by the owner, Claude Valette, with 65% Merlot, 25% Cabernets and 10% Malbec. Here, too, vinification is in stainless steel fermentation vats. The wine is sold chiefly to Belgium, the United States, and Britain. M. Troplong was Speaker of the Senate under the French Emperor Napoleon III.

Château L'Angélus, *Grand Cru Classé, St-Emilion*
This velvety wine matures in the modern cellars of L'Angélus. Nowadays it is stored in new wooden casks for six months. The grape varieties in the vineyard (69 acres) are Merlot (45%), Cabernet Franc (50%) and Cabernet Sauvignon (5%). The yield is normally between 70 and 140 *tonneaux*.

Château Cadet-Piola, *Grand Cru Classé, St-Emilion*
Some very generous wines of high quality are made at Château Cadet-Piola, owned by the Jabiol family. The vineyard covers 17 acres and is planted with 51% Merlot, 28% Cabernet Sauvignon, 18% Cabernet Franc and 3% Malbec. The wine is normally left to mature for 12 months in wood. A quarter of the casks are renewed each year. The yield

List of Further Important Growths

varies from 18 *tonneaux* (1975) to 40 *tonneaux* (1982).

POMEROL

Château Nenin, *Pomerol*
The attractive Château Nenin is surrounded with 67 acres planted with 50% Merlot, 30% Cabernet Franc and 20% Cabernet Sauvignon. They produce a yield of 50 to 110 *tonneaux,* depending on the year. The wine matures for up to two years in cask after being vinified in concrete or steel vats. The director and co-owner is François Despujol, the manager Pierre Esben.

Château Petit-Village, *Pomerol*
The wine from Petit-Village can be drunk young but will continue to develop for a long time. The Merlot grape predominates in the vineyard (80%), followed by the two Cabernet varieties: 10% Cabernet Franc, 10% Cabernet Sauvignon (originally 28%). The wine — average 35 *tonneaux* — matures in wooden casks of which at least half are new. The owners of the château (uninhabited) are the Prats brothers. Bruno Prats manages the business.

Château La Conseillante, *Pomerol*
The silver lining round the label nicely matches the gleaming stainless steel fermentation vats. The wine fetches very high prices, evidence of an excellent reputation. The owners, Nicolas, have altogether planted 29 acres with 45% Merlot, 45% Cabernet Franc and 10% Malbec. The average yield is 50 *tonneaux.*

Château L'Evangile, *Pomerol*
Together with Vieux Château Certan and La Conseillante, L'Evangile is often put at the top of the Pomerols (after Pétrus, of course). It belongs to the Ducasse heirs. Between 35 and 85 *tonneaux* are produced each year, about one-third of which is matured in new casks. The vineyard covers 33 acres, two-thirds of which are planted with Merlot and one-third with Cabernet Franc.

Château Gazin, *Pomerol*
Gazin is a former holding of the Knights Templar. The present owner is Etienne de Bailliencourt. On this 50-acre vineyard he produces between 35 and 120 *tonneaux* each year. Approximately half the grapes are Merlot, a quarter Cabernet Franc and a quarter Cabernet Sauvignon. The must ferments in concrete vats disguised to look like wood.

Château La Fleur-Pétrus, *Pomerol*
This 20-acre property (18 of which are planted with vines) lies close to Château Pétrus and is similarly managed by the firm of Jean-Pierre Moueix. At Pétrus the shutters are turquoise, here they are egg-yolk yellow. The grapes, (75% Merlot and 25% Cabernet Franc) thrive on a very gravelly soil which makes them ripen very quickly. The yield is between 13 and 38 *tonneaux,* shipped mainly to the United Kingdom and the United States.

Clos L'Eglise, *Pomerol*
Clos L'Eglise lies at the edge of a clay plateau. The château derives its name from the church at Pomerol which once stood right next to it. The vineyard extends over 15 acres and produces 10 to 35 *tonneaux* a year. One-tenth of the casks are renewed each year.

Château Trotanoy, *Pomerol*
Trotanoy belongs to the firm of Jean-Pierre Moueix, like La Fleur-Pétrus and several other châteaux in Pomerol and St-Emilion. Trotanoy has a great name (thanks to the aromatic strength of its wine) but a small vineyard (17 acres). Average yield approximately 25 *tonneaux.* This impressive wine matures some 20 months in casks, of which half are new.

Château Clos René, *Pomerol*
This property lies towards the edge of the commune of Pomerol, only half a mile or so from the area of great names. The owner is Pierre Lasserre, *Chevalier du Mérite Agricole.* His vineyard is 26 acres in size and is planted with 60% Merlot, 30% Cabernet Franc and 10% Malbec. His highest yield in recent years was in 1970 (80 *tonneaux*), his lowest in 1977 (25 *tonneaux*).

The page numbers in italics in this index refer to the pages where the relevant château is discussed extensively.

Index

Right:
The fine old castle of the
Château de Lamarque is a
landmark in the Médoc.

Index

Right:
Château Fonréaud, a cru bourgeois superieur *in Listrac.*

Index